FOLK ART

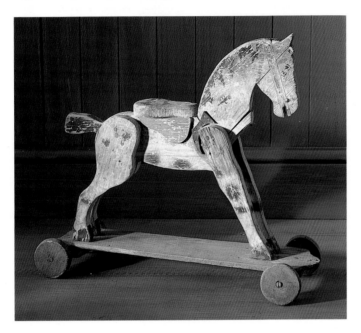

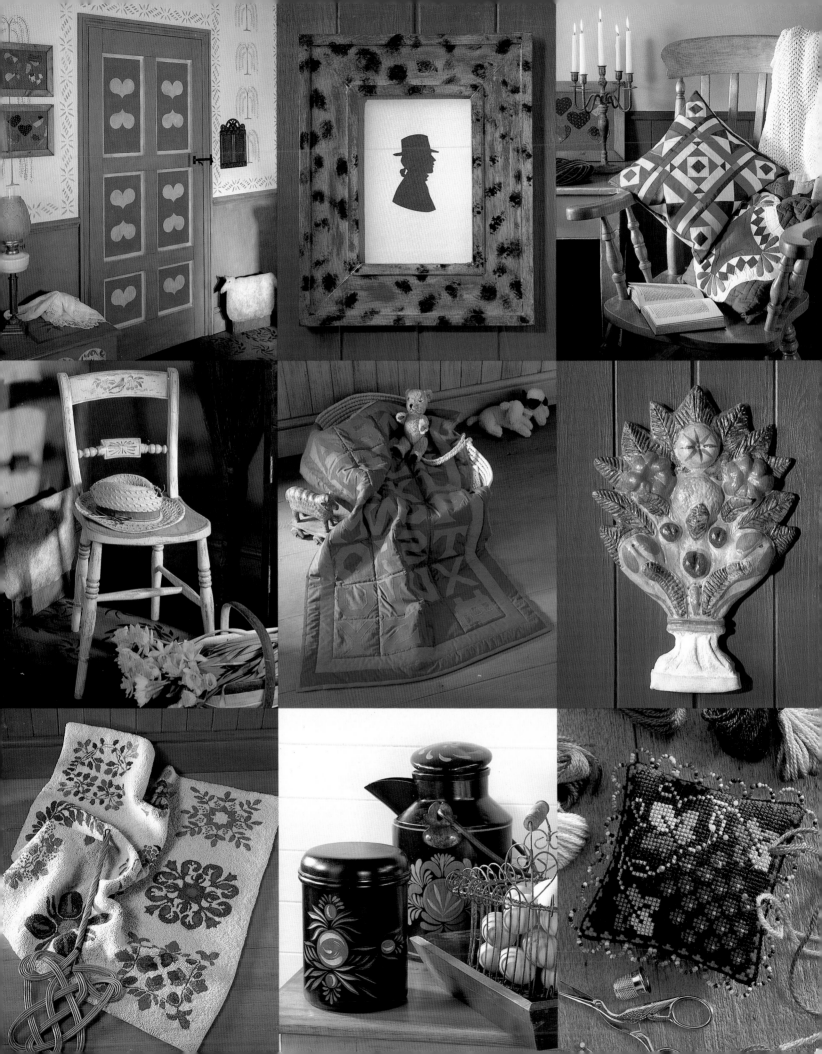

FOLK ART
STYLE & DESIGN

STEWART &
SALLY WALTON

Special photography by
Steve Tanner

Sterling Publishing Co., Inc.   New York

FOR STEPHANIE

Produced by
Anness Publishing Limited
Boundary Row Studios
1 Boundary Row
London SE1 8HP

Library of Congress Cataloging-in-Publication Data.

Walton, Stewart
    Folk art: style & design / Stewart & Sally Walton: special photography by Steve
Tanner.
        p.   cm.
    Includes index.
    ISBN 0-8069-0408-9
    1. Folk art——Themes, motives.   I. Walton, Sally.   II. Title.
N5313.W36   1993
745——dc20   93-4661
                                                                 CIP

10 9 8 7 6 5 4 3 2 1

Published 1993 by Sterling Publishing Company, Inc.
387 Park Avenue South, New York, N.Y. 10016

© 1993 Anness Publishing Limited

Distributed in Canada by Sterling Publishing
c/o Canadian Manda Group, P.O. Box 920, Station U
Toronto, Ontario, Canada M8Z 5P9

Typeset by MC Typeset Limited, England
Printed and bound in Hong Kong

ISBN 0-8069-0408-9

Page one: An old folk toy.

CONTENTS

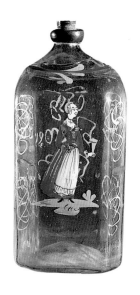

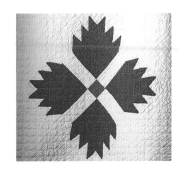

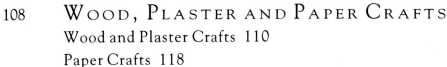

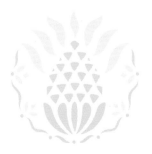

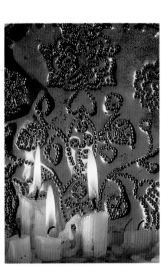

INTRODUCTION

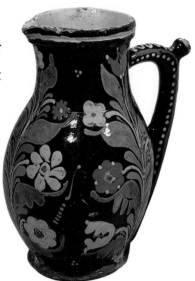

FOLK ART HAS A UNIQUE APPEAL. WE LOOK AT IT, LOVE IT, and then we can participate in and make it. It is our heritage and, because it is not elitist, it offers positive proof that the creative spirit moves within everyone.

Folk artists have their own design traditions to draw on, they have hands-on skills and above all they have chosen to allow their practical and creative natures to work in unison. Art education was not available to the European peasants any more than it is, for example, to the Panamanian Indians whose brightly coloured cut-out appliqué work has won worldwide recognition and admiration. Small isolated communities such as theirs, with a traditional form of decoration, pass down their skills through generations until art becomes second nature to them and completely without pretension; it is simply "what they do" and a part of their way of life.

A ceramic jug from
Alsace, France.

The creativity of folk artists demonstrates how limited resources contribute to ingenuity. Natural pigments provide a small but harmonious palette, while climate and local availability dictate the choice of materials. Custom also plays a constraining role in folk art, with the elders of the community keeping a

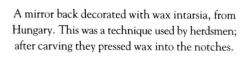

A mirror back decorated with wax intarsia, from Hungary. This was a technique used by herdsmen; after carving they pressed wax into the notches.

Opposite: A wooden cabin in Scandinavia.

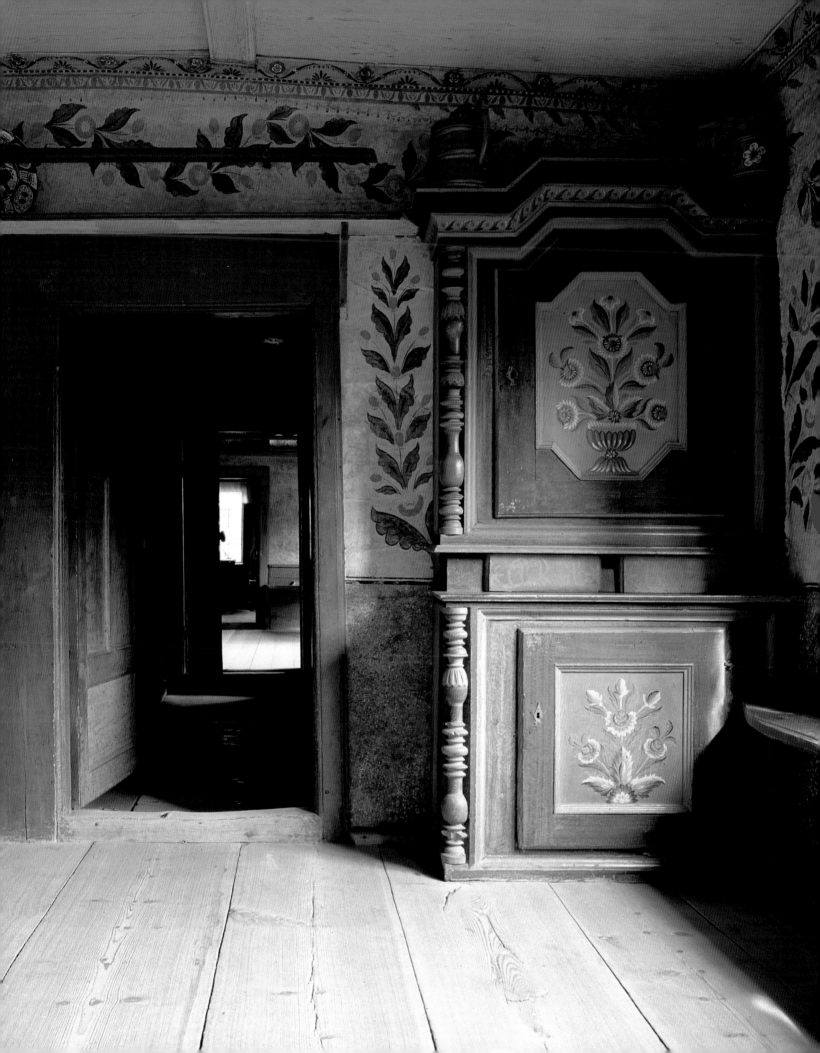

watchful eye on innovators: if the traditional colour for a barn is red, it is a brave and impetuous man who chooses to paint his barn blue.

Age has added credibility to the work of simple men and women, and ordinary household objects are now placed in museums, so that everyone can recognize their beauty and importance. But folk art is not only about the past. The work of rural artisans today shows the same attention to decoration, individuality and celebration of colour. The common motivator seems to be love rather than money; as soon as the dictum "Time is money" is applied, then the loving creativity of the artist disappears as time flies by.

Sadly, the desire by people in the West to possess beautiful handmade objects made by "ethnic" peoples today has led to the plundering of these peoples' cultures on an unprecedented scale, and the exploitation of rural craftsmen to mass produce traditional goods. These people are subject to the fashions of the moment, for the consumer society soon tires of the same recipe. Folk art should be seen from a different perspective than simply being a "nice style for the living room"; instead of taking for granted the luxuries of today, looking back to the past and the ways of previous generations can help society to value the present.

It is often the patina of age on folk art, the wearing away with use, that gives the objects their intrinsic appeal. There is a nostalgic element in the admiration of a simpler, more basic lifestyle, but perhaps it is more spiritual than sentimental to feel pleasure in seeing natural earthy colours on walls and feel the warmth and comfort of a beautiful hand-stitched patchwork quilt.

The quilts, stencilling, painted furniture, braided rugs and painted tinware that we recognize as being American folk art today were mostly made by the Pennsylvania Dutch and other immigrant communities who settled on the eastern seaboard of North America from the

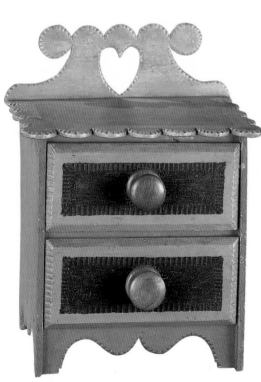

A painted and chip-carved chest, possibly from New England, c.1840.

seventeenth century onwards. They came from Europe to escape the bitter destiny of poverty, wars and religious persecution. The American folk art that is so distinctive is the result of a gathering of skills and traditions from all over Europe, poured into the melting pot of colonial life. Scandinavian folk culture celebrated courtship and marriage with traditionally crafted gifts, while German folk artists decorated their furniture with carvings and painted patterns. French and Italian glassmakers, Dutch painters and English weavers and quilters all had national and local styles, motifs and conventions which governed their self-expression. Their skills and traditions travelled with them.

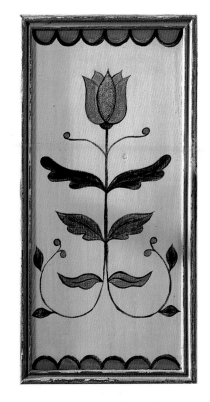

A modern-day folk art design, inspired by Pennsylvania Dutch patterns.

Once the settlers arrived in the New World a gradual homogenizing of styles took place, as disparate elements became fused together. This merging was further influenced by the itinerant painters, decorators and woodcarvers who roamed the countryside, providing specialist craft services. They were probably more responsible for the emergence of a distinctive American folk art style than any other group, taking patterns, colours and techniques from one isolated community to the next. That is not to say that the settlers turned their backs on their cultural history – quite the contrary. The tulip, which had been so celebrated in the folk art of Holland and Germany, became the most common floral motif; the heart, a symbol of love so much a part of Scandinavian rural art, was widely adopted. Each cultural contribution enriched the mixture of arts and crafts.

Ironically, the creation of new traditions means the smothering of indigenous styles – for example, in Australia as well as America the immigrants rejected the ancient culture of local peoples and chose to look backwards to Europe for their cultural references. Recently, however, the Aboriginal

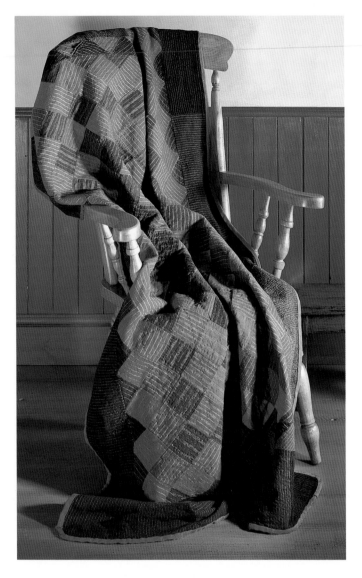

A late nineteenth-century Welsh quilt.

Australians have regained a pride and awareness of their ethnic art which is now crossing over into mainstream Australian art and decorating styles. But when cultures cross and intermingle a new folk art style is born, such as happened in Mexico where the result is a glorious mixture of Spanish and Central American symbols, stylized pattern and vibrant colour schemes.

Traditional skills were largely influenced by the common constraints of the rough and ready lifestyle that the immigrants were confronted with. Floors were covered with canvas taken from sails, which were stencilled to imitate richly woven carpets, and walls were painted and stencilled to look like fine printed wallpaper. The pieced quilts that are so much a focus for lovers of folk art, began as a recycling venture, using up scraps of cloth. The earliest are of English origin, using chintzes from the East, but sadly, few examples have survived – as with so much folk art, they were not considered to have intrinsic value and last year's quilt often became next year's filling.

Most folk art was home-based and the decoration of objects and making of crafts was very much a way of life. A girl began to patch and quilt when she was three years old; she would be given squares to join and the same squares would be sewn and unpicked many times until her stitchwork was approved by her mother. Each girl would aim to make twelve quilts before her betrothal, and then she would sew her finest, the thirteenth, for her marriage bed.

In the kitchen, decoration abounded, from the fancy cast iron stove plates to the hand-carved and painted salt boxes. *Sgraffito* pottery and slipware dishes were often dated and they provide a wonderful record of what life was like for the settlers, with designs depicting both custom and costume, as well as commemorating particular events.

Painted tin called toleware, from the French *tôle*, or sheet iron, became very fashionable in the early 1800s and tinsmiths produced a huge range of household items which were peddled door-to-door by tinkers. The designs, with their hand-painted floral shapes on dark backgrounds, were reminiscent of Norwegian *rosemaling* and English bargeware.

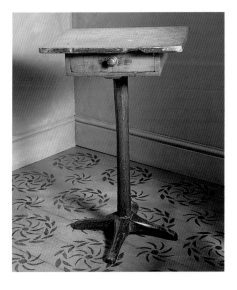

A candle table with a drawer for keeping lighting devices and books in.

Folk art was by its very nature undervalued and undocumented. The progress of industrialization which eased the burdens of daily life also saw the undermining of traditional skills and pleasures. It was not until 1924 that the first exhibition of American folk art took place at the Whitney Studio Club in New York, showing pieces loaned by contemporary artists, who were among the first avid folk art collectors. More exhibitions followed and perhaps it was at this point that the tide turned and country people began to think carefully before throwing out old worn quilts, painted chests or chipped commemorative plates.

There has been a resurgence of interest in the simpler lifestyle of the past. We can now have everything we want at the touch of a button and, given the time for reflection, we can see what has been lost along the way. Making copies of folk art pieces is not "faking" the past, but rather picking up the threads. Folk artists always used and copied particular motifs, styles and colours, and to gain inspiration from them or reproduce them now is simply to acknowledge their value.

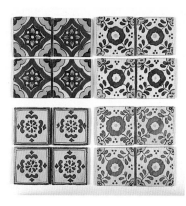

Mexican village tiles.

STYLE AND DESIGN

TRADITION • MOTIFS • PATTERN • COLOUR

Art is always difficult to define and folk art is no exception; an individual's cultural history plays such a large part in their appreciation of visual language.

Folk art style could be described as rustic, utilitarian and traditional but these terms scarcely begin to describe the enormous creative energy and richness of the art form.

The apparent absence of sophistication came from folk artists' lack of formal art education, which allowed a great freedom of expression. No doubt the talent of the folk artists could have been tamed by theoretical studies and the patronage of the art establishment, but the essential beauty of their work lies in the fact that it was not. The spirit remained intact and the art remained an integral part of people's everyday lives.

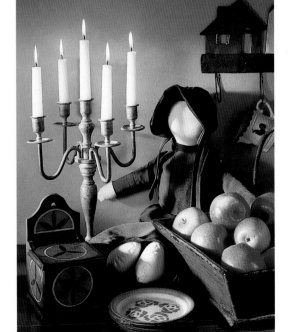

The many different shades of green are all popular colours used in folk art.

Opposite: This quilt design, the Double Irish Chain, was a popular pattern in both the British Isles and North America. The indigo blue and white fabrics are especially fresh and appealing. Indigo blue was a common and inexpensive dye for fabric.

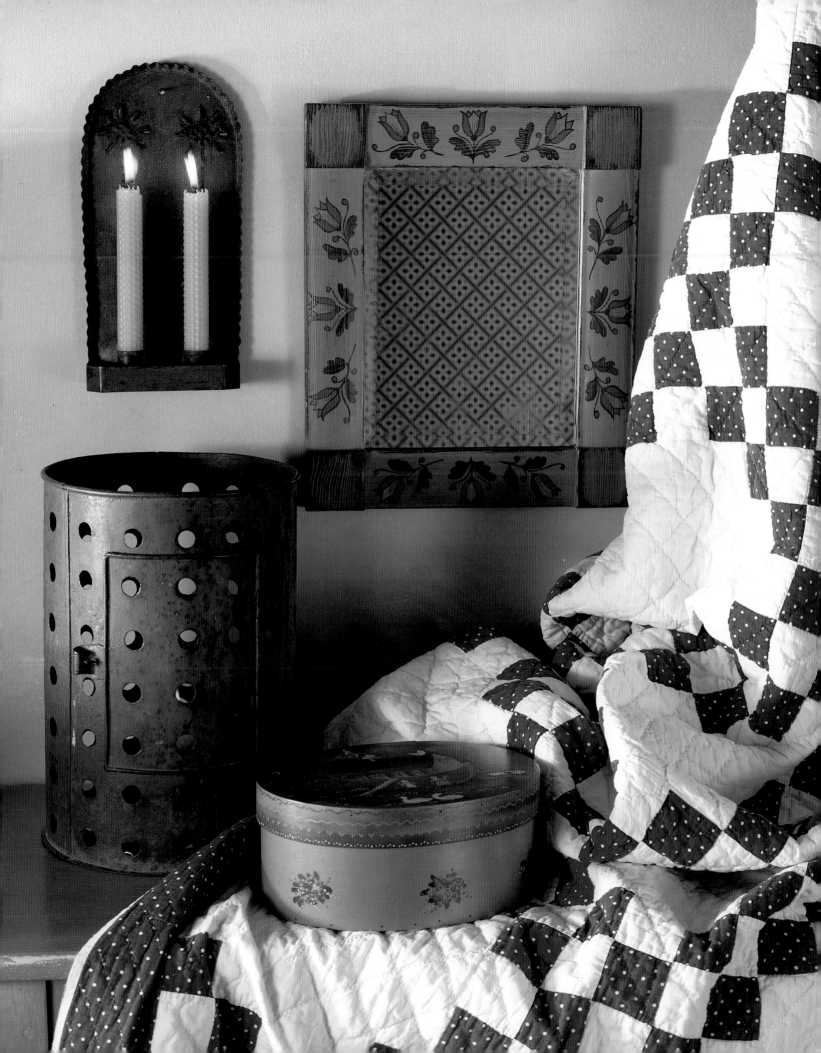

ART FROM NECESSITY

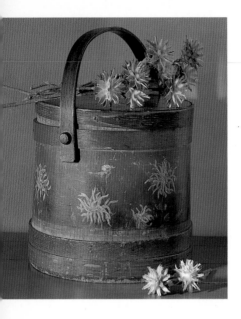

THE RUSTIC NATURE OF MOST FOLK ART COMES FROM IT BEING A LOCAL ACTIVITY. FOLK ARTISTS WERE NOT WEALTHY PEOPLE, AND THE MATERIALS THEY USED WERE USUALLY FOUND WITHIN THEIR LOCALITY. FINE, EXOTIC WOODS SUCH AS MAHOGANY WERE, FOR INSTANCE, SIMPLY NOT AVAILABLE TO THEM, SO THEY USED MORE COMMON PINE, AS WELL AS FRUIT WOODS SUCH AS APPLE AND CHERRY. LOCAL MATERIALS DICTATED THE STYLE OF LOCAL CRAFTS. FOR EXAMPLE, THE SAILORS WHO SAILED ON THE LONG WHALING EXPEDITIONS PASSED THEIR TIME BY CARVING WHALES' TEETH AND TUSKS, KNOWN AS SCRIMSHAW, AND ISOLATED WOMEN ON REMOTE HOMESTEADS SATISFIED THEIR CREATIVE URGES BY CONSTRUCTING BRILLIANT PICTORIAL HOOKED RUGS FROM STRIPS OF OLD RAGS.

Very little early folk art was made without a purpose – if someone needed a piece of furniture, a rug, an implement or a container, they made it, and the decorative elements were just a natural extension of their craftsmanship. Objects were made with the naive confidence that breeds creative originality.

Folk art was traditional in that it drew on the motifs, patterns, methods and styles that were the common property of the community, and before widespread literacy, everyone was required to learn traditional craft skills in the same way as they learnt to grow crops and tend animals. The boundaries between art and the rest of life were nonexistent, and traditional decoration was as much a part of a community's identity as their spoken language. In design terms most folk art is utilitarian, with form following function. There would have been no place in a household for articles whose decoration interfered with their efficiency.

Folk designs are as rich and varied as the cultures they represent, but if a generalization must be made then a folk style interior would have a slab stone or wooden board floor; walls of uneven texture painted with chalky earth colours featuring applied decoration; panelled doors and small paned windows. The floor coverings would be hand-woven hooked or braided rugs and the lighting would be low. The only form of heating would be the open fire or the cooking range and the insulation would depend upon the climate. In colder climates the winters were long and the furniture and household items were heavy in form and decoration, while in warmer regions a lighter, more ventilated style was practical. The heavier traditional folk style of Bavaria, for example, is very different to the airy style of sunny Provence in the south of France, but each is well suited to the particular climate and lifestyle of the region.

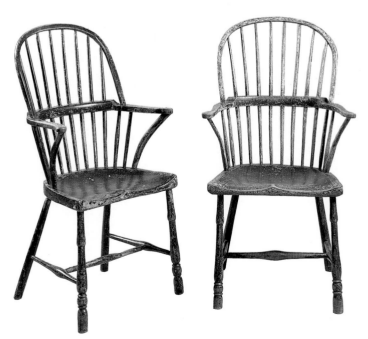

Above: The Windsor chair is both practical and elegant.
Top: A wooden box painted with floral decoration.

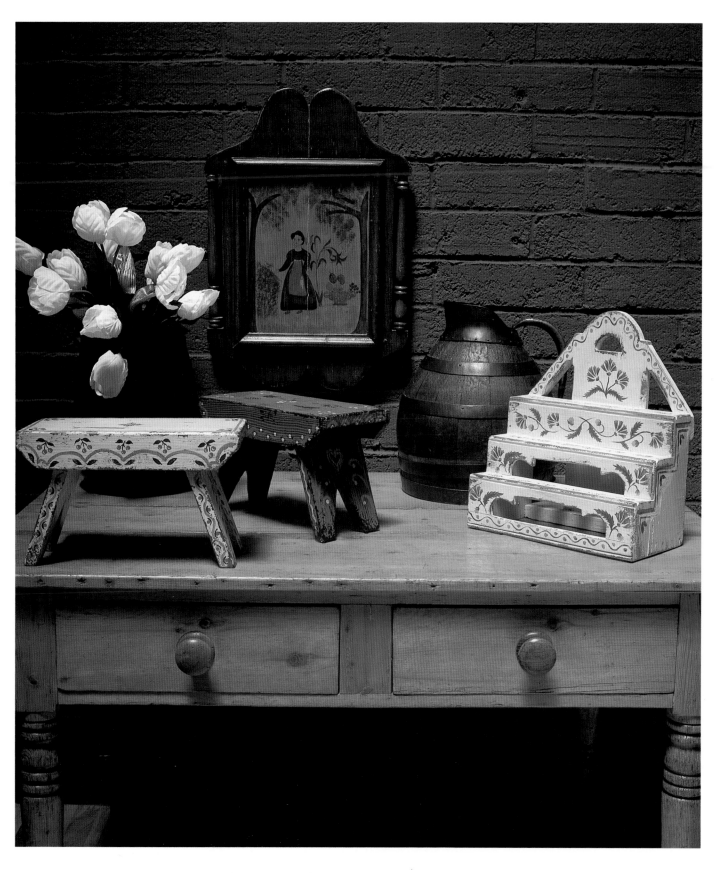

A collection of painted reproduction country furniture and objects,
made in Somerset, England.

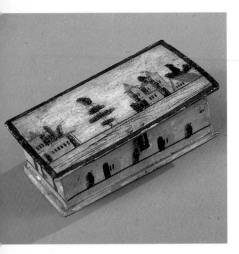

AMERICAN FOLK ART

THE SETTLERS WHO SAILED TO AMERICA IN THE EARLY SEVENTEENTH CENTURY HAD NOTHING BUT THE LAND TO TAME. THEY CAME FROM CIVILIZED COUNTRIES AND BROUGHT WITH THEM A RICH CULTURAL HERITAGE AND SPECIALIST SKILLS COMBINED WITH A STRONG DESIRE TO MAKE A BETTER LIFE FOR THEMSELVES AND THEIR OFFSPRING. THEY SAILED WITH PEOPLE OF THEIR OWN NATIONALITY WHO SPOKE THE SAME LANGUAGE AND A BOND GREW BETWEEN THE STRANGERS AS THEY SHARED THE TRIBULATIONS OF THE JOURNEY.

It was natural that when the immigrants reached their destination, they continued to travel as a group until they found land suitable for a settlement. At first, the English settlers were predominant, with Dutch communities along the banks of the Hudson River, but the settlers who were to have the greatest influence on the development of folk art were the Germans who settled in Pennsylvania, New

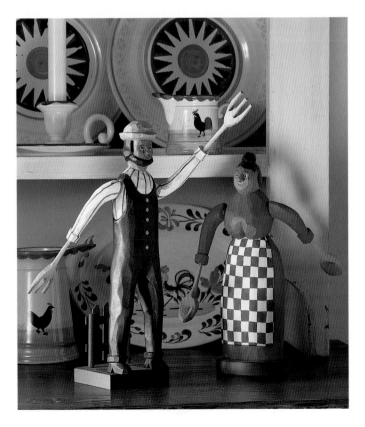

Above: Whirligigs are wind-driven toys.
Top: A painted and decorated American box.

England and North Carolina. Initially, all the settlers remained within their national groups but intermarriage and trading gradually caused the cultures to mix.

Early American folk art was essentially European and each community retained the traditions of its particular homeland. The Germans more than any other group continued to make furniture, textiles and crockery in the style of their homeland for many generations, and it is sometimes only the indigenous American woods that distinguish their objects from those made in Alsace, Switzerland or Germany. There were also devout religious groups such as the Shakers, Amish and Mennonites who chose not to integrate; instead they formed strong communities of their own where they appreciated the freedom from religious persecution which America granted them. The Shakers were of a break-away religious movement who were driven out of their native England and found refuge in the New York area. Their designs demonstrated their belief in harmony, regularity and order, and austerity is their trademark. The Amish and the Mennonite communities survive today, but very few Shakers remain to take the credit for the distinctively plain and practical style of furniture which their community developed, and which is now world famous.

· When the settlers built and furnished their homes, they used building procedures and tools they had brought with them from their homelands, or made modified versions of the tools to better suit the new environment. Naturally, not all men were skilled builders and carpenters, but most were craftsmen whose roles were less clearly defined than

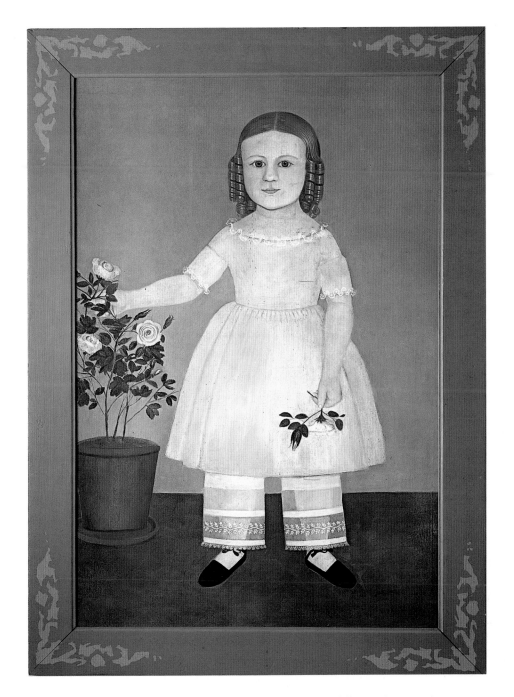

Portraits are one of the most popular forms of American folk art. They provide
a record of the American people, from before photography became widespread.

in later years, and a practical man was able to turn his hand to most things.

The woman's role as homemaker was paramount. Men built the structures but it was the women who softened the edges with textiles, painted furniture and decoration. Large families were hoped for, with the boys helping their fathers on the land and the girls learning their life-skills from their mothers. The children lightened their parents' workload, and provided the incentive needed to build for the future.

Many of the early American folk art objects probably travelled over from Europe with the settlers, but as soon as a certain level of comfort had been achieved craftsmen began to design and make new furniture and household accessories. The chests, cradles, weathervanes, butter-moulds and other objects would all have been designed in

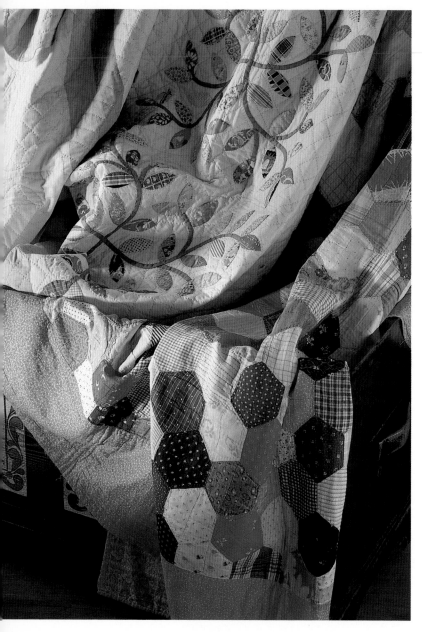

their freedom – the flag, the eagle, the Lady Liberty and George Washington – were now subjects which nobody seemed to tire of and after that, any new invention that improved people's lifestyle could be seen reflected in contemporary folk art. Similarly, the coming of the railroad brought irreversible changes to the continent, making travel and trade possible over long distances, and the locomotive too became a favourite folk art subject.

The glory-days of American folk art were from 1750 to 1850, before industrialization took hold with its side-effect of obsolescence. When everything was hand-made, decoration was a natural extension of the making process and objects were handed down within families, mended when broken and never abandoned until beyond repair. Everything was made to last as long as possible and to give pleasure to the user by the nature of its decoration. It was art made in the home, for the home.

American folk art has undergone a revival in recent years and has attained a value beyond anything the humble men and women who made it could ever have imagined; but it is right that it should be preserved for the nation, and in 1961 the Museum of American Folk Art, New York City, was opened to the public, as a permanent showpiece for these humble treasures. Today folk art pieces are exhibited around the world, fetching high prices in auctions, and more accessible reproductions of these wonderful objects are now widely available.

An American appliquéd quilt (c. 1940), and a late-nineteenth century pieced quilt from Pennsylvania.

A side chair decorated with simulated woodgraining, and stencilled and free-hand patterns, c. 1835.

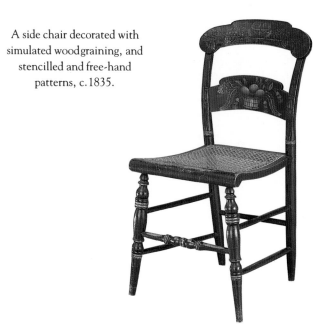

the material from which they were made. There were no drawn plans to translate and this gave objects an appropriateness of form for function. Practicality was balanced with beauty as the new Americans began to make things to suit their own tastes and requirements, rather than simply to follow the dictates of custom within the community, as was the case in much European folk art.

With the creation of the Republic in 1776, America's new citizens felt a surge of creative energy which expressed itself in almost every area of their lives. The symbols of

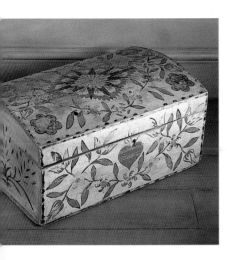

THE EUROPEAN TRADITION

THE FOLK ART OF EUROPE WAS ESSENTIALLY THE ART OF THOSE PEASANTS WHO REMAINED ILLITERATE SERFS AND TENANTS UNTIL ABOUT THE SIXTEENTH CENTURY, WHEN SOME WERE GRANTED THE RIGHT TO OWN LAND AND TRADE FREELY. STYLES WERE TRADITIONAL AND DID NOT CHANGE MUCH OVER THE YEARS, BUT GREAT ART MOVEMENTS SUCH AS THE ROMANESQUE, GOTHIC AND RENAISSANCE AND LATER ROCOCO AND EMPIRE, DID FILTER THROUGH TO PEASANT ARTISTS.

The effect of great art movements on folk art varied from region to region, with particular styles finding more favour in some areas than others. The Norwegian Viking style blended with the Romanesque style, which remained dominant for centuries, but it seemed to lack appeal for their Swedish neighbours, whose greatest artistic and cultural influence came from the Italian Renaissance.

Although the major force of these movements was felt in the towns and cities, there were always tradesmen and itinerants who spread new ideas as they travelled between the towns and the isolated farm communities. French folk artists were always less isolated than their counterparts elsewhere in Europe because of the way French society worked. Towns and markets were great meeting places where the country people would take their produce to sell and stay to socialize and exchange gossip and ideas. Their folk art never existed in isolation and did not vary so much from region to region, but found its inspiration in the popular styles of the upper classes, which country people imitated in a distinctively rustic manner.

National boundaries have little to do with defining the communities who make a particular style of folk art. They are political divisions which are often decided by wars, whereas the people who live near these borders sometimes have more in common with communities on the outside than those on the inside. To cite one typical example, the much disputed French province of Alsace borders Switzerland and Germany and the people of Alsace have their own styles and traditions which are a unique blend of all three cultures. They have suffered many wars and have seen the national boundaries move from one side to the

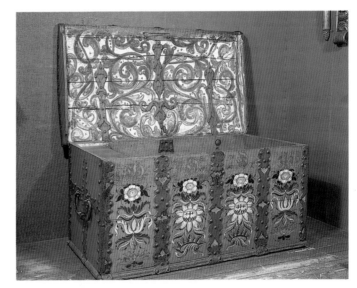

Above: A brightly painted Norwegian chest.
Top: A French marriage casket, c. 1770.

other over the centuries. It was often for reasons such as this that many Europeans emigrated to America, and thousands of Alsatians emigrated to America in 1870 rather than endure newly imposed Prussian rule. One famous man who fled to exile in Paris, Auguste Bartholdi (1834–1904), created the Statue of Liberty to represent the freedom that he and his countrymen were denied.

SCANDINAVIA

Scandinavia is geographically separate from central Europe and the folk art of the region reflects this. Heavily forested land made wood the most plentiful material for buildings, furniture and household objects. The Viking influence lasted many centuries and social structures did not alter much until the Reformation, which brought religious changes but never quite extinguished the primitive belief in magic and superstition. The woodburnt patterns found on kitchenware and farm equipment are made up of ancient runes and magic symbols from the prehistoric past.

One style that is synonymous with Norway is *rosemaling* (literally rose painting), which may have begun as a painted imitation of ornate Romanesque woodcarvings. The *rosemalers* who travelled the towns and countryside painting their distinctive floral brushstroke designs were not academically trained artists, but self-taught tenant farmers who discovered they had skills that were worth exploiting. This is one area of folk art where a style filtered up from the peasants to the elite, rather than the other way around.

There was a strong tradition of embroidery among Scandinavian women and many customs surrounded marriage and the particular garments or household linens that were made for the celebrations. There were finely embroidered shirts for the groom, fine lace caps and kerchiefs for the bride, as well as woven coverlets, embroidered sheets, towels, pillowcases and cushions. All cloth was homespun from flax and decorated with traditional patterns and motifs that mixed ancient characters from saga and fable with religious symbols, local emblems and dates and initials. Flemish weaving patterns were absorbed into

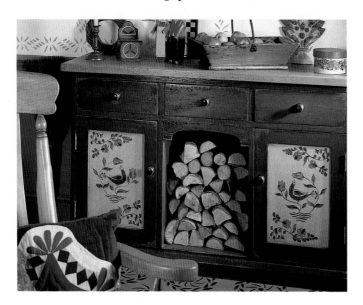

Dog's kennel dressers were designed so that dogs could sleep in the middle section of the chest.

Scandinavian folk art, and the influence is particularly obvious in the colourful embroidery that was used to decorate another marital offering, the marriage cushion.

GERMANY

In Germany, as in most folk cultures, there was also a great exchange of traditional gifts to celebrate a marriage, the largest being the dower chest which a bride took with her to her new home. Other articles, such as mangle boards, the equivalent of our washing machines, were intricately carved by the groom as a gift to his new bride. A home was filled with equipment in the form of handcrafted love tokens.

In the north of Germany most furniture was made out of oak and never painted, and it is sombre-looking compared with the painted pine of Bavaria, which shows the influence of Renaissance inlay work in its decorated panels. The subject matter was usually naturalistic — flowers in urns, birds on flowering shrubs, sunflowers, grapes and the tulip which was often shown with three stems. This is the folk art style that the immigrants took with them to America, where it became known as Pennsylvania Dutch and achieved a far wider recognition than it ever knew in Europe.

ENGLAND

Some of England's folk art skills similarly thrived better when transplanted to the fertile soil of the New World, the most notable example being the art of quiltmaking. The patchwork quilt, which arrived as a seed of an idea, grew into a brilliantly coloured tree of many branches.

English carpenters did not make elaborately decorated furniture like their European cousins but, instead, specialized in a simple country style that can be seen as the roots of the Shaker style which developed later in America. The simplicity of designs gave them a timeless quality, and some, such as the Windsor chair, are still made today and retain their original character. Another graceful folk character was the grandfather clock, with its long cabinet supporting a large clockface decorated with country landscapes and shipping scenes.

There was no real tradition of furniture painting in England, the exceptions being the painted caravan art of the gypsies and the bargeware produced by canal boat

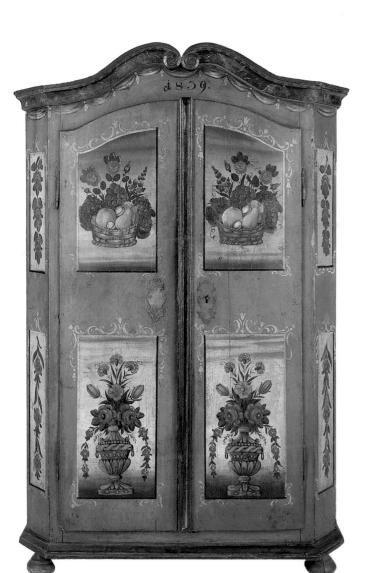

A nineteenth-century cupboard, probably made in
eastern France, near the border of Switzerland.

made into plates, bowls and dishes which are painted and
decorated with animals and flowers in brilliant glazes.

Pottery was also the greatest achievement of the Italian
folk artists whose history in this area goes back to
pre-Christian times. Styles varied between districts, but
one particular design can still be found in production,
unchanged over three centuries – a distinctive Venetian
pottery that features the seasons and months of the year.
In other areas, drinking vessels and oil lamps were
traditionally made in human and animal form, and with
Christianity came another symbolic shape, that of the
fish. Cooking was done in glazed terracotta ware and each
region had its own style of decoration for eating and
drinking vessels.

Italian folk painting was largely of a religious nature; in
particular there was the custom of painting plaques to be
displayed in the churches of pilgrimage. The plaques
represented hopes and prayers, and promised devotion in
return. Other folk painting surrounded the *commedia
dell'arte* – the travelling troops of entertainers – and the
trade and inn signs of the market towns where their shows
were performed. Perhaps though, the form of folk painting
that most belonged to Italian country people was the
traditional decoration of farm carts. Each area adopted a
different style, but the most spectacular examples were
from Sicily where the cart was covered with carving,
scenic panels and brightly painted patterns. The carts of
Tuscany, by way of contrast, were painted a simple brick
red while the Romagnese examples featured paintings of
the Madonna, and St. George slaying the dragon.

Traditions of the European folk artists have so many
regional variations, they stand as evidence of people's
need for both individuality and conformity. Families and
communities banded together and declared their identity
by means of dialect, costume, colours and decorative
devices. Attributing a particular style to any country is
difficult, because each locality had its own unique form of
folk art expression.

Today, as in eighteenth-century America, traditional
folk art often flowers among immigrant communities.
Strangers in strange lands, their folk art allows them to
share their cultural memories, and reassures them with the
familiar symbolism that reaffirms their identity and binds
them together.

people; and neither of these groups were in fact typical of
English countryfolk as they came from isolated travelling
communities.

SOUTHERN EUROPE

Southern European folk art shows a strong Catholic
influence, and much of it is devotional, although it still
bears all the hallmarks of traditional peasant art with its
bright colour and exuberant interpretation. In southern
Spain the Moorish influence from North Africa pervades,
while the more typical Spanish style of bright floral
pattern is seen farther north and on the Balearic Islands.
Furniture is still carved and painted, and pottery, the
traditional form of expression for Spanish folk artists, is

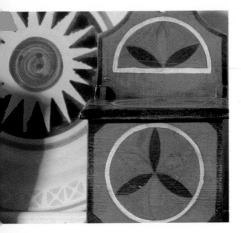

THE MOTIFS

THE MOST FAMILIAR MOTIFS USED IN FOLK ART HAVE BECOME HIGHLY STYLIZED, AND ALL HAVE THEIR OWN SYMBOLIC SIGNIFICANCE. CERTAIN MOTIFS, SUCH AS THE HEART, APPEAR IN THE FOLK ART OF MANY CULTURES AND THEIR MEANINGS REMAIN CONSTANT. THE AMERICAN SETTLERS RETAINED THESE SYMBOLS BECAUSE OF THEIR EUROPEAN ANCESTRY, AND IN EUROPE IT WAS THE SPREAD OF CHRISTIANITY, AS WELL AS THE COMMON LIFESTYLES OF THE PEASANT PEOPLES, WHICH PLAYED A PART IN THEIR DEVELOPMENT.

There are many interesting definitions attached to common symbols, but with constant use the shapes were conventionalized and refined to the point where their original meaning lost significance and they became simply design elements. In Sweden, for example, the letters AM were used in reference to the Madonna for many generations, until they became just a part of the pattern women used for embroidery.

Religion provided the symbolic meaning for many folk motifs: for example, the sheep represented Christ's flock, the peacock stood for the Resurrection and the five-pointed star announced the birth of Christ. The tree of life had its branches reaching up to Heaven and its roots down to Hell, and Adam and Eve were often featured with it.

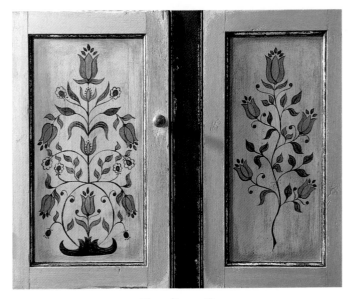

The tulip motif.

Secular motifs often represented love and friendship. The stag was associated with gentleness and pride, the owl with wisdom and the parrot with gossip. The lion illustrated strength and the dog fidelity.

THE TULIP

The tulip was the most popular of all floral motifs. The plant was introduced to Europe from Asia in the sixteenth century and achieved tremendous popularity in England and throughout the Low Countries and Germany. The bulbs were traded almost as a currency, and the fashion for them took hold to such an extent that the term *tulpenwuth*, literally "tulip madness," was applied. A religious significance has been attributed to the use of three tulips which are thought to represent the Trinity, and this may account for the popularity of the motif among the devout Pennsylvania Dutch.

FRUIT

A basket of fruit represents love and the cornucopia spilling out a variety of fruits shows the rich bounty of nature. Both were popular as stencilled images, used in theorem painting and bronzed Hitchcock chair decoration. The pomegranate, which also featured heavily in old Turkish designs, often appeared on painted tinware. The rich red fruit with its plentiful seeds was a symbol of fertility and immortality. The apple was never forgiven for the temptation of Adam in the Garden of Eden and was used to signify evil. The acorn, often featured with oak leaves in border patterns exemplified strength and endurance, and the grapevine referred to Christ.

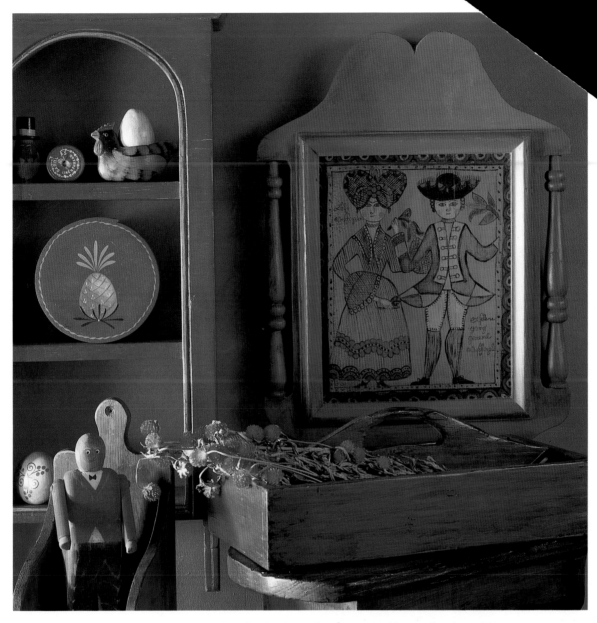

A reproduction portrait of Lord and Lady Washington inspired by a *Fraktur* from 1800.

The Folk Man and Woman

These figures appear in folk art throughout Europe and America and the only real variation is in the costumes they wear. A couple together symbolizes the union of marriage and is often featured on traditional wedding gifts. A man alone stands for marital fidelity and a woman on her own, often holding a palm branch, is the symbol of life and fertility.

Patriotic America

The bald eagle with its wings outstretched was approved by Congress as the national emblem of the USA on June 20 1782. (One notable voice in opposition to this was Benjamin Franklin who favoured the turkey because he felt it was a more respectable bird, more truly a native of America and more deserving of the honour.) Folk artists immortalized the eagle in every possible medium, and it was the most popular subject by far in nineteenth-century America.

The American flag was an overnight success with folk artists and the red and white stripes with white stars on a blue ground seemed adaptable to many forms, and could be mixed up in countless ways without losing their power as a symbol. Almost any combination of the essential elements can be read as the American flag. Whirligigs,

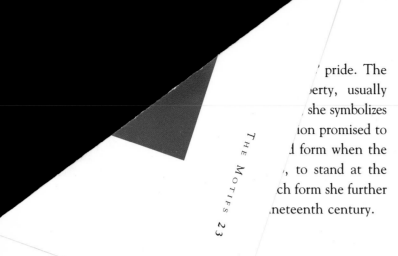

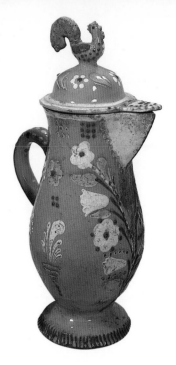

A French jug displaying the rooster.

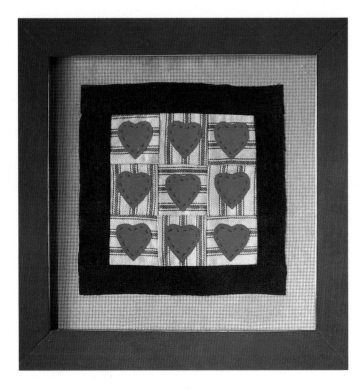

A modern appliqué picture, showing the heart, the symbol of love.

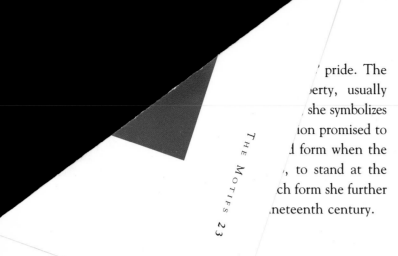

...pride. The ...erty, usually ...she symbolizes ...ion promised to ...d form when the ..., to stand at the ...ch form she further ...neteenth century.

The hea... ...ny folk cultures and can be seen on costu... ...objects and furniture all across Europe, from Engla... ...o Eastern European countries such as Romania. The Scandinavians were particularly fond of the heart motif and a red heart is still one of the most popular Danish Christmas decorations. The heart shape varies a lot, but remains recognizable whether cut from paper in a *scherenschnitt* from Switzerland or chip-carved out of wood in a Dutch cutlery holder. The heart symbolizes divine love and love between men and women, and as many decorated folk objects were given as tokens of love the heart was the most appropriate motif.

THE ROOSTER

The rooster's symbolic significance dates back to Christ's prophecy to St. Peter in the Bible. He said that Peter would deny him three times before the cock crowed twice. Peter's denial was marked by the crowing of the cock and when he heard it his faith was reaffirmed. As such the rooster was seen as an appropriate form for the weathervane, declaring the faith on the rooftops, outlined against the sky. In American folk art the rooster was celebrated for its pride and beautiful plumage, and the motif's religious significance became less important as time went by.

GEOMETRICS

The compass-drawn pinwheel designs can be seen on painted chests, boxes and, on a larger scale, on the barns of the Pennsylvania Dutch. Known as hex marks, they were used to ward off evil. They were painted in white on the red barns but on the furniture the general colour scheme dictated their colour. Itinerant stencil painters favoured many such compass-drawn patterns and mixed these up with naturalistic images, such as the willow tree or pineapple, framed within border panels. The Scandinavian chip-carvers used a lot of geometric motifs on their traditional betrothal gifts.

THE PINEAPPLE

The pineapple is the sign of hospitality. In Ancient Greece the resin from pine-cones was applied to wine casks, to give flavour to retsina. It became associated with generosity and conviviality. The Georgian period saw a Classical revival and the pine-cone was replaced by the pineapple, having similar characteristics but a better decorative shape. The motif was much used in New England and although the historical meaning was known, its decorative qualities alone would have been enough to ensure its popularity.

THE BASKET

The basket motif was particularly popular with embroiderers who used it in samplers to display flowers. The basket pattern used for pieced quilts dates back to the early nineteenth century and is still a favourite with quiltmakers today. The pattern uses contrasting triangular patches for the body of the basket, with a single curved patch handle. The pieces are used to construct diamond-shaped blocks. The symbol of the basket probably signifies the act of "giving."

FLOWER

Most flower motifs have become highly stylized over centuries of use, but in folk art even the most static of traditional floral shapes has life and individuality.

The carnation is one of the oldest floral motifs, particularly popular in Turkey on rugs and textiles. It shares its symbolic meaning of Divine love with the rose.

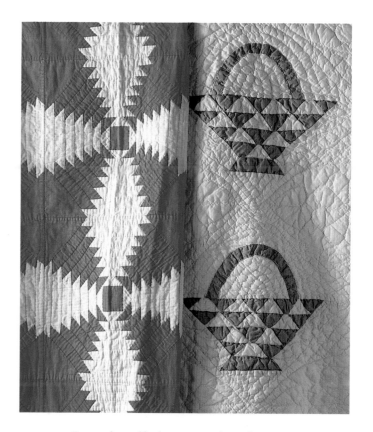

Pineapples and baskets are popular quilt patterns.

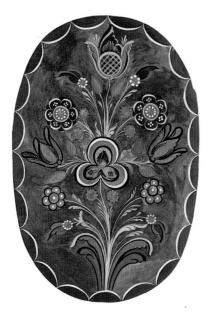

Floral design from Rogaland, Norway, 1827.

The Tudor rose was also a symbol of England, and was used there, interwoven, as a border pattern. The lily is the "flower of heaven" and proclaims purity, while the daisy stands for humility and honeysuckle was used to avert evil. The Amish were fond of the forget-me-not and the pansy, both of which were used in their rug and sampler patterns. Flowers were often used purely for decoration, with simple unidentifiable floral shapes arranged and coloured with no thought to their symbolic significance.

There are many more folk motifs, some with symbolic meaning and others associated with particular areas or professions. Motifs such as the mermaid or the unicorn have their roots in magic and legend and the sunburst has always given people cause for celebration. Sailors produced a wealth of art and craft work, and the Native Americans, among many other indigenous communities, have a rich and wondrous folk art of their own which demands more attention than a general book can give.

Whatever the source of inspiration – tradition, patriotism or nature's bounty – it is the unsophisticated and vibrant use of the motifs that gives them their unique folk art character, and allows them to retain their appeal.

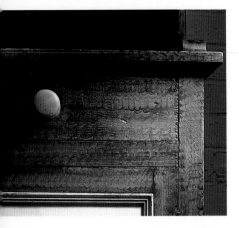

FOLK PATTERN

ALL THROUGH HISTORY YOU WILL FIND THAT THE SAME PATTERNS HAVE BEEN USED AGAIN AND AGAIN BY DIFFERENT CULTURAL GROUPS. PROGRESSIVE ARRANGEMENTS OF SPOTS, SQUARES, TRIANGLES, CROSSES AND CHEVRONS APPEAR WITH STRIPES, EITHER STRAIGHT, WAVED OR ZIG-ZAGGED, USED VERTICALLY, DIAGONALLY AND HORIZONTALLY. THESE ARE THE BASICS OF PATTERN MAKING, AND EACH CULTURE HAS ITS FAVOURITE NATURALISTIC AND COLOUR ELEMENTS TO ADD.

European and subsequently American folk art pattern is quite sophisticated and styles can be traced back through the Renaissance and earlier Romanesque periods to Classical Rome and beyond that to Ancient Greece. The influences of these great cultural upheavals spread across the continents and permeated even the remotest folk cultures. In the north, the Viking influence passed down through generations and the patterns of ancient runes and symbols were never relinquished in favour of popular new patterns from the south; these were simply assimilated and the decoration became all the richer.

The stencilled wall paintings of New England feature stylized festooned columns and this pattern can be traced back through England and France to the wreath-clad pillars of the Roman Empire, which themselves echoed the floral garlands and harvest offerings that were draped around the columns in Ancient Greece.

Cross-stitch sampler patterns were often derived from oriental carpets; patterns copied by one culture, whose subsequent embroidery motifs were incorporated into another country's folk art, and in this way little girls in America sewed the same carnation borders that had been woven into the rugs of the Ottoman Empire.

The character of a pattern is influenced by the medium to which it is applied so that a linked border of leaves woven on a loom, or embroidered in needlepoint, takes on the angularity of the grid upon which it is worked, and so stencilled swags are far more static than those which are hand-painted.

In American folk decoration pattern was used in the same way as conventional wallpaper with the addition of columns, friezes and panels to break the monotony. It was considered perfectly acceptable to mix several patterns and have, for example, a frieze which imitated a rope of leaves combined with a swag and bell tassel running along below it. The verticals could be blocks of diagonal stripes and the skirting pattern a wave of oak leaves and curved stems. All of these patterns together would make panels which could then feature a combination of large single motifs such as pineapples, pinwheels and sunbursts. A contemporary decorator would need exceptional confidence to convince a client to accept such a hotchpotch today. These pattern arrangements worked, however, and their success was due both to the charismatic nature of the application and to the limited, harmonious palette that the painters used.

The woodgraining and marbling of folk furniture was not intended to deceive but rather to give a richer look to something plain. After the excavation of Pompeii there was a great surge of interest in Classical patterns and inlays in Europe. Folk artists who used turkey feathers to paint imitation marble, and sponges and combs for woodgraining did so with their unusual vigorous lack of pretension, not in the least intimidated by the glory of Rome, or the grandeur of European cabinetmaking.

Folk artists drew upon centuries of pattern-making history but were still in touch with many of their pattern elements; after all a tulip may have had deep symbolic meaning but when a man walked in his garden and saw a row of them waving in the sunshine, their suitability as a decorative device in his home was obvious.

Top: Paint effects can give a richer look to something plain.
Opposite: Bedcovers displaying typical folk patterns.

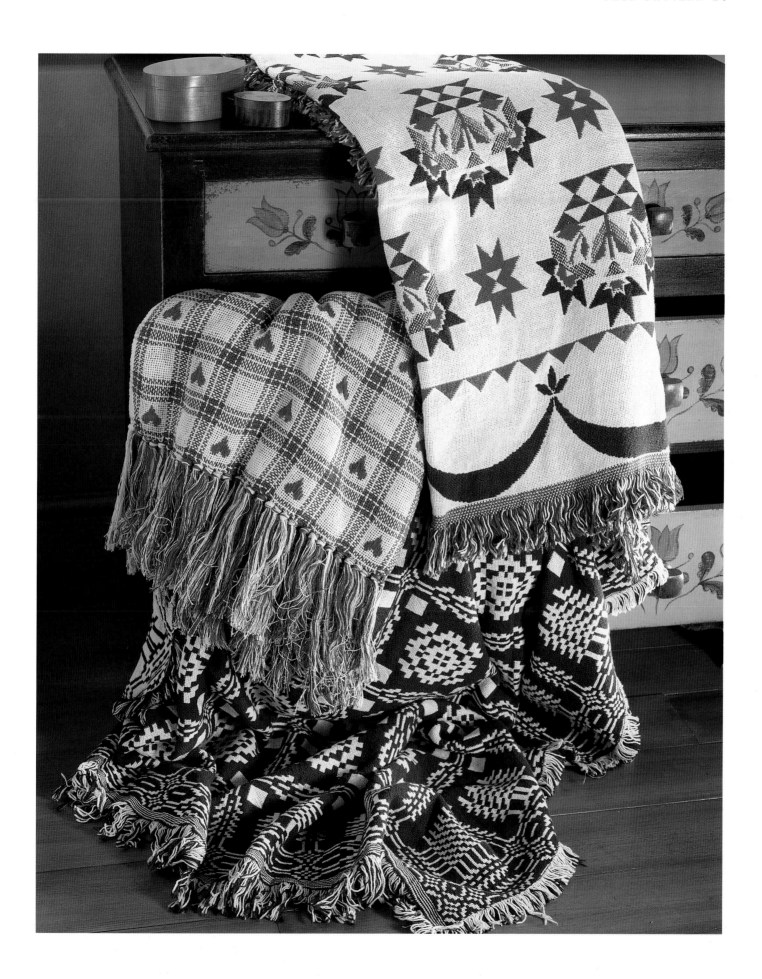

FOLK COLOUR

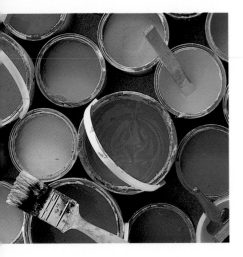

THE VERY EARLIEST FORM OF FOLK ART MUST HAVE BEEN CAVE PAINTING, AND IT IS APPARENT FROM SURVIVING EXAMPLES THAT PREHISTORIC MAN KNEW HOW TO MAKE COLOURS FROM NATURAL PIGMENTS. THEY MADE BLACK, WHITE, YELLOW AND RED OCHRE, AND THEY CERTAINLY MADE THEM TO LAST! THE FOLK PALETTE USED FOR THE PROJECTS IN THIS BOOK INCORPORATES THESE SAME COLOURS WITH THE ADDITION OF GREEN – WHICH ANCIENT MAN MAY WELL HAVE USED, BUT BEING A PLANT DERIVATIVE IT DID NOT HAVE THE LONGEVITY OF THE EARTH COLOURS.

The manufacture of paint pigments was a long and complicated procedure, taking days to prepare each colour from a range of ingredients. The resulting pigment had still to be mixed into a medium such as oil, varnish or skimmed buttermilk before being used as paint.

Among the natural colour sources the roots of the madder plant made a deep red, boiled walnuts gave a rich dark brown, boiled chestnuts produced a buff brown, and powdered brick dust and baked yellow clay both made a reddish brown. Differing shades of yellow came from flowers or clay and black was mixed from soot.

EUROPEAN COLOURS

In Europe, the regional differences were more apparent in the colour schemes than in the folk motifs. In Norway, the *rosemalers* used a restricted palette to identify their work. Thus the men from Hallingdal painted in bright colours with predominant red shades while their neighbours in Glomdal only used shades of blue-green, with the slightest of highlights for contrast. The *rosemalers* demonstrated the great passion for colour and pattern that is commonly found in people from northern snow-covered landscapes. Bavarian folk art features the green of the forest and contrasts it with bright red, and in southern Europe the backgrounds are often white with flashes of yellow or blue, like the ripened fruits, the sun, the sea and the sky. Surrounded by living colour they had less incentive to decorate their homes and furniture with heavy pattern and colour, although in churches they did this to the glory of God.

AMERICAN COLOURS

The early American folk palette is made up of vermilion, brick red, deep red, straw yellow, pumpkin yellow, yellow ochre, dull green, sage green, dark green, red ochre, medium brown, black, white and grey. These are the colours that were used before "shop paint" became available, but oddly enough, even after manufactured paints became available a lot of customers still requested colours they were familiar with, so suppliers continued with the colour scheme that nature had provided. Some of these colours were easier to come by, and being cheaper to produce in large quantities, they became the background colours – for example yellow ochre, off white and plaster pink, which were then highlighted with stencilled pattern in greens, blues, vermilion, red, pumpkin yellow or black.

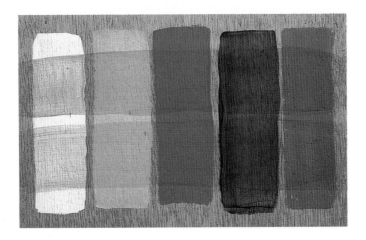

All colours can be mellowed with tinted varnish.

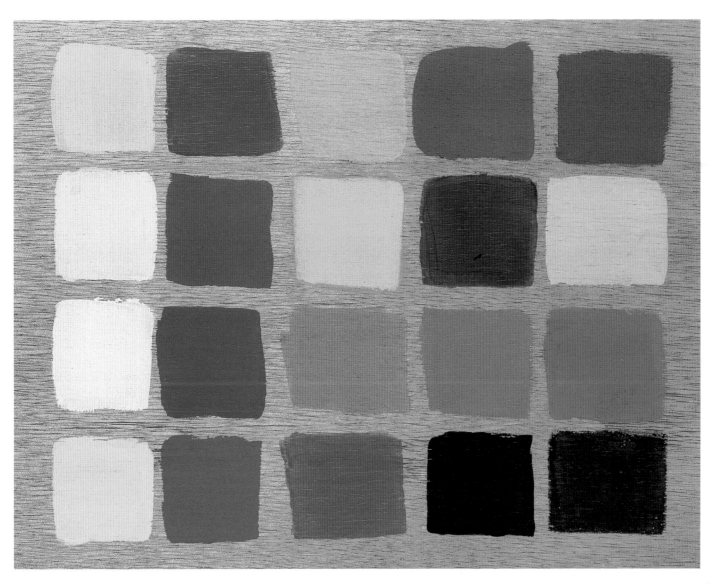

This bright patchwork features the most popular colours in the folk art palette.

These days most paint companies have expanded their colour ranges to include an in-store mixing facility which enables the customer to match any shade they choose, so there should not be a problem finding folk colours among the huge array on offer. When selecting shades for a folk interior look at an old quilt, a piece of painted furniture or any folk art object to find a colour combination that you find particularly pleasing. Choose, for instance, your background colour from the traditional range of ochres, pinks or creamy whites, and then stencil or paint the pattern with your favoured colour combination.

The colours of old folk art pieces will in fact have faded with age, or if protected by varnish, then they will have yellowed to dull the colour beneath. The result is a soft,

warm colour that is very appealing. Newly painted walls can look clean and fresh, but also rather clinical, so if you want a soft effect apply a colourwash, which is several coats of thinned emulsion (latex) paint, brushed on with random strokes to give a slightly patchy finish. This is, of course, a means of creating folk art colours as they appear now, rather than as they would have looked when they were freshly applied.

In a similar way, on smaller objects and furniture a small amount of colour can be added to the first coat of varnish to achieve a mellowing effect. The colours most used to tint varnish are raw umber and burnt umber over the colder colours such as blue, green and white, and raw sienna and burnt sienna over the yellows, reds and browns.

INTERIORS
AND
FURNITURE
WALLS • DOORS • CHESTS • CHAIRS

THE RUSTIC NATURE AND SIMPLICITY OF FOLK INTERIORS AND furniture have an enduring appeal and they have never been more popular than they are today. This revival of interest is partly due to the fusion of the eminently practical and the exuberantly visual nature of folk decoration.

The soft harmonies of the colours of the walls and stencil patterns are complemented by the massive armchairs, with their simple turned front legs and solid backs, sawbuck tables and long benches, and open cupboards and painted chests, which are all sturdy, practical pieces of furniture, many of which have stood the test of time. Often decorated with brilliant colours, folk furniture displays, as much as other smaller objects in the home, the folk artist's inherent love for pattern and colour.

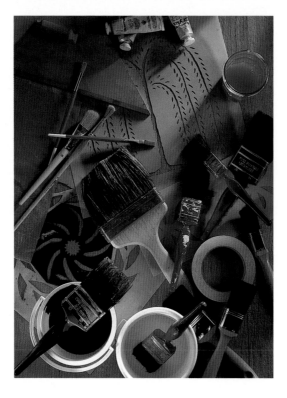

You will find the stencilling and patterning much easier if you have a good range of paintbrushes.

Opposite: A corner cupboard from Alsace, France, 1830.

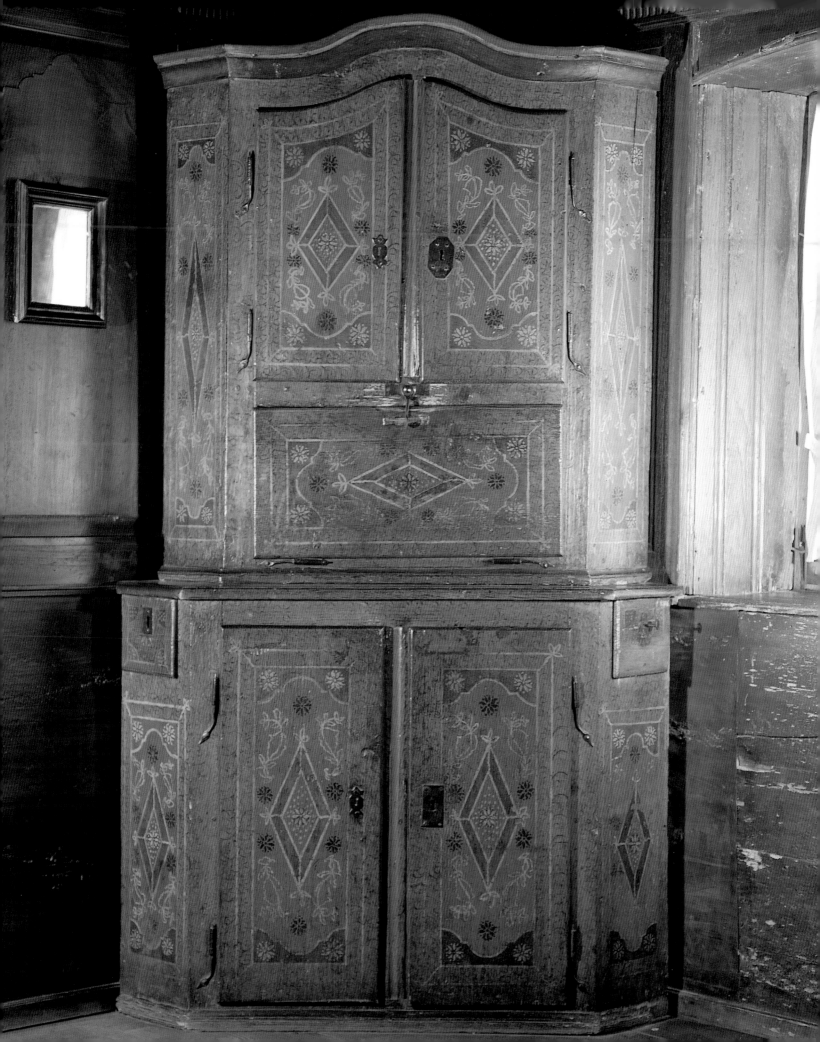

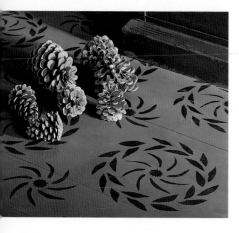

FOLK INTERIORS

No doubt early folk artists would have been delighted to choose from the vast array of decorating materials available today, but instead, they had to invent their own materials. They brewed up the most extraordinary concoctions from diverse and unlikely ingredients. As these early paints were neither hard-wearing nor damp-proof, walls had to be redecorated time and again to prevent them from becoming chalky-textured and faded.

PAINTS AND PAINT TECHNIQUES

The most common decorating materials were plaster made from crushed oyster shells mixed up with sand and seawater, producing a monotonous beige wallcoating which the decorator then covered either with a whitewash made from quicklime or, alternatively, with a forerunner of modern emulsion (latex) paint ingeniously made from a mixture of strained stale buttermilk, sifted river sand and vegetable pigment.

Oil paints had been used in Europe since the fifteenth century, but they were expensive and not widely available. The early settlers in America borrowed skills from the Native Americans who knew how to extract oil from walnuts and mix colours from different earths. Flax, grown to provide linen for clothing, was also a source of linseed oil, an excellent paint base into which the earth colours, vegetable pigments and minerals such as verdigris were blended. Advertisements in newspapers for ground powder colour pigments to be mixed with oil, show that by the early eighteenth century innovative decorators in North America had found ways of making superior oil-based paints.

These new paints changed people's attitudes to home decoration and soon specialist painters were in huge demand among the better-off settlers. There was a strong European tradition of graining – the painting of common woods like pine to look like rare mahogany or walnut – particularly among the Dutch who were expert painters. Marbling also became popular as the real stone was far too heavy and costly to be transported from its source. Specialists would work from small samples of marble, copying the colour and adding the veining with the stiff tip of a feather.

Expert grainers and marblers were expensive to employ however, and, with a growing demand for special effects, new and simpler techniques were soon invented to give similar results more cheaply. In fact, some of the most charming examples of faux painting of the time were done by amateurs who made little attempt to reproduce wood or marble faithfully, with results that were more like copies of copies, unconstrained and full of fun.

Other new paint effects included "stippling," "ragging," and "glazing." Glazing involved applying two coats of paint, the first a flat colour which was left to dry before being glazed with a different colour top coat. The glaze was made of buttermilk applied to a base of coloured oil paint which would resist the coating and form a raised pattern on the surface, which would then be varnished to a high sheen. Stippling was done by jabbing at the wet paint with a coarse bristled brush to remove specks of the top coat and allow the background colour to show through. Ragging or mottling was similar except a piece of cloth was used in place of a brush, with more of a rolling movement to remove some of the paint. Many of these old painting techniques have now been revived, and are extremely fashionable, as is stencilling, also a very traditional form of folk decoration.

Stencilling was often used by folk artists to decorate walls and floors, with both simple stylized motifs and

Opposite: An old farm kitchen or living room in
Sweden, displaying a wide variety of painted objects.

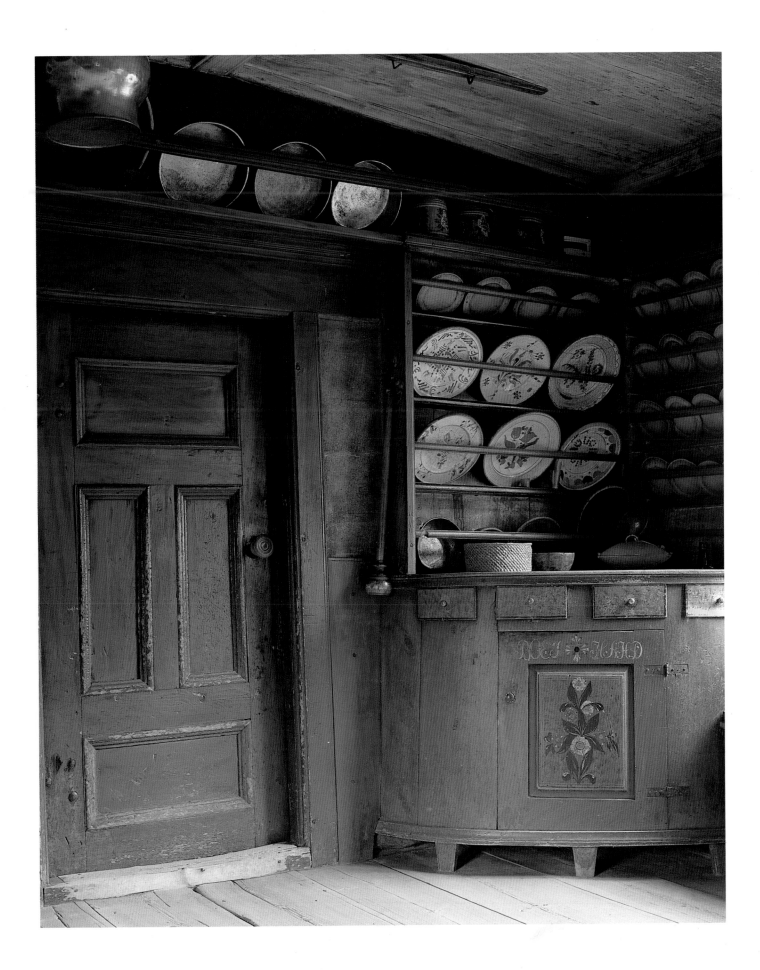

geometrical patterns repeated around the room. The stencil was introduced to Europe from the East and became a very popular form of church decoration during the Middle Ages. Richly coloured patterns were applied directly to plastered walls or wooden screens, often featuring gold embellishments which were added by stencilling a pattern of adhesive to hold the gold in place. Sometimes stencils were also used to introduce mock architectural features such as dado (chair) rails, plaster friezes and panelling, and also to emphasize existing ones such as doorways, window frames and mantelpieces.

In France, stencillers called "domino painters" travelled around the market towns painting and selling sheets of playing cards and patterned papers which were used as a crude form of wallpaper. Later special wallpapers were produced which had woodblock outlines filled with stencilled colour or purely stencilled coloured patterns.

The "Busy" Folk Style

Up until the sixteenth century, the majority of European peasants lived in extreme poverty, but after that date they began to see a gradual improvement in their circumstances. Homes had been very basic structures made of clay, wood and stone, with furniture consisting mostly of planks that were raised off the ground by means of trestles to make tables, benches and beds. As the burden of poverty eased, rural craftsmen began making peasant furniture out of local woods which were carved or painted in imitation of the furniture of the wealthy classes. Great pride was attached to owning furniture, pottery and tin or silver plate, and all were displayed in the home – most European cultures had strong marriage customs which involved the showing-off of all exchanged gifts. The "busy" decorative folk style sprung from a combination of improved circumstances and the desire to show the family's social status, along with a natural love of colour and decoration.

Folk art was not generally recognized as being valuable until the 1920s and for this reason, sadly, few original interiors remain. There are however, some excellent points of reference, thanks to the cult of the family portrait. Many early nineteenth-century families considered it important to have a portrait painted to signify their social status. The family would be pictured seated in the parlour wearing their finest clothes and surrounded by

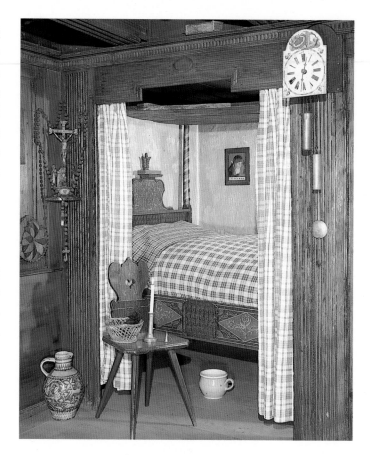

A living room in Alsace, France, 1796.

their best furniture and ornaments, with every detail of the home decoration recorded. It was thought far more important for the picture to stress the family's respectability than to achieve any sort of personal likenesses: letters survive in which portraits were commissioned by post, with a list of possessions to be included in the picture and a very general description of the family members to be featured; no sitting was in fact required.

These family portrait paintings clearly reveal the riot of colour that was flamboyantly applied to all the surfaces of a room. Add to this the decorated furniture, patchwork chair throws, painted tinware, glassware and braided and hooked rugs, and you begin to get an idea of the richness and vibrancy of the folk art style. To decorate your home in this style it is important not to be too precious – in fact this is one style where bumpy plasterwork and sloping floors are a positive advantage. If your home is perfectly sound and symmetrical, however, colourwashing will soften any hard edges, particularly if you choose a colour scheme to harmonize with one featured folk art piece such as a patchwork quilt or a painted chest.

PAINTING WALLS

This first project shows you how to set the scene for your folk art interior by colourwashing the walls ready for stencilling. Up until the 1950s the only water-based paint for interior walls was distemper, which was uneven in texture and gave a poor covering. New paint technology has solved these problems for the modern decorator, but if you are trying to reproduce a folk style, you need to re-create the soft, patchy background of old-fashioned distemper; you can do this by colourwashing.

In this technique the base coat is white matt emulsion (flat latex), either freshly applied, or washed down for a grease-free surface. The colourwash is made by mixing four parts water to one part emulsion (latex) in whatever quantity you need for the whole room. It is important to mix it all at once, as colour variations will occur in different batches, and also you need to work quickly with a wet colourwash to get the right effect; by stopping to remix you would risk spoiling the final finish.

You will need:
- White matt emulsion (flat latex) paint
- Cream matt emulsion (flat latex) paint or whatever colour you require for the wash
- A paint kettle or bucket
- A 6in (15cm) or 8in (20cm) brush (whichever is easiest to hold)

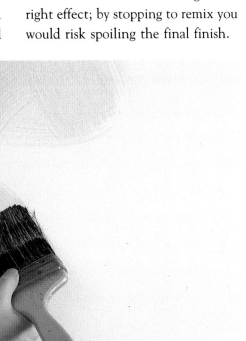

1 First apply base coat of white emulsion (latex) and allow to dry. Mix the cream paint with water in a paint kettle as described and brush on using random strokes over a small area, no more than 1 sq yd (1 sq m) at one time. Use the paint sparingly; do not overload the brush, or the colour will run. If this happens, pick up the run with the next brushstroke, rather than dabbing it with a cloth.

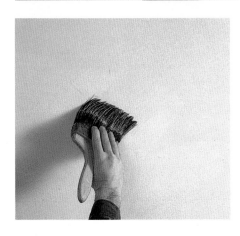

2 ◄ Apply a second coat in the same way on to the dried colourwash. This gives you the chance to go over patchy areas and blend them into the rest of the wall.

3 ► When the second coat has dried, if you are satisfied with the texture, you are ready to stencil, but if the colour needs further softening, dilute the wash with one more part of water and apply another coat using random brushstrokes.

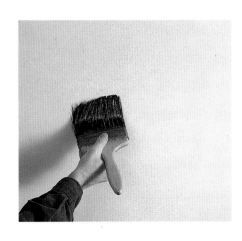

PAINTING DOORS

As with all other aspects of folk interiors, doors were often elaborately decorated with both painting and relief or chip-carving. Grand homes, palaces and churches set the style, which was copied on a humbler scale in the peasant homes of Europe from the Middle Ages through the Renaissance to the highly elaborate Rococo era. The materials used often affected the type of decoration – the heavy, dark oak doors of Germany were an ideal surface for carving, while the pine doors of Scandinavia were suited to painting.

Pine doors were painted because the wood was not deemed interesting enough in its own right. The design would have been mostly a symmetrical representation of flowers in a vase, with the style depending on the fashion of the day. Pine was also used for all internal walls, with little definition being made between the doors and the rest of the room's decoration.

Decorative door panels, stencilled or freehand, were a particular feature of Pennsylvania Dutch homes. The tulips that were so prevalent in their work were used throughout the Low Countries, Scandinavia, Holland, Germany and Eastern Europe. Other stencil motifs were often simple and stylized, with hearts, birds, fruit, flowers, ribbons and baskets all being popular.

Doors come in many shapes and sizes, with or without panels and mouldings. Follow the step-by-step instructions below, making adjustments to suit your own door, and the result will be true to the spirit of folk art – your own rendering of a traditional idea.

You will need:
- Matt emulsion (flat latex) paint: olive green, cream and brick red
- A medium-sized household paintbrush and two artist's brushes – one square and one pointed
- An enlargement of the pattern on page 148
- Tracing paper and pencil
- Stiff paper and scissors
- Low-tack masking tape
- A soft pencil
- A straight-edge
- Tinted or antiquing varnish (optional)
- Raw umber artist's acrylic (optional)
- Varnish brush (optional)

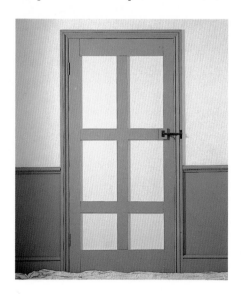

1 Paint the door surround and the door frame green, and when dry, fill in the panels with cream. If you are working on a plain flush door, you could attempt to create trompe l'oeil panels, or less ambitiously simply paint cream rectangles.

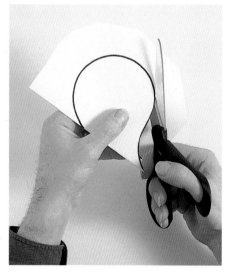

2 Trace the half-heart template (page 148) on to a folded sheet of stiff paper, cut and unfold. The panels on this door are 12in (30cm) wide and the heart is 7in (17.5cm) wide.

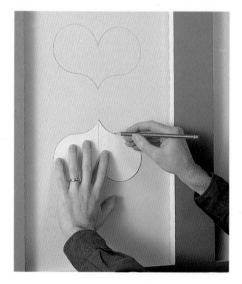

3 Position your heart on the cream panel, making sure that there is room for the inverted heart below, and stick it with masking tape. Draw around it in both positions using the soft pencil.

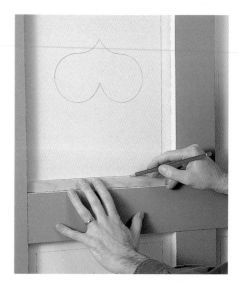

4 Use a straight-edge, such as a ruler, to draw a border around the panel; the example shown is 1in (2.5cm) wide. If your door has a moulding around the panels, you could leave this cream instead of drawing another border.

5 Fill in the red background using a square-tipped artist's brush, but use a fine-tipped one for the sharp points of the hearts. Try not to get too fiddly, or your painting will lose its vigour.

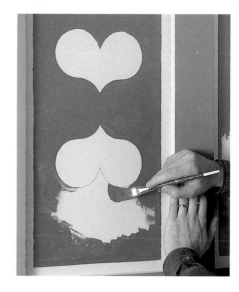

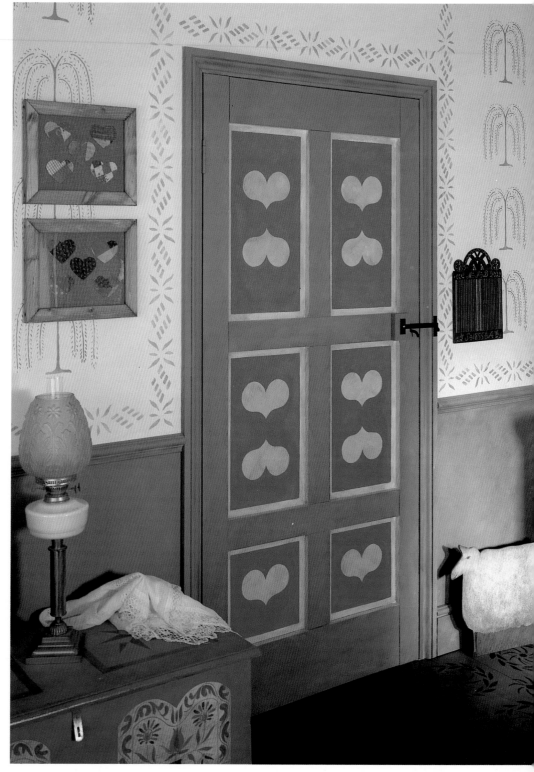

6 If you would like to "age" your door, give it a coat of antiquing varnish, either a proprietary brand, or mix your own. One small can (8fl oz/250ml) of water-based varnish will need a small amount of raw umber artist's acrylic colour – about ¾in (2cm) squeezed from an average tube – which must be thoroughly mixed. Simply paint all over the door and frame to dull the colours and also give the paintwork a protective coating.

STENCILLING WALLS

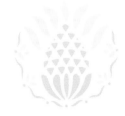

This combination of stencil designs is typical of those used by the itinerant painters who worked in the American colonies in the early nineteenth century. The stencils were painted on to coloured plaster walls using contrasting darker shades. Walls were divided by border patterns and larger single motifs filled the spaces between them.

When stencilling, there was little anxiety about whether patterns turned the corners accurately or whether two different borders blended where they met: it was the amount of decoration and the harmonious colour schemes that made the result so successful. Remember that while a printed wallpaper gives a regular pattern, the irregularities of folk stencilling will add to its authenticity.

If you cut your stencils from acetate they will be easier to align than stencil card, and a light spraying of an aerosol adhesive gives you just enough tackiness to hold the stencil in place while you apply the paint while allowing it to peel off easily.

You will need:
- An enlargement of the stencil on page 148
- Acetate sheet or waxy stencil card
- A craft knife or sharp scissors
- Spray adhesive
- A plumbline
- A spirit level or straight edge
- Stencil paint or artist's acrylics: brick red and dull green
- Two stencilling brushes – one for each colour
- Absorbent paper towel

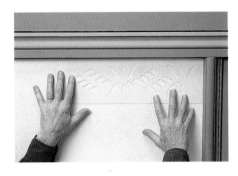

1 Cut out the stencil (see page 147). Spray lightly with spray adhesive and align it with either the picture or the dado (chair) rail. Alternatively you can draw a horizontal line as a guide, using a plumbline and a straight-edge at 90 degrees, but do check the horizontal with a spirit level.

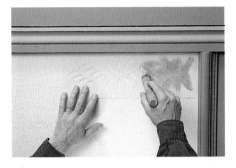

2 The very worst thing a stenciller can do is use too much paint. Put a small amount of colour on the brush – rub it on absorbent paper towel before you start – and then apply the paint using a circular motion. Do not try to paint solid colour; even the lightest covering stands out when you remove the stencil.

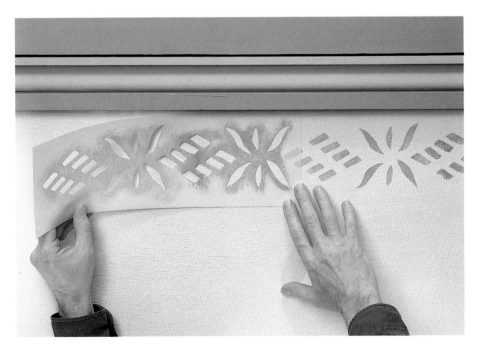

3 If your stencil is acetate sheet you will be able to see where the second stencil meets the first; if you are using waxy stencil card then place it above the first and lift the bottom corner to check that it is in position.

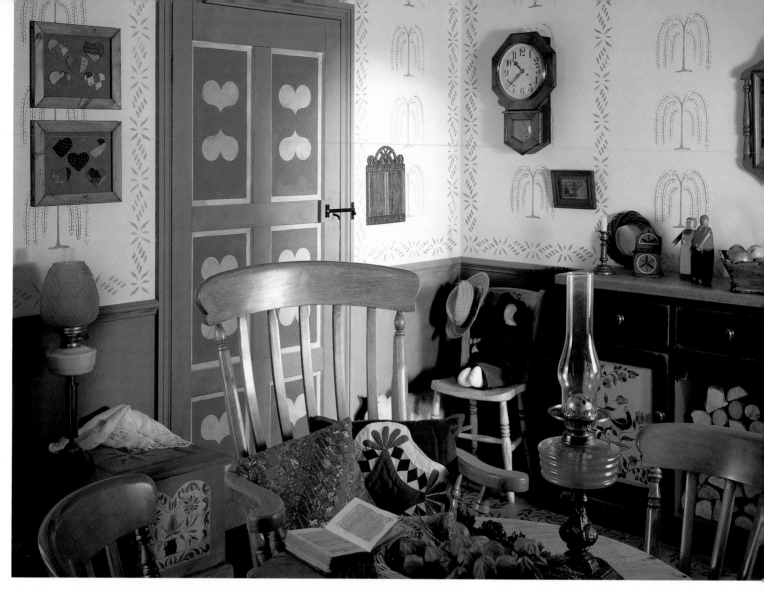

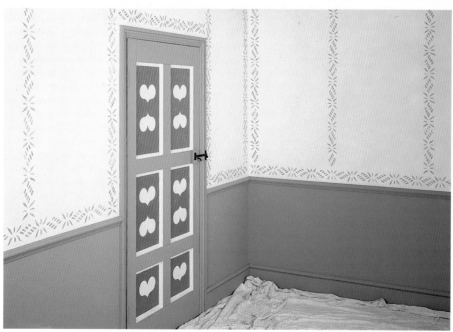

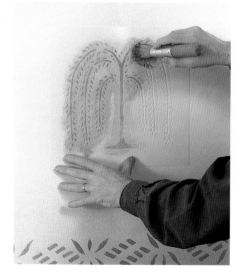

4 Turn the stencil to continue the border panels, using a plumbline from the ceiling to check the patterns are aligned.

Repeat to frame the room with as many panels as you need. This will depend on how busy you want the effect to be.

5 Stencil willow trees in the centre of your panels, one above the other. Again there is no hard and fast rule for spacing, although the willow looks best with a bit of space around it.

STENCILLING FLOORS

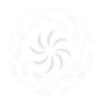

Floor stencilling began in imitation of expensive oriental rugs, in the same way that stencilled walls imitated the fine printed European wallpaper the colonists were unable to obtain. Some early Pennsylvania Dutch houses used oak flooring, but more usually floorboards were of pine which was painted with many layers of oil paint to prevent it from splintering, and then stencilled with borders and repeat patterns. These patterns were often more intricate and vibrantly colourful than those patterns on walls, and on a larger scale, sometimes 12in (30cm) wide.

It will take a long time to complete this project if you use slow-drying oil-based paint, but if you use emulsion (latex) for the base coat and pattern it will dry quickly and you can seal the floor with several coats of hard-wearing clear polyurethane varnish. Make sure you buy hard-wearing floor varnish; you can choose between matt (flat), semi-gloss and gloss finishes.

You will need:
- Sugar soap or all-purpose cleaner
- Olive green matt emulsion (flat latex) paint
- Two medium-sized household paintbrushes and a stencil brush
- An enlargement of the stencil on page 148
- A tape measure or a ruler
- Acetate sheet or waxy stencil card
- A craft knife or sharp scissors
- Spray adhesive
- Black matt emulsion (flat latex) or stencil paint
- Masking tape
- Hard-wearing polyurethane varnish

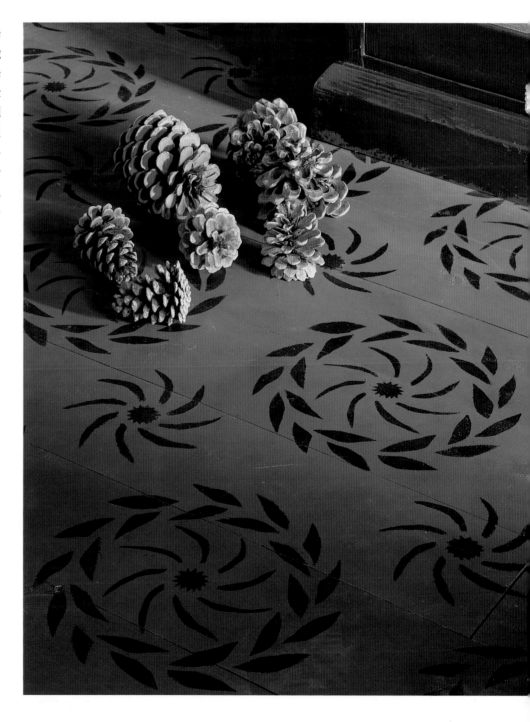

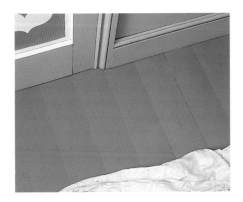

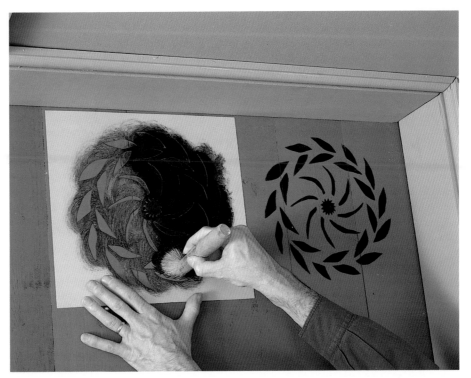

1 Prepare the surface for painting by washing with sugar soap or all-purpose cleaner, to remove any grease, and when it is dry, paint with green emulsion (latex). If you like a worn, old surface then thin the emulsion (latex) half and half with water and wipe it on with a cloth. The paint will stay in the grain and give a patchy effect. Otherwise, apply two full-strength coats. Allow to dry.

2 Measure your floor space to judge how many medallions will fit comfortably between each corner: if ten fit snugly, then it would be better to use nine and space them out a bit. Cut the stencils out of acetate or card (see page 147) and spray lightly with spray adhesive. Begin by stencilling a medallion in each corner and one midway between the two. Paint alternate sides of the central medallion, spacing by eye until you reach the corner motif. Use a circular brushstroke and if you have chosen the worn look for the background then match the stencilling to it by using light uneven strokes.

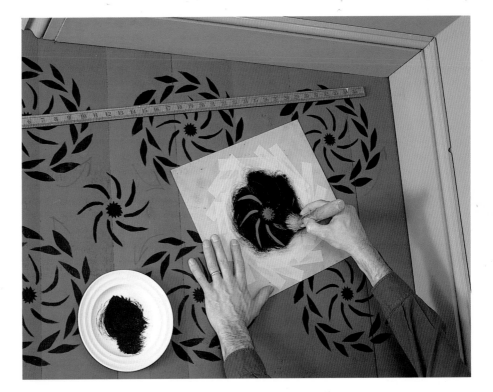

3 Stencil one row of medallions all around the room first, as these will act as a guide when positioning the other rows. The grid of large medallions can be broken up by using the centre of the motif between each block of four. Use masking tape to isolate the centre and make a smaller stencil to fill in the gaps. Finally, to preserve all your hard work, paint the floor surface with two or three coats of polyurethane varnish.

FLOORCLOTH

Floorcloths became tremendously popular in America during the eighteenth century, although very few early examples now survive because of the daily wear and tear they received. The ingenuity of the settlers was clearly demonstrated by their adaptation of sailcloth canvas which they painted to imitate chequered floors with marble or slate veining, or more often the geometrical designs of rich oriental carpets.

The floorcloth, which began as a substitute, soon became a fashion in its own right – old newspapers carry advertisements for ready-painted floorcloths as well as entries by tradesmen providing the service of carpet painting.

The stencil pattern (see page 148) of this floorcloth is adapted from an Amish quilt and the colours are also Amish inspired, but naturally you can use any combination. It is made from painter's canvas, available from any art supplier, and the surface needs priming with several coats of matt emulsion (flat latex) paint and sealing with at least three coats of varnish.

You will need:
- Heavy artist's canvas
- A craft knife or sharp scissors
- White acrylic primer or matt emulsion (flat latex) paint
- Two medium-sized household paintbrushes and stencil brushes – one for each colour
- Medium-grade sandpaper
- A pencil, ruler and spoon
- Strong fabric adhesive
- Acetate sheet or waxy stencil card
- Spray adhesive
- Artist's acrylics or stencil paints: blue, brick red, purple, light blue, dusky pink and light emerald green
- Clear water-based varnish
- Small tubes of raw umber and raw sienna artist's acrylic paint

1 Cut a piece of canvas 5ft by 3ft (1.5m by 90cm). Turn the canvas over and apply three coats of the primer or emulsion (latex). Rub lightly with sandpaper between coats. If you want to secure it, staple it down.

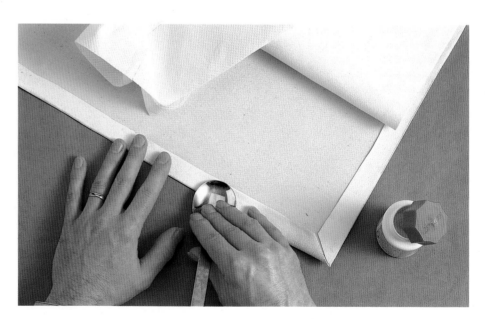

2 Draw a border 1½in (4cm) wide around the edge; mitre the corners. Apply strong fabric adhesive to the border and fold it flat, using the back of a spoon to apply pressure and smooth any bumps.

3 Mark out the pattern in pencil (see page 148) except for the stars, and paint the framework following the colour scheme.

4 Cut three simple geometric stencils from acetate sheet or waxy stencil card.

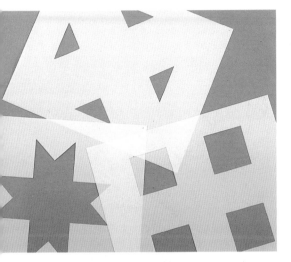

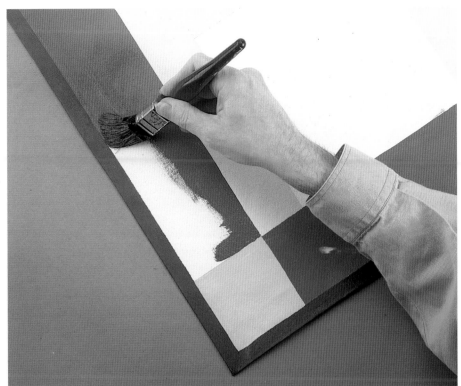

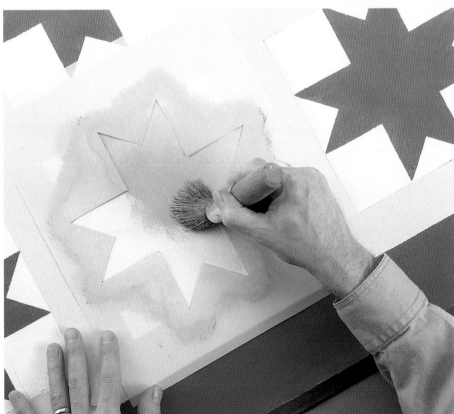

6 ▼ When the stars are dry add the purple and light blue triangles. Lightly spray the back of their stencil with adhesive and place it over the star, aligning the white space with the stencil cut-out. ▶

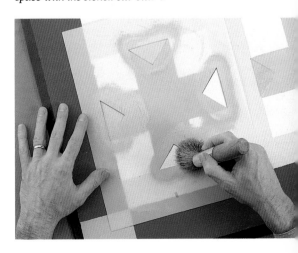

5 ▲ Stencil the red and blue stars in the centre of the large squares. Give the back of the stencil a light coat of spray adhesive to keep it in place as you paint. Use the paint sparingly on a dry brush but try to get a flat colour finish.

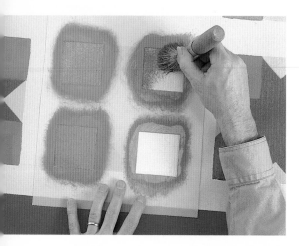

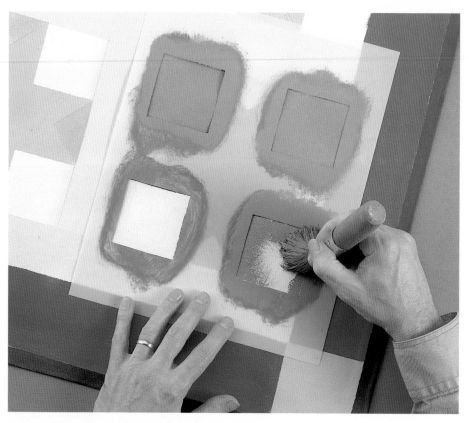

7 *The corner boxes are done in alternate colours. Begin by painting half of them using dusky pink.*

8 *Finish off the colour scheme by painting the rest of the corner boxes light emerald green.*

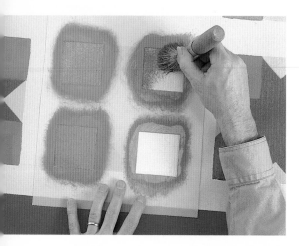

9 *Apply one coat of varnish tinted with a squeeze of raw umber and raw sienna acrylic paint to mellow the colours; then apply two coats of clear varnish, allowing adequate drying time between them.*

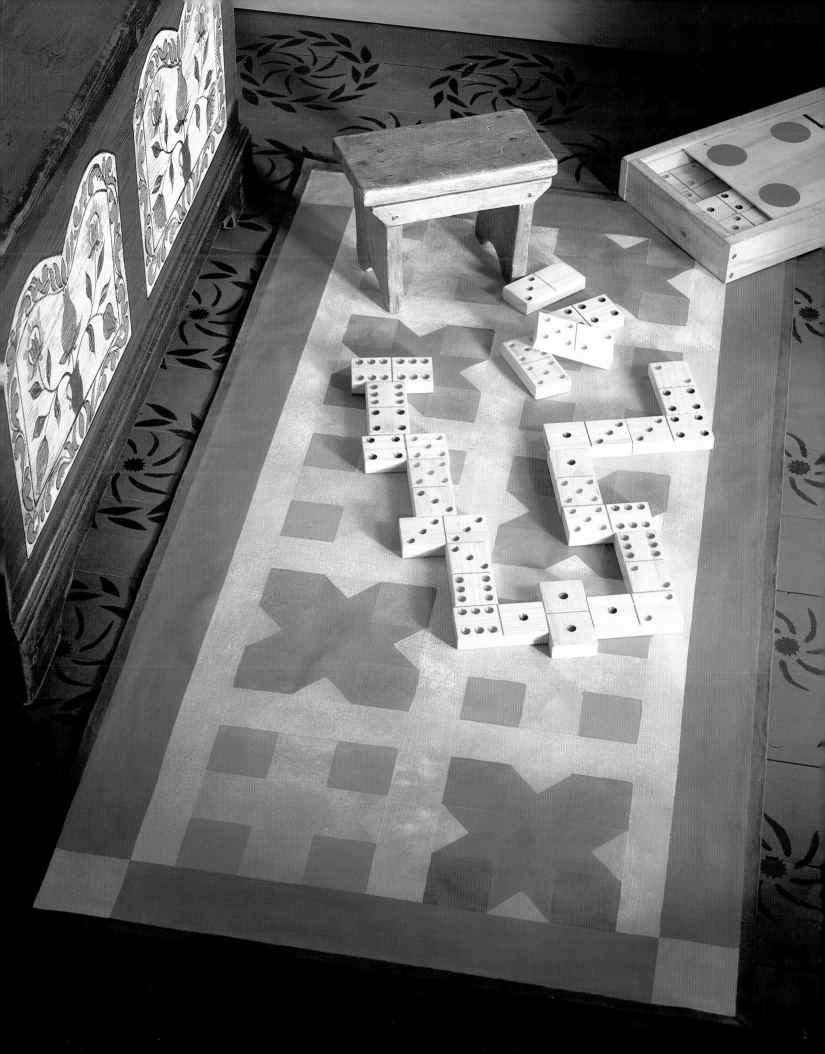

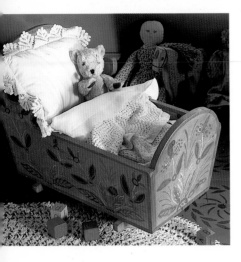

FOLK FURNITURE

MOST OF THE ARTICLES OF FURNITURE WHICH ARE NOW COMMON TO HOMES AROUND THE WORLD WOULD NOT HAVE EXISTED OUTSIDE THE WEALTHY CLASSES UNTIL AROUND 1700. PEASANTS USED PLANKS OF WOOD AS BENCHES, TABLES AND BEDS, AND EVEN THE CHAIR WAS UNCOMMON BEFORE THIS TIME. WHEN FOLK FURNITURE BEGAN TO BE PRODUCED IT VARIED ENORMOUSLY BETWEEN DIFFERENT AREAS. THE LOCAL WOOD SUPPLY WAS ONE OF THE MOST IMPORTANT DETERMINANTS OF THE STYLE AND DECORATION, WITH HARDWOOD BEING CARVED AND SOFTWOOD PAINTED.

The Scandinavians built much of their furniture into the walls, particularly the beds, which were still being built this way in rural areas up to early this century. In the Netherlands and Scandinavia during the middle of the eighteenth century the wardrobe took over from the chest as a storage place for clothing and household linen, although settler homes in America used such chests until a much later date.

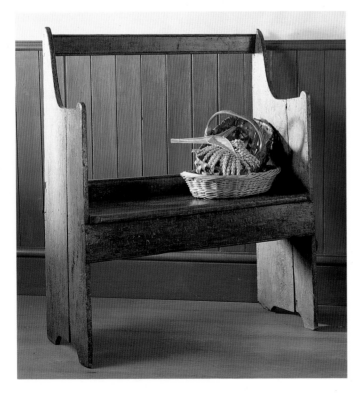

Small open-back love seat with shaped plank ends and old blue painted surface. British, c.1760.

One small item of furniture that was common to all European folk cultures was the cradle. It was made from wood and always lovingly decorated. In the mountainous regions of Italy shepherds decorated their cradles with carvings of animals, particularly roe deer. In other neighbouring regions painting protective religious devices such as the Lamb of God was popular. In Germany cradles are particularly noted for their variations in style, with some designed to rock from side to side and others lengthways. Those that were made in the south also tended to be lower than those from the north.

COLONIAL FURNITURE

Most early colonial furniture was copied directly from European patterns; in fact some early pieces are so like European prototypes that only the use of native woods identifies their origins. Walnut was sometimes used, especially for chairs, but plain timbers such as pine were also common and then the finished pieces were often painted over and decorated with stencilwork. Lavishly patterned painted furniture was especially popular with the Pennsylvania Dutch communities. For some religious groups such as the Shakers and the Amish, however, plainness was part of their way of life. Both these sects disapproved of decoration and ornament and although the Amish did paint their furniture, they allowed themselves mostly plain colours such as red, blue and yellow ochre, and the only patterning a subtle woodgraining.

Inspired Amish craftsmen such as Henry Lapp (1862–1904) still found ways of expressing their individuality

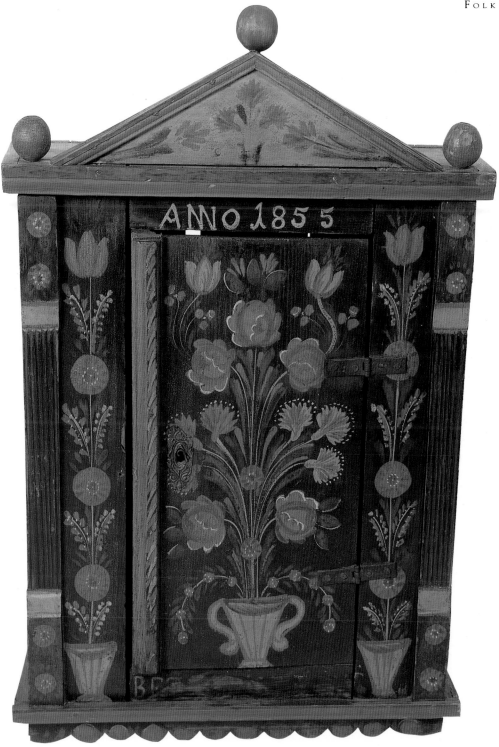

Wall cupboard from Hódmezövásárhely, Hungary, 1855. The motifs and colours
varied according to the region.

through exceptionally fine design and subtle, distinctive colour schemes. Lapp was a highly versatile carpenter who made items ranging from small sewing boxes and cutlery trays to large cupboards, bridal chests and drop-leafed tables. His drawer fronts often featured yellow woodgraining and the handles were of white porcelain, but the main exterior colour was a deep red with a contrasting duck-egg blue inside cupboards and drawers.

Shaker furniture is unpainted but recognizable for its superb practical elegance and wonderful craftsmanship. Their philosophy forbade the display of household or personal accessories, which were all stored in specially built units. Shaker homes often featured rails with pegs at picture-rail level from which chairs were hung when not in use. Although they mainly worked with pine, the Shakers also used fine-grained woods such as rock maple and fruitwoods like cherry and apple for furniture, and ash and hickory for bending into boxes. There is now a revival of interest in Shaker designs; although few Shakers survive, the design skills live on.

The one item of furniture common to almost all folk art culture is the dower or bridal chest, a large wooden box with a hinged lid to contain all the needlework that the bride had sewn in preparation for marriage. In Norway, even the poorest peasant families would provide a chest and wealthy families employed expert *rosemalers* who were famous for their distinctive flourishes and colourways. The Dutch favoured stencilled motifs of cherubs, ribbons, bowknots and opulent floral garlands, while the Pennsylvania Dutch who were mostly of German extraction, held the tulip in the highest esteem. Other popular motifs were the heart, turtle doves, ribbons, flowers and unicorns, which since medieval times had been regarded as the guardians of maidenhood.

Early colonial tables were often of simple, easily built sawbuck design, and cupboards (closets) were of an open style with shelves. Canvas sailcloth was used as a floor-covering, stretched over a padding of straw and tacked into the floorboards. This was then painted with many layers of oil paint to give it strength, before a painted pattern was applied as a final coat. When it came to chairs, most folk artists were happy to leave their construction to expert carpenters. Early lathes provided turned legs but generally chairs were simply designed. Massive walnut armchairs were made with solid backs and seats, while other chairs were either rush- or plank-seated and were often individually painted and stencil patterned. Large rocking chairs were made for women, to accommodate mother and child together. By the end of the seventeenth century inexpensive chairs were being mass-produced by rural craftsmen and larger town-based factories. Some of these styles, such as the Windsor chair, have endured to the present day.

Much wonderful painted furniture was discarded or destroyed in the name of progress during the Industrial Revolution. Mass production, assembly lines and new

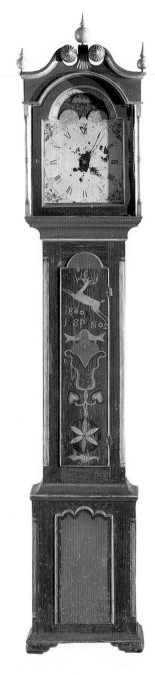

A tall case clock of painted yellow pine, c.1800, decorated by Johannes Spitler (1774–1837). The painted composition on the door is the least geometric of Spitler's known designs.

materials all contributed to the belittling of folk art furniture as family heirlooms. It is rare to find examples being used and enjoyed in homes today – surviving pieces are mainly in museums.

For the following projects you can use any plain country-style chair or chest to paint in folk art style. If you want to try the crib, but lack carpentry skills, you could make local enquiries – for a small fee woodwork teachers will often make up just such a simple piece. The floor-cloth, although not strictly a piece of furniture, but an early forerunner of linoleum, is fun to make and will add greatly to the authenticity of your folk interior.

PAINTED AND STENCILLED CHAIR

Painted and decorated chairs became so popular in the early 1800s that they were soon mass produced. One man, Lambert Hitchcock from Connecticut, was said to have employed more than one hundred chair painters at his factory, with the result that the Hitchcock chair became a generic name for all chairs of that style. A country-style kitchen chair is ideal for painting and stencilling: the curved backrail carries most of the pattern and the spindles, plank seat and turned legs all lend themselves to decoration.

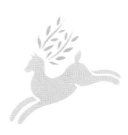

It is usually easy to find an old chair at a reasonable price. Use paint stripper to remove thick layers of old paint, or have the chair dipped. If existing paint is in reasonable condition simply sand it and apply a base coat. The stencil is a design from an American folk stencil sourcebook. Perfect lining with a paintbrush takes practice and it is important to relax your wrist. If your lines wobble a bit, do not worry, the other patternings will draw the eye away from less-than-perfect stripes.

You will need:

- Matt emulsion (flat latex) paint: pumpkin yellow and white, and brick pink (optional)
- Two medium-sized household paintbrushes, a stencil brush and a selection of artist's brushes – including a long-haired brush
- A cloth
- An enlargement of the stencil on page 149
- Acetate sheet or waxy stencil card
- Craft knife or sharp scissors
- Spray adhesive
- A selection of artist's acrylics or stencil paints
- Pale-coloured chalky pencil
- Fine-grade steel wool
- Clear water-based varnish
- Small tubes of raw umber and raw sienna artist's acrylic paint

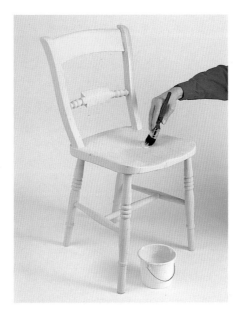

1 If your chair is bare wood, apply a coat of light pumpkin yellow (add a touch of white to lighten it); if you are covering old paint, first apply a coat of brick pink paint as a base.

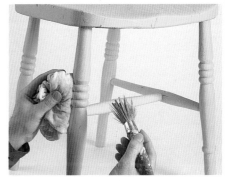

2 Thin the pumpkin yellow with equal parts of water and apply it to the chair. Use a damp cloth to wipe some of it off. It will remain in the grain to emphasize the mouldings. Cut the stencil from acetate sheet or stencil card (see page 147).

3 Spray the back of the stencil lightly with adhesive and position it centrally on the chairback. Apply the colours sparingly, rubbing the paint through the stencil with circular brushstrokes. ▶

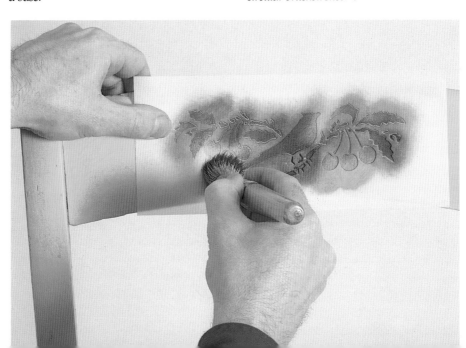

4 Use a pale-coloured chalky pencil to draw radiating guidelines in the centre of the lower chairback. Practise the strokes on paper using a long-haired artist's brush. Starting with the tip of the brush in the centre, draw it towards you, pressing down in the middle of the stroke to achieve a teardrop shape.

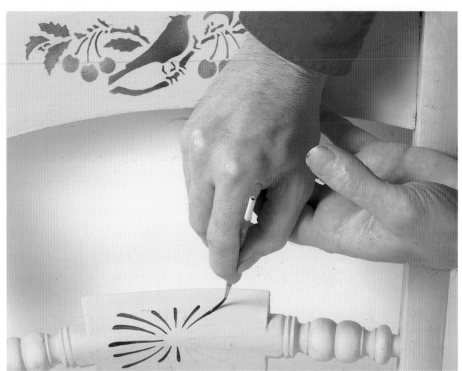

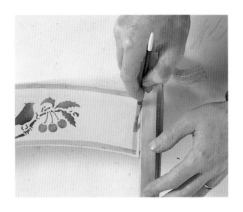

5 Line the chair with thick and thin stripes. Add water until the paint flows easily off your brush, and support your hand with your ring finger on the brush hand.

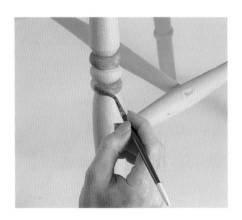

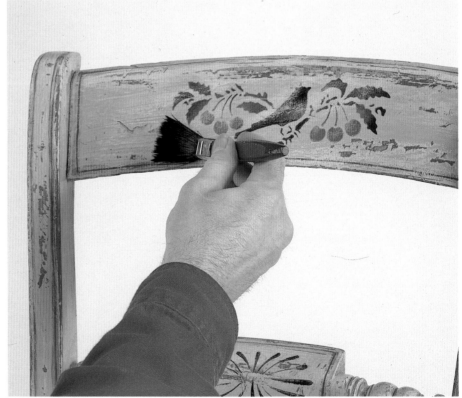

6 When lining, try to complete the whole line with one brushstroke. Begin with the shortest and least conspicuous lines, progressing to the more obvious ones as your skill and confidence grow. Add rings of colour to highlight any turned features, perhaps incorporating a colour from the stencilled pattern. The amount of lining depends upon the features of your chair.

7 Rub back the paint with fine-grade steel wool to simulate wear and tear. Try not to overdo it, just concentrate your efforts on the edges. Finally tint the clear varnish with a small amount of raw umber and raw sienna acrylic paint and apply two coats. Allow plenty of drying time between coats and then apply one last layer of untinted varnish.

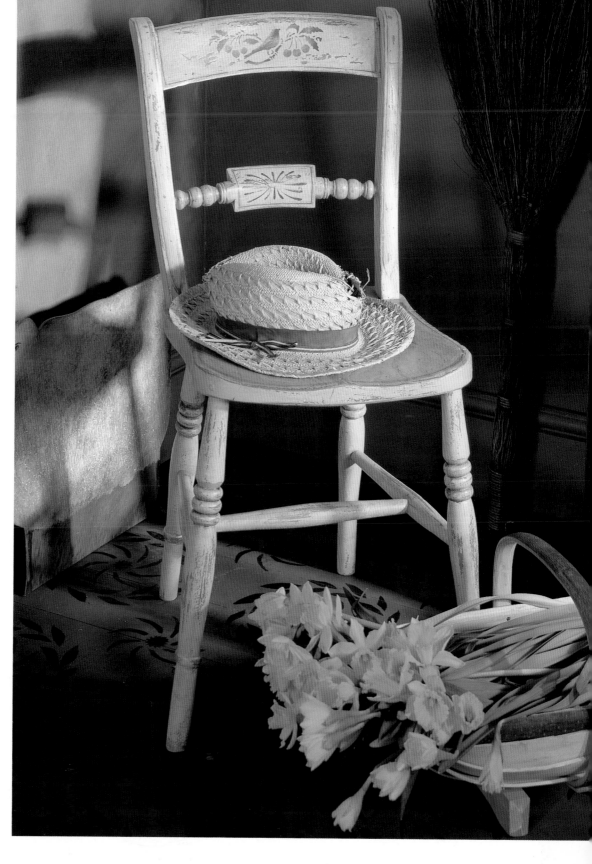

Below: This Hungarian chair shows how painted decoration can be applied more extensively. Adapt the patternings and stencils to suit your own chair and taste.

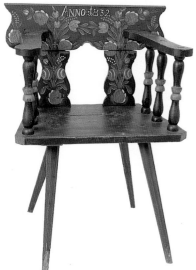

BRIDAL CHEST

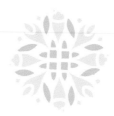

For hundreds of years all over Europe, a father traditionally would present his daughter with a painted chest when she married. The chest contained the needlework, linen and lace she had spent her girlhood preparing. In some parts of Europe, the chest was a present from the groom to his bride but, either way, dower chests were precious possessions and many remain in good condition today.

This design is based on traditional German chests which were painted with a dark background of red, blue-green or even black, and lighter stencilled decorative panels. A distinctive feature of many of these chests was the symmetry of the patterns. The tulip motif was a favourite of the Germans, and the Pennsylvania Dutch settlers.

You will need an old pine chest, or have one made up roughly to the proportions of a blanket chest and preferably with small feet. The chest illustrated measures 37in (94cm) long by 18in (46cm) wide by 12½in (32cm) high.

You will need:
- Matt emulsion (flat latex) paint: pumpkin yellow, dark reddish brown and creamy yellow
- Two medium-sized household paintbrushes and a selection of artist's brushes – a 1in (2.5cm) square-tipped brush and several fine-pointed brushes (nos. 2, 4 and 5)
- A cloth
- An enlargement of the pattern on page 149 drawn on tracing paper
- Chalky-backed transfer paper
- A soft pencil, a sharp pencil and a ruler
- Low-tack masking tape
- Artist's acrylics or stencil paints: reddish brown, red, brown, blue-green and yellow ochre

- A raised wooden batten (a straight-edged strip of wood). Cut two squares and tack them under each end. This acts as a guide for your brush for the striping
- Clear water-based varnish
- A small tube of raw umber artist's acrylic paint

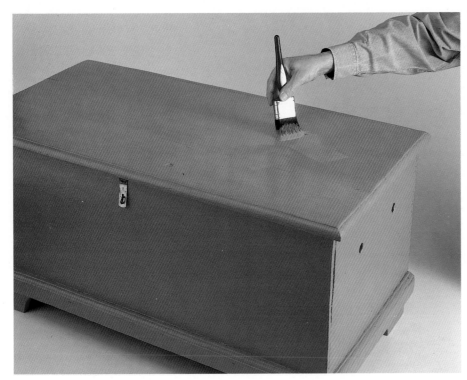

1 Paint the whole chest with one coat of pumpkin yellow emulsion (latex).

2 Thin the darker reddish brown emulsion (latex) with an equal amount of water and apply it to the dry base coat. Use the brush vigorously, changing direction often – aim for an uneven texture. Wipe some of the paint off to simulate wear and tear.

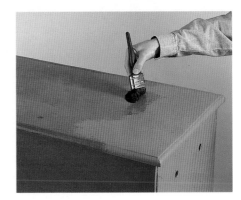

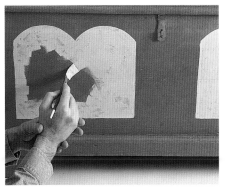

4 Fill in the background of the panels using a creamy yellow emulsion (latex) paint. Support your wrist with your spare hand.

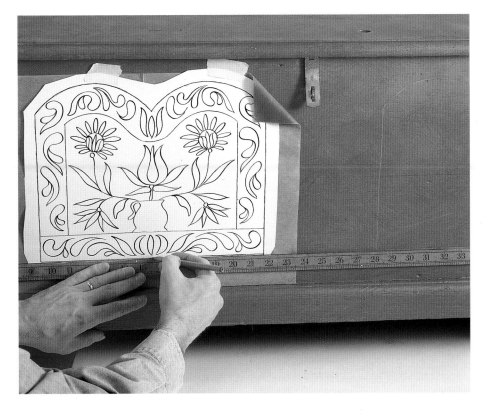

3 Use the pattern enlargement to draw the panels on the front of the chest. Position the pattern in the centre of each panel on either side of the chest. Place transfer paper between the pattern and the chest and draw around the outside. Repeat for the other side using a straight edge to ensure that the baselines are the same.

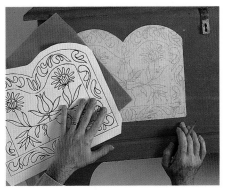

5 When the background is dry reposition your pattern and transfer paper, securing them both with masking tape. Carefully trace all the pattern on to the panel. It will be easier if you tip the chest on to its back.

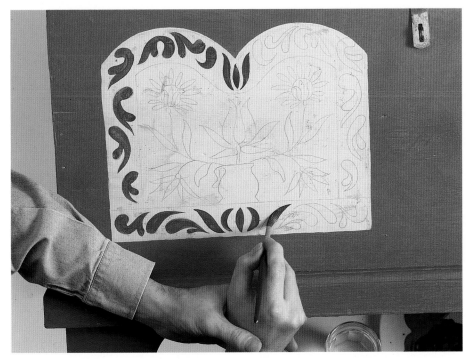

6 Practise brushstrokes until your wrist has loosened up and then work around the border using the reddish brown acrylic thinned with water. Support your wrist. Try not to labour over the brushstrokes – better that they are irregular than too stiff.

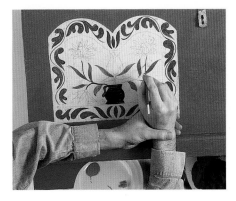

7 Thin the red paint with water and add the fine curves to the border using a fine-tipped artist's brush, a no. 2 is ideal. Use the same brush with thinned brown to paint the leaves and stems as illustrated. ▶

8 ▶ Change to a no. 4 or 5 artist's brush and paint the alternate petals and lower leaves using thinned blue-green paint.

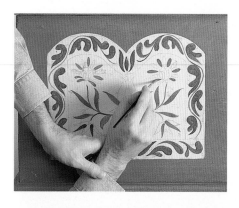

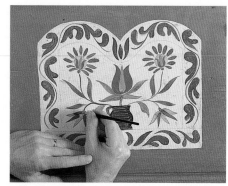

9 ▶ ▶ Now complete the flowers, filling in the red petals and the yellow ochre lower petals. Check the pattern to make sure you have painted all the elements.

10 Outline the inner panel using a fine brush and the thinned reddish brown paint – you may need to add more water than before to get a really smooth line. Practise until you feel confident and support your hand and the brush with a straight edge. If you do make mistakes it is better to let them dry and then paint them out with the background colour than to try to wipe them away.

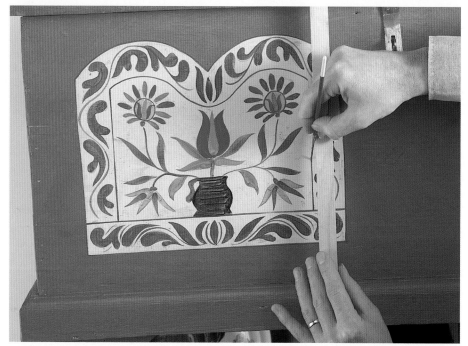

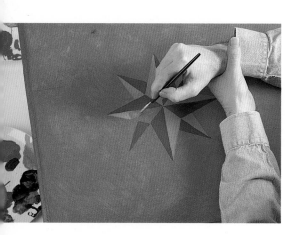

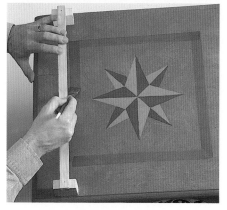

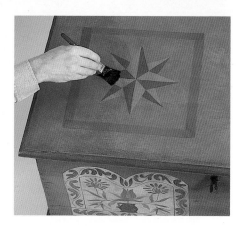

11 Position the stars on the top of the chest using the same method as for the panels; trace them down and then paint alternate sections with brown and pumpkin yellow emulsion (latex).

12 Mark a square to surround the star using a pencil; align it with the panel on the front. Using the batten, paint a border of the thinned brown acrylic paint with a square-tipped 1in (2.5cm) artist's brush. Repeat on the other side.

13 Finally, add a touch of raw umber to the clear varnish and apply two even coats to the whole chest using a household paintbrush. Allow the varnish to dry thoroughly between coats and then add one final coat of untinted varnish.

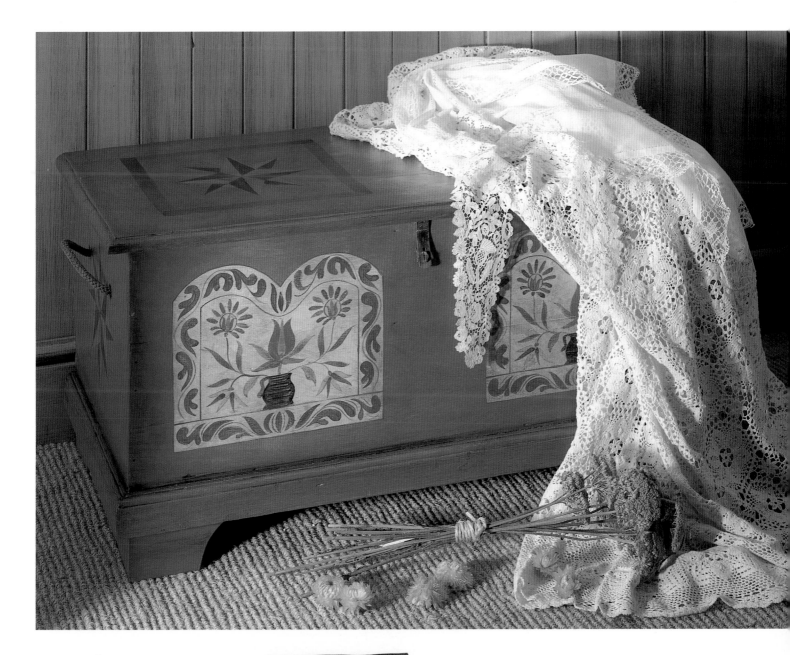

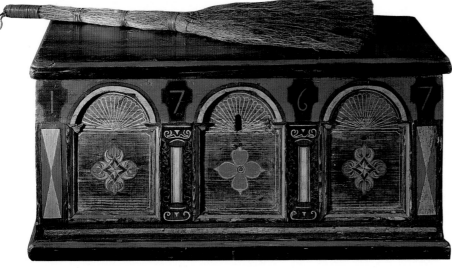

Left: The painted decoration has been used to enhance the inset panels of this eighteenth-century chest from Switzerland.

CRADLE OR CRIB

The wooden rocking cradle has a long history in Europe and though there are variations in the style, height and direction of the rocking, it seems that they were always decorated with carving or painting. The cradles must have been almost permanently in use in colonial homesteads where families were large. And to encourage early maternal instincts miniature dolls' cribs were made for girls, who used them to display their first attempts at quilting.

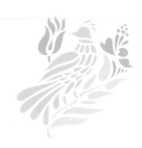

The shape of the cradle in this project is taken from an Amish doll's crib and made up of recycled pine. You can either ask a local carpenter to make one for you or buy an old one. The decoration is taken from an old Swedish hanging crib and painted freehand on to the natural wood. When painting the pattern on to unpainted wood, give it a coat of varnish first to prevent the paint spreading into the grain.

Practise your brushstrokes on paper until you are confident about their regularity but do not be too fastidious; this kind of decoration needs to be bountiful and energetic. You can either follow the pattern shown in this project or select your own motifs.

You will need:
- Shellac
- Chalk or coloured pencil
- Two medium-sized household brushes and a selection of artist's brushes – including one 1in (2.5cm) square-tipped brush
- Thinned artist's acrylic paints: green, red, yellow, white and brick red.
- Fine-grade sandpaper
- Clear water-based varnish
- A small tube of raw umber artist's acrylic paint

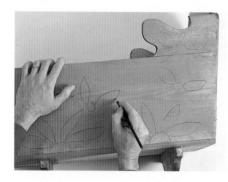

1 Prepare the crib for painting by applying a single coat of shellac, and leave it to dry. Decide on appropriate motifs to fit the shape of your crib and sketch the rough outlines using chalk or coloured pencil.

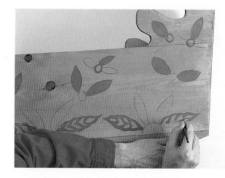

2 Begin filling in the green shapes, which are the most static feature of the design, and then the outlined leaves – try to use one brushstroke for each segment and support your painting hand with your spare hand.

3 Repeat the process with the red areas, filling the flat shapes first and then adding the more fluid brushstrokes. Your confidence will increase as your wrist loosens up, but as you have a shellac basecoat you will be able to wipe off obvious errors. Try not to do this too much as it will spoil the rhythm of your painting.

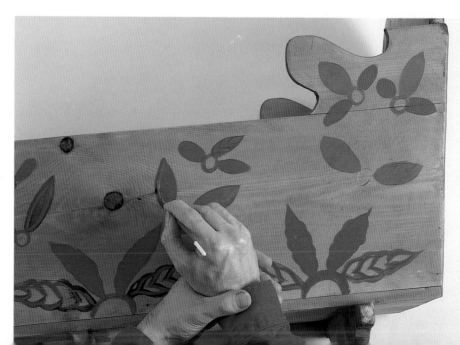

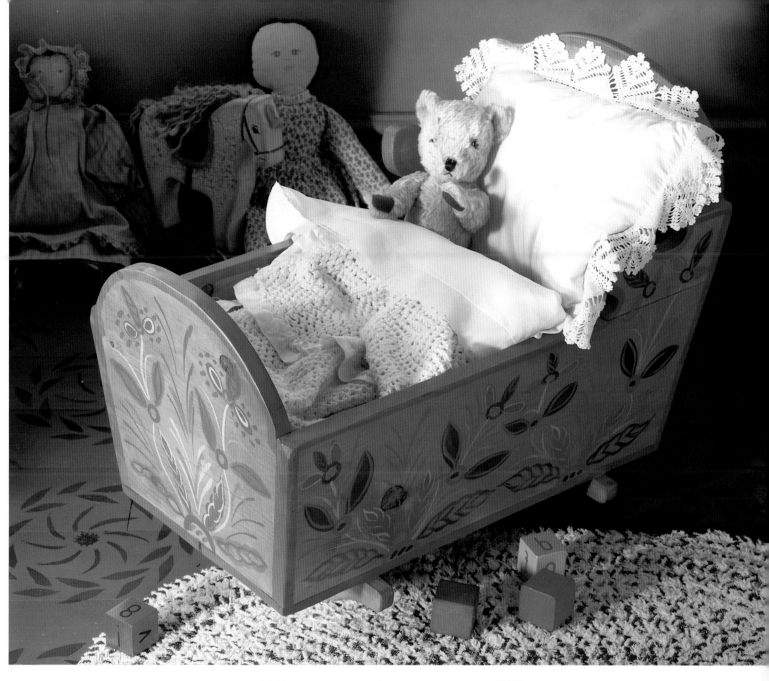

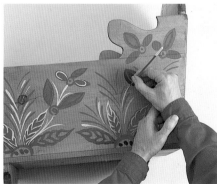

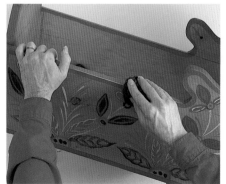

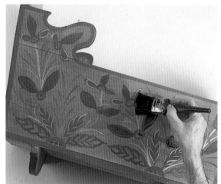

4 The white brushstrokes need real vitality; practise on paper until you can paint a long curve with a single brushstroke. Remember, this is an energetic country pattern and freshness is more important than accuracy.

5 Using a 1in (2.5cm) square-tipped brush and brick red, first paint the top edges and then a 1in (2.5cm) striping along all the edges. When it is completely dry, rub the edges gently with sandpaper, to "age" the crib. Do not overdo this.

6 Finally, apply two coats of varnish tinted with a small amount of raw umber and one coat of clear varnish. It is important not to rush this last stage, as the first coat of varnish must be bone dry before receiving the second.

FOLK
DECORATION

BOXES • TINWARE • GLASSWARE • FRAMES

IN TRADITIONAL FOLK INTERIORS EVERYTHING WAS WORTHY OF decoration – the walls, floors, chests, boxes, tins and glasses. In particular, the most practical objects were made to be beautiful. If a woodworker fashioned a spoon or a box he took time to carve a pattern into it, and if a tin merchant was selling a pitcher, he knew his market well enough to paint it with brightly coloured patterns.

The projects in this chapter show some of the simplest and most effective forms of folk art decoration. In these days of mass production, unfortunately, decorative patterns often have been refined to the point of sterility and blandness, so perhaps it is not surprising that the work of old folk artists is a source of pleasure and inspiration. The objects themselves can be picked up cheaply in old junk stores. Try one of the paint techniques described, or the patterns and motifs shown on pages 148–151. Equally, patterns and references can be found in old design sourcebooks.

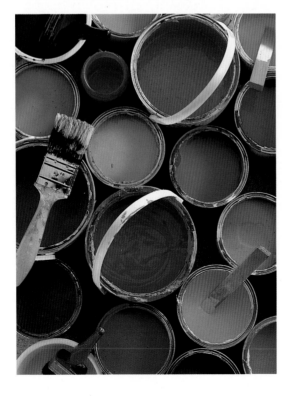

Do not feel bound to using the colours suggested for each project; you can always choose tones to suit your own colour scheme.

Opposite: Nineteenth-century "rose-painted" marriage box and ale bowl from Norway. Marriage boxes often contained woven and knitted items for a future baby. The ale bowl would have been filled with dark beer and passed around at festive occasions.

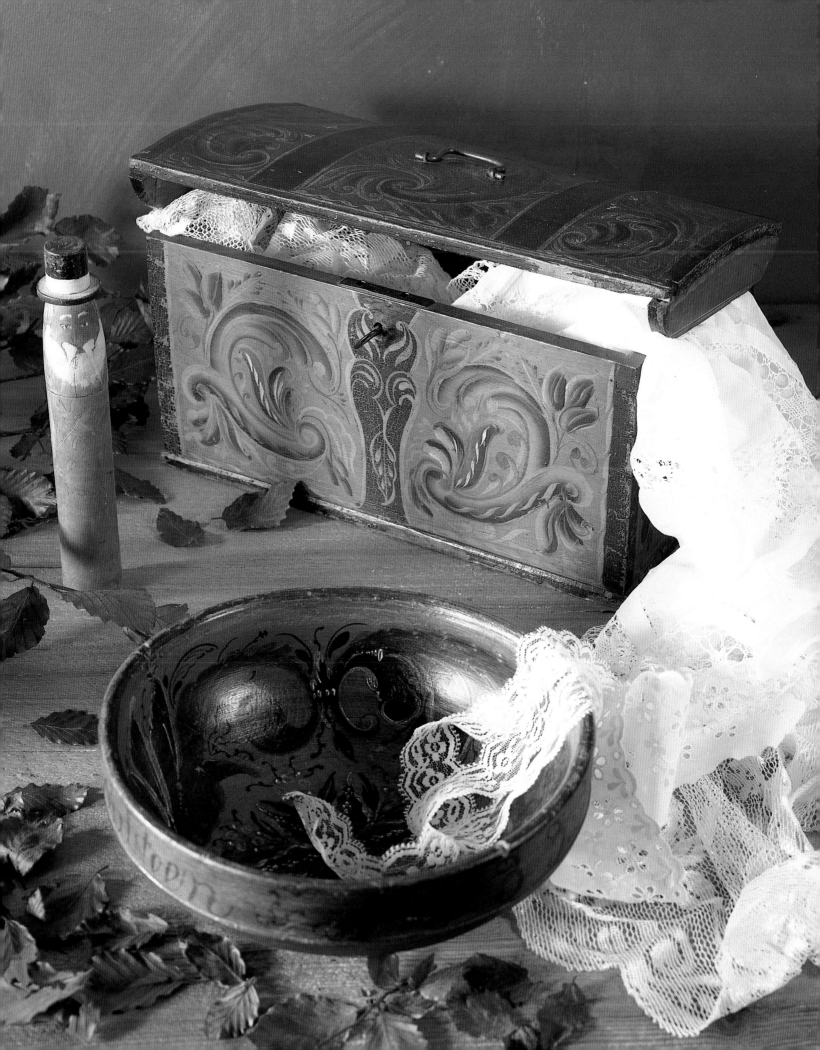

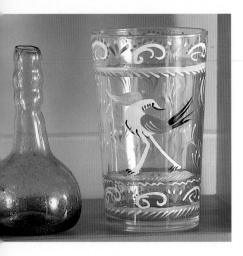

PAINTED OBJECTS

IN EUROPE MANY HOUSEHOLD OBJECTS WERE GIVEN AS PART OF THE MARRIAGE CUSTOMS. ON THEIR WEDDING DAY THE GROOM WOULD PRESENT HIS BRIDE WITH DECORATED SPOONS, BOWLS, TUMBLERS AND BOXES. THE MOTIFS USED WERE THOSE COMMON TO ALL EUROPEAN ORIGIN FOLK ART: TULIPS, BIRDS, RIBBONS, STYLIZED HUMAN FIGURES, AND SOMETIMES PORTRAITS. PORTRAITS WERE PAINTED BY TRAVELLING ARTISTS; BEFORE THE ADVENT OF PHOTOGRAPHY THE LIKENESS OF A SEPARATED LOVED ONE PAINTED ON A BOX WAS A PRECIOUS KEEPSAKE.

Perhaps the most common form of painted object in folk art is the box. Boxes were needed for every kind of storage and transportation, and throughout Scandinavia, Germany, Holland and later colonial America, they were made in many sizes out of bentwood. The wood was cut into thin flexible strips which were bent around an oval base, and where the sides overlapped, stitched with roots. Snap-on lids were made to fit snugly on the top and the result was a strong but light-weight container which was then painted and decorated. There were two kinds of box specially used by women: one was the church box which European women carried to Sunday services to hold their Bibles and gloves; and the other was the bride's box, given on the wedding day and decorated with a painting of the bride, and sometimes her groom, the date of the marriage and the bride's initials. This brightly painted love token was a private place for the bride to keep her most personal possessions – lace, letters and jewellery – while the larger bridal chest held the shared possessions.

Tin was also used to make boxes, mainly document boxes with a latch and a handle on the lid. These were painted black and decorated with bands of scrolls, leaves and flowers in bright colours. Tin trays were extremely popular and were hung from the walls like paintings.

Another popular vehicle for folk art was glass. Glass-making in Europe during the seventeenth century had reached a high level of sophistication, but even window glass was rare in America until entrepreneurs such as Henry Wilhelm Stiegel set up factories. Stiegel's name is synonymous with a whole range of glassware in

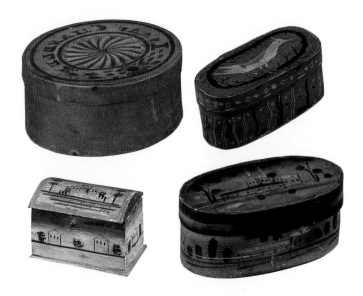

A selection of American painted boxes.

eighteenth-century America. Although he never actually blew any glass himself he imported experts from England, Germany and Poland to work for him.

Much of the most creative glassware came from the tradition of "after hours ware" in which a man, having completed his allotted task for the day, could use the left-over materials to make his own glassware, to sell or take home. This is the glass that shows the most exuberant use of folk art patterns and styles. Early spirit bottles from different parts of Europe were decorated with very similar motifs, indicating perhaps that these treasured items were taken on journeys and passed around at the other end. These historical European influences come together in American folk glassware.

AMISH SEWING BOX

Amish craftsmen worked within the restrictive confines of The Ordnung, a code governing all aspects of life. Decoration for its own sake was forbidden, "plainness and practicality" were the qualities to strive for and pride was to be avoided at all costs. This discipline produced the simple beauty of objects such as the sewing box that inspired this project. It is based on a box attributed to Henry Lapp, an Amish carpenter who owned a shop supplying furniture, household objects and paint to his own community in the late 1800s.

This is a simple design, an oblong with a lid, hinged to allow access to the largest compartment used for storing spools of thread, and a small drawer at the bottom for smaller sewing paraphernalia. The colouring and decoration is typical of the style of Henry Lapp – red paint, yellow graining, pale blue interiors and white ceramic handles. The box was commissioned from a local craftsman who used a photograph as a guide, but simpler wooden boxes could be adapted for the project.

You will need:
- Matt emulsion (flat latex) paint: duck-egg blue, brick red and beige
- A 1in (2.5cm) artist's brush, two thick-bristled varnishing brushes and a small household paintbrush
- Clear water-based varnish
- Small tubes of raw sienna and burnt umber artist's acrylic paint
- A cloth
- A small white ceramic or plastic knob
- A screwdriver

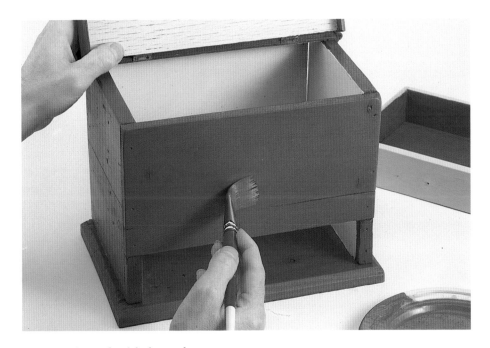

1 Paint the inside of the box with two coats of duck-egg blue, and apply a base coat of brick red to the outside, and beige to the drawer front.

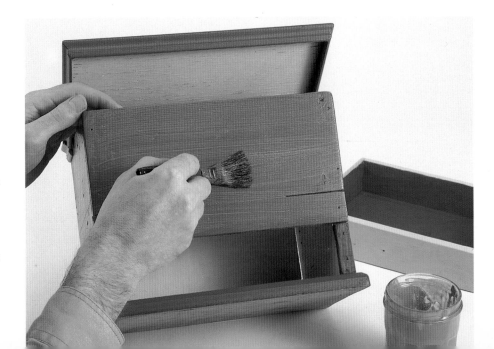

2 Tint the varnish with a small squeeze of the raw sienna and burnt umber and paint the outside of the box. Apply it with a thick-bristled brush, using pressure to leave visible brushstrokes, sideways across the box and lengthways across the lid. ▶

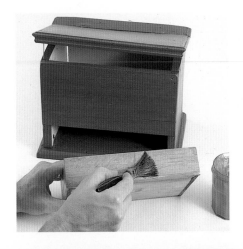

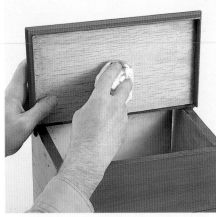

3 ◀ ◀ Apply the same varnish over the beige base coat on the drawer and while it is still wet, use a dry thick-bristled brush to lift some of the glaze to imitate woodgrain. Do not try for a realistic graining effect, but one like lines of static interference on a television screen.

4 ◀ Apply a coat of tinted varnish to the inside and while it is still wet wipe off patches of it with a damp cloth to imitate wear and tear. Follow this with a coat of clear varnish over the whole box.

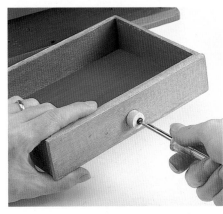

5 Finally, screw on the white knob. If you have bought a new one try making it look a bit scruffy by scratching the surface and rubbing it with a dab of burnt umber to "age" it.

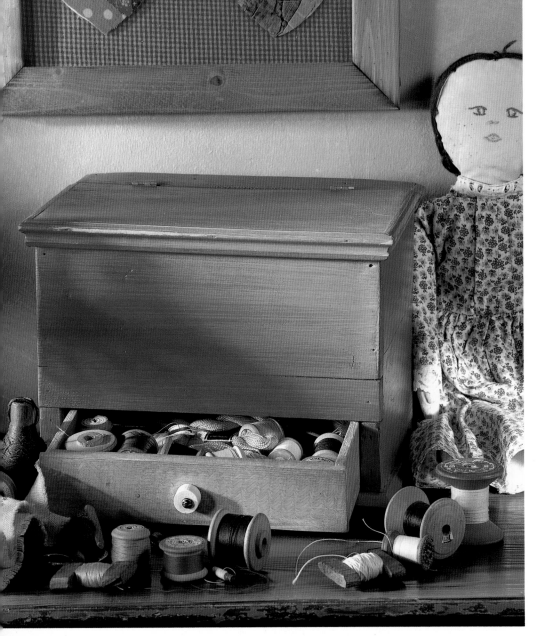

PAINTED SEWING BOX

In the days before factory-made clothing, every woman's sewing box was in daily use, keeping needles, threads and thimbles safe and close at hand. It is objects such as these that show the wonderful rich patina of age which develops with constant use. Sewing boxes were decorated by their owners, often with pretty feminine patterns, then marked with initials and dates.

This sewing box was inspired by one made by an Amish woman as a wedding gift. The legs are aptly made from old wooden cotton reels. The painting is done with freehand brushstrokes over a traced pattern that you will find on page 149. If you wish to personalize your box you can paint your initials on it. Either use letters from the alphabet on page 151 or select others from a pattern source book. The birds on the front hold date cards which you can adjust to commemorate a personal anniversary. Any oblong wooden box with a hinged lid is suitable for decoration in this way.

You will need:
- Four wooden cotton reels (spools)
- A hammer, thin nails and wood glue
- A selection of artist's brushes – including a 1in (2.5cm) and a ⅜in (1cm) brush
- White matt emulsion (flat latex) paint
- An enlargement of the pattern on page 149 drawn on tracing paper
- Chalky-backed transfer paper
- A soft pencil
- Low-tack masking tape
- Artist's acrylics or stencil paints: emerald green, deep and light red, yellow ochre, cobalt blue, white, blue, rose pink and light blue
- A raised wooden batten (see page 52)
- Clear water-based varnish
- Small tubes of cobalt blue, raw umber and raw sienna artist's acrylic paint

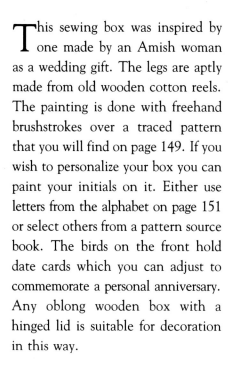

1 Attach the cotton reels (spools) to the corners by hammering thin nails through the base of the box. A dab of wood glue will make them more secure. Tint the white emulsion (latex) with a squeeze of cobalt blue and raw umber artist's acrylic paint.

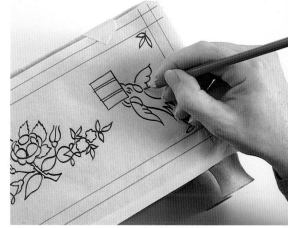

2 Apply the emulsion (latex) to the outside of the box and the inside of the lid. When dry trace down the pattern with a soft pencil, using transfer paper between your pattern and the box. Secure the tracing with masking tape if necessary.

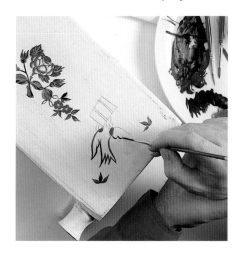

3 The decoration on the box is very informal and painterly. Let your brushstrokes flow and embellish the decoration to suit yourself. Emerald green, deep and light red, yellow ochre and cobalt blue tinted with white are used here.

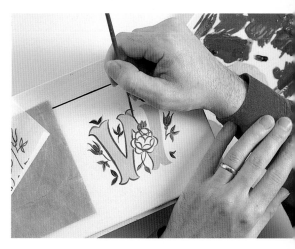

4 Select initials from the alphabet and paint them as solid shapes in blue. Allow them to dry and then outline edges in dark red. Decorate the letters as shown. ▶

5 ▶ Use the ⅜in (1cm) brush with thinned rose pink to paint the thick stripes. Practise on paper until you can complete the longest stripe with a single brushstroke. This is more important than getting a completely straight line. Support your brush hand on a raised wooden batten.

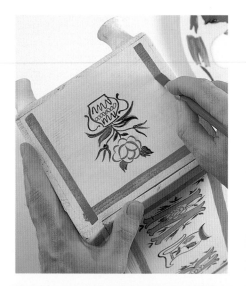

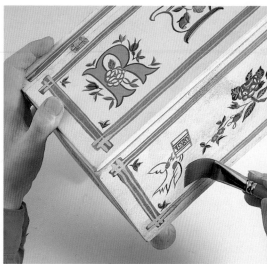

6 ▶▶ Allow the red stripes to dry and then use a fine brush and thinned light blue paint to outline the red, crossing over to form boxes at the corners. Tint the varnish with a squeeze of raw umber and raw sienna and then give a final coat of clear varnish.

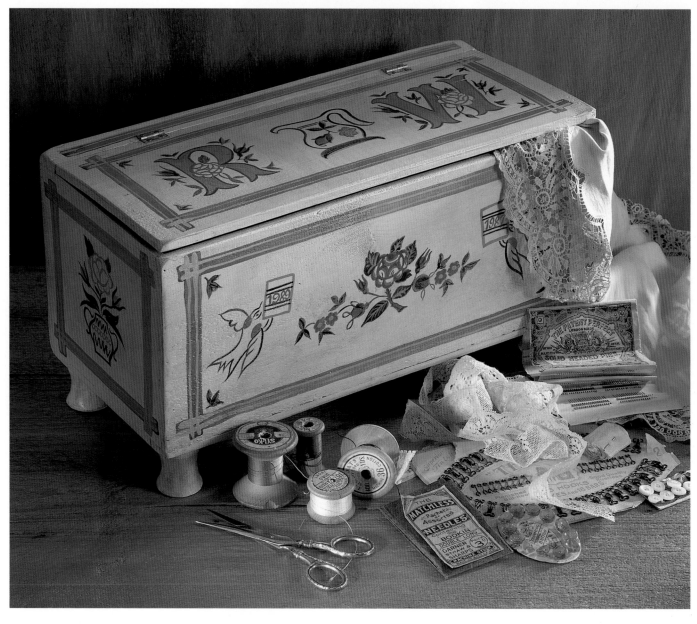

PAINTED PICTURE FRAME

Folk art frames were often made of common woods painted and grained to imitate something much grander, such as walnut or bird's eye maple. Some of the most appealing examples of woodgraining bear little resemblance to the real thing and seem to be almost a pastiche. The paint is vigorously applied, usually in a dark colour on a light background, using a piece of sponge, crumpled paper or a cloth. The paw print in particular was a popular pattern in which the surface was covered with spots resembling animal tracks.

The frame for this project was painted in a naive energetic style. It is an old frame from a junk shop and quite rustic, both in construction and texture. A silhouette was framed here, itself a typical folk technique. If you do not have anything suitable to go in the frame, try a mirror. Take the frame along to a glass merchant and have the mirror cut to fit, as old frames can be very quirkily shaped.

You will need:
- Matt emulsion (flat latex) paint: red ochre and pumpkin yellow
- 1½in (4cm) decorator's brush, a stencilling brush and a small household paintbrush
- Black artist's acrylic or stencil paint
- Absorbent paper towel
- Fine-grade steel wool
- Clear water-based varnish
- Small tubes of raw sienna and burnt sienna artist's acrylic paint

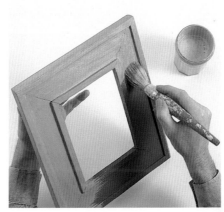

1 Paint the frame with a base coat of red ochre, allow to dry and then apply a coat of pumpkin yellow.

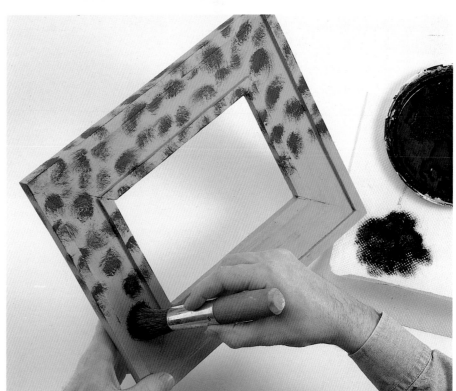

2 To paint the spots use black paint undiluted on a dry stencilling brush. Too much paint will "blob," so rub the brush on paper towel between dipping and painting. Hold the brush in a vertical position and push down slightly while twisting it on the frame. The effect needs to be more wild than restrained. ▶

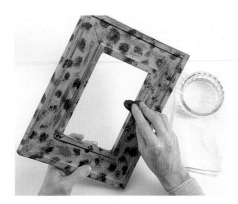

3 *When the paint is completely dry, rub the edges lightly with steel wool to simulate wear and tear.*

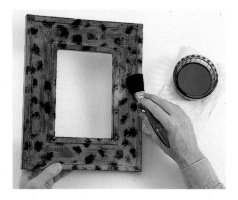

4 *Tint the clear varnish with a small amount of both raw and burnt sienna and apply to the frame. Add a finishing coat of clear varnish.*

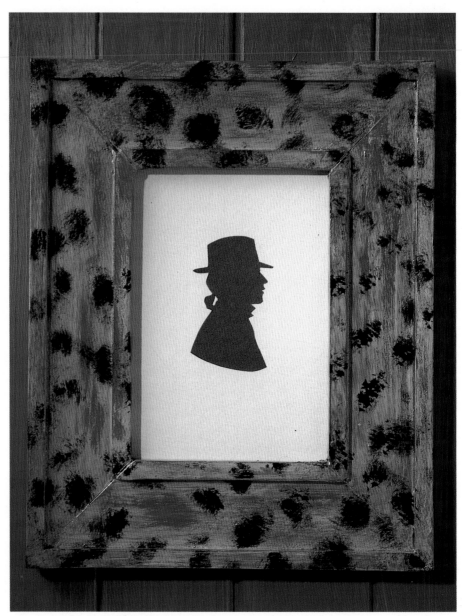

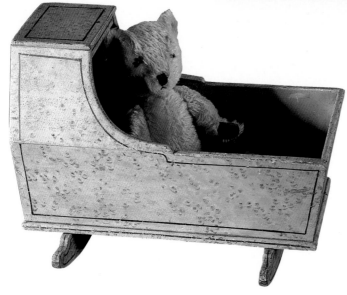

This crib shows another example of the bird's eye maple pattern.

PAINTED TIN OR TOLEWARE

The first tinsmiths to ply their trade in America imported sheets of tinplate from England, where the craft was well established. They made cooking pots and baking dishes from heavy-grade tin and a huge array of painted display objects from thinner, lighter tin. There was hardly a household accessory that the tinsmith did not turn his hand to making, and almost all these items were then painted with bright patterns and decorations.

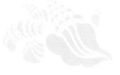

Like the canal boat painting in England and *rosemaling* in Norway, the toleware decoration relies on strong contrasts, bright colours and handpainted brushstrokes for its distinctive character. For this project an assortment of tin and aluminum containers was collected and painted using the new water-based acrylic paint colours and varnish instead of traditional oil colours. Purists might baulk at the idea, but the results speak for themselves. Although the finish on the tinware is permanent, it is not as durable as enamelled tin, and is best used for decorative storage containers rather than heavily used household objects.

You will need:
- Coarse-grade steel wool
- Black matt emulsion (flat latex) paint
- A small household paintbrush and a selection of artist's brushes – including one 1in (2.5cm) and one long-haired brush
- An enlargement of the pattern on page 150 drawn on tracing paper
- Chalky-backed transfer paper
- A soft pencil
- Low-tack masking tape
- Artist's acrylic or stencil paints: red, forest green, white and yellow-green
- Clear satin water-based varnish
- Small tubes of burnt sienna and raw sienna artist's acrylic paint

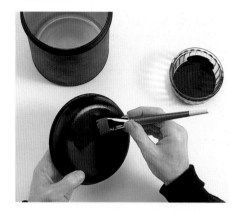

1 Clean the tin to a grease-free surface and rub down with steel wool to allow the paint to key in. Apply two coats of black emulsion (latex) paint and leave to dry.

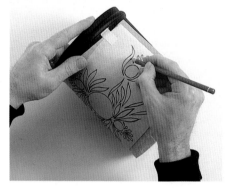

2 Using transfer paper and a soft pencil, copy the pattern from the tracing to the tin, holding it in place with low-tack masking tape if you find this awkward.

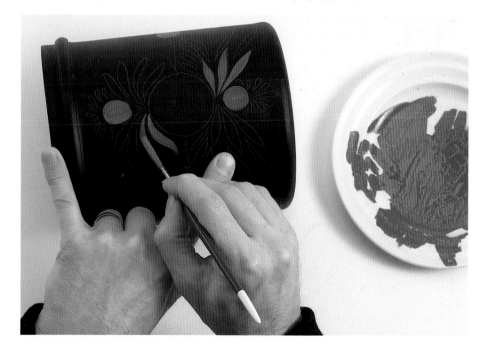

3 Thin the red paint until your brush glides along easily, and begin by filling in the round, red shapes. Practise brushstrokes on paper beginning with the fine point of your brush and a light touch,

draw the brush towards you, applying pressure to spread the brush for the thicker end of your stroke. It is better to flick the brush along the surface than to labour over achieving a perfect-shaped stroke. ▶

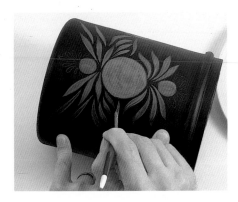

4 The green strokes are finer and longer, so practise these sharper curves with thinned green paint before adding them to the design.

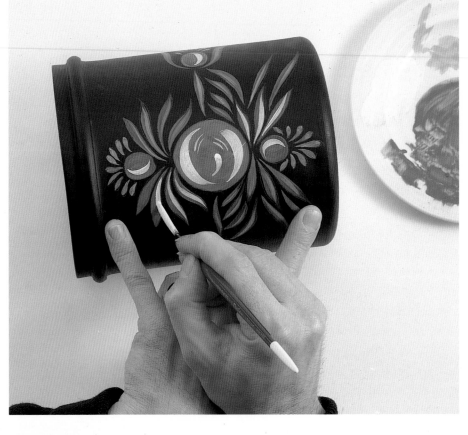

5 The highlights must not be overdone; just skim the surface with your brush, following the curves of the pattern. Use white on the red and yellowish-green on the green shapes.

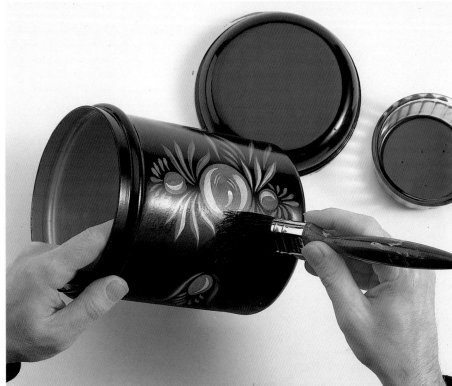

Below: This American tin box from the nineteenth century shows further ideas for decorating tinware, still using the same bright colours and floral motifs.

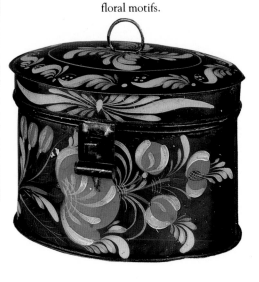

6 Tint some of the satin varnish with a small amount of both burnt and raw sienna and apply two even coats followed by one coat of clear varnish.

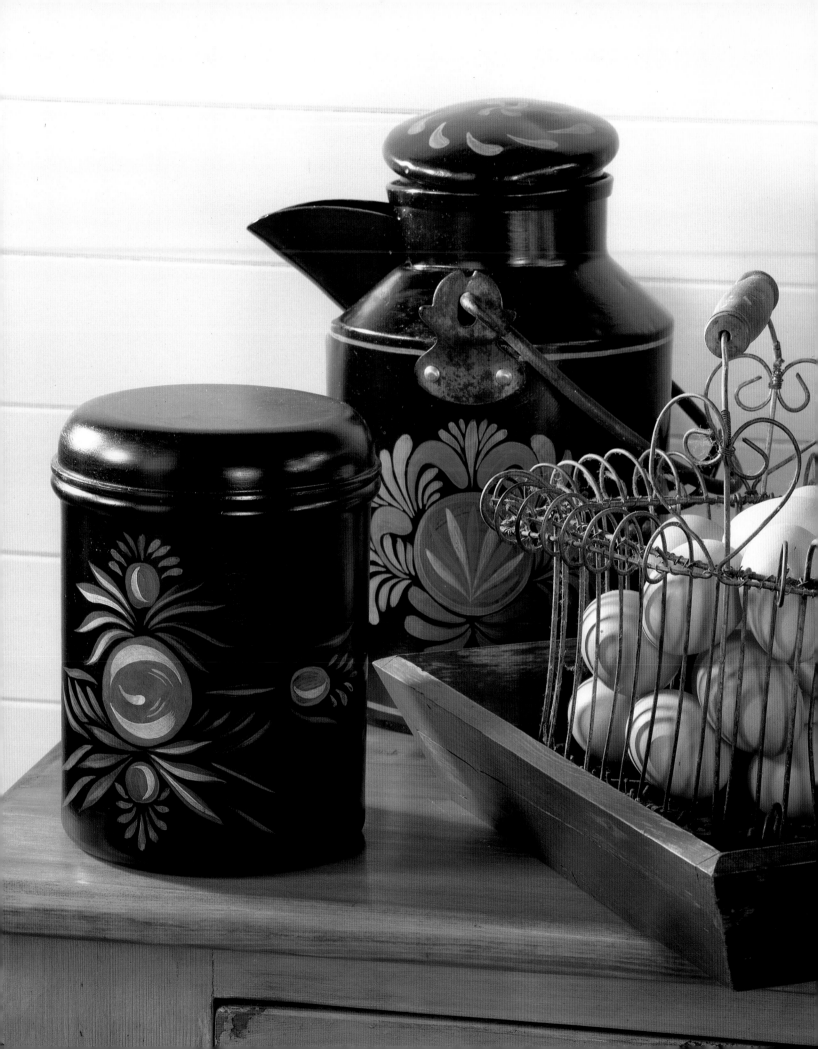

PAINTED GLASS

Painted glassware was a popular folk art form in Europe, with bright figures used to adorn bottles of spirit and drinking tumblers from France to Hungary. When emigration to America began in the early seventeenth century, glassmakers from Poland, Holland, England and Germany crossed the sea to make their fortunes, and some of them succeeded. Henry Wilhelm Stiegel was the most influential glass manufacturer of his time. His name is still used to describe the type of enamel-painted glass featured in this project.

Painting on glass is not difficult provided that you thin the enamel paint sufficiently and relax enough to let the brushstrokes flow. Do not slavishly follow your tracing – use it as a positional guide for the main motif, but let the shape of your glass suggest the detailing. Enamel paints are available from most hobby shops.

Try to find old glasses in junk or antique shops – a glass with a slight imperfection will cost next to nothing, but is perfect for folk painting.

You will need:
- A tape measure
- An enlargement of the pattern on page 150
- Tracing paper and pencil
- Low-tack masking tape
- A soft cloth
- Enamel paint thinners
- A selection of small pots of enamel paint: red, green, yellow, blue, black and white
- Two fine, short-haired artist's brushes
- An elastic band

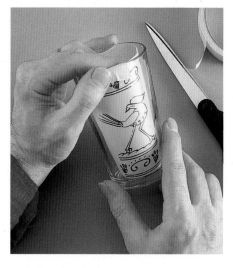

1 Measure around your glass, top and bottom, and cut a piece of tracing paper to fit inside it. Draw the pattern on to the tracing paper and put it into the glass, using masking tape to secure it if necessary.

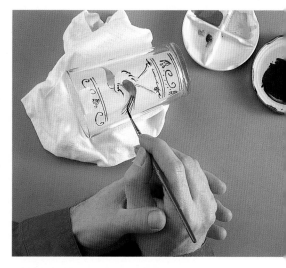

2 Rest the glass on a cloth and support your painting hand with your other hand. The paint should be thinned enough to make it flow nicely and be slightly transparent; if it is too thin it may run. Try to avoid over-painting, or the design will lose its freshness. Aim for light animated brushstrokes.

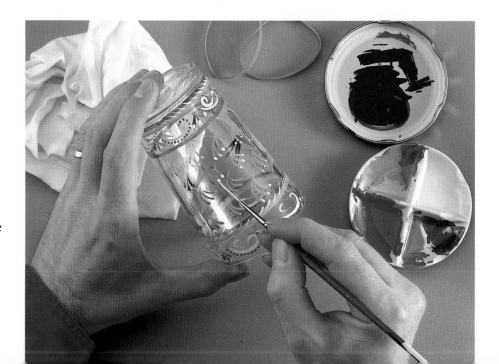

3 Add the small dots and motifs to suit your glass; if you have a fluted base, emphasize this with your pattern. Allow one side of the glass to dry first before painting the other, unless you can support the glass on its rim by using your other hand splayed inside the glass.

4 ▶ *When the pattern has dried, place an elastic band around the glass to act as a guide, and paint stripes of colour around it. Support the glass as described in the previous step.*

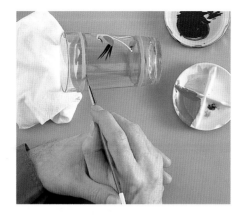

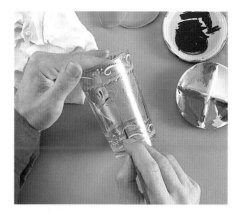

5 ▶ ▶ *Finally, introduce some individuality by adding embellishments of your own, perhaps just a few squiggles, some dots or even your initials.*

Below: This eighteenth-century painted brandy-bottle illustrates the effectiveness of a central motif bordered by free brushstrokes and patterns.

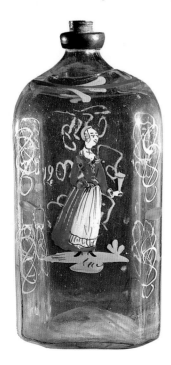

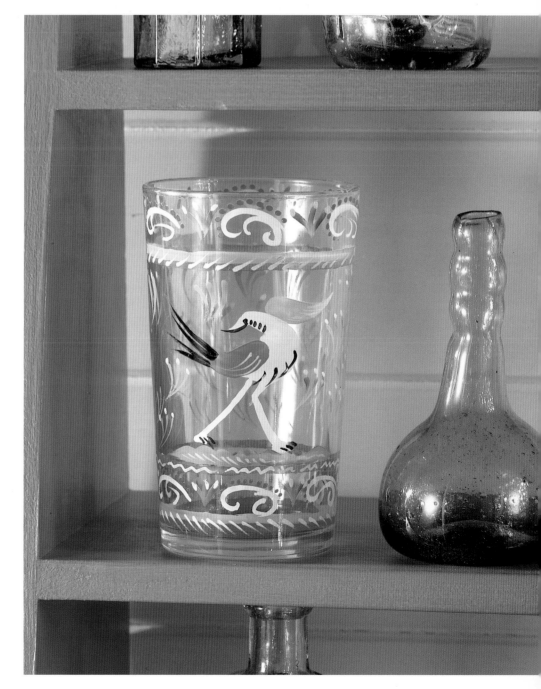

HANGING SALT BOX

Salt was even more important to cooks 300 years ago than it is today. It was the main preservative for meat and fish, which were salted down and stored ready for lean winter months. The hanging salt box is common to many European folk cultures, and the design is fairly standard. Decoration of the boxes varies; in Norway, for example, it usually featured a woodburnt repeat pattern using symbols and runes which date back thousands of years. In other parts of Europe, and later America, it was customary to paint the box with the year it was made, bordering the numerals with traditional motifs such as hearts or tulips.

Scandinavian-style kitchenware is now widely available and you should not find it difficult to buy a plain pine hanging salt box like the one featured in this project. But if you are a keen woodworker you could easily make a box; the design is relatively simple.

The geometric motif used here was very popular with painters of American folk furniture and objects. The design was drawn with a pair of compasses and the segments painted different colours. This box is painted with a green background, but natural wood, or any folk colour would suit equally well.

You will need:
- Emerald green matt emulsion (flat latex) paint
- Two 1in (2.5cm) and one long-haired artist's brush
- A pair of compasses
- Artist's acrylics or stencil paints: brick red, off white and black
- Clear water-based varnish
- Small tubes of raw and burnt umber artist's acrylic paint

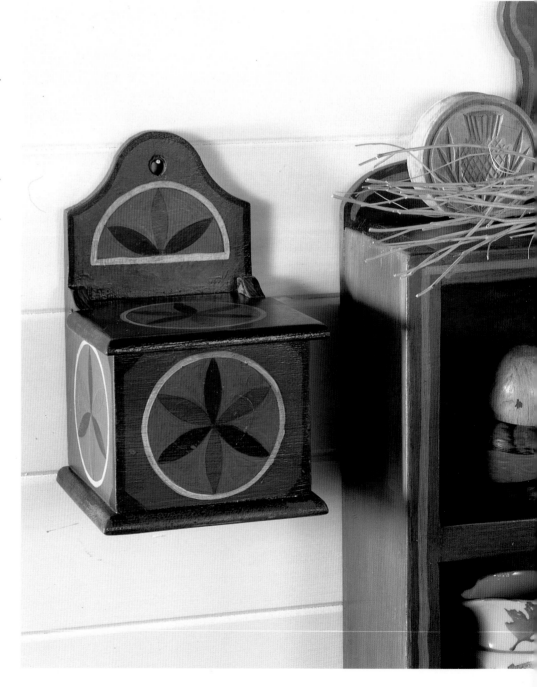

1 Apply the base coat of green emulsion, and allow to dry. Using the compasses draw a circle on the lid. Without adjusting the radius, move the compass point to the edge of the circle and draw an arc to intersect both sides of the circle. Move the point to one of these intersections and draw another arc; continue around the circle until you complete the pattern.

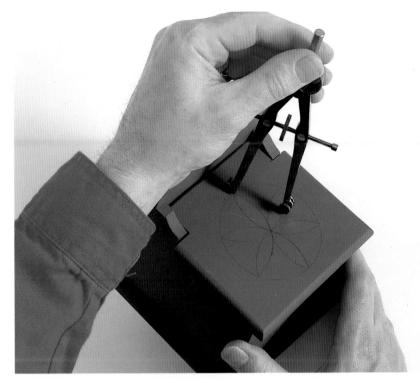

2 Repeat the pattern on the front and sides of the box and draw half of it on the backing plate. Fill in the background of the motif using brick red paint. Support your brush hand with your spare hand.

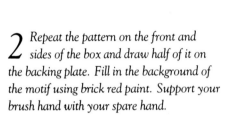

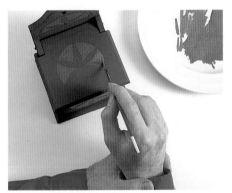

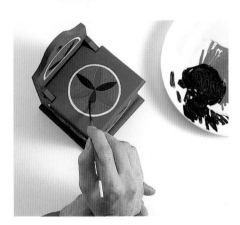

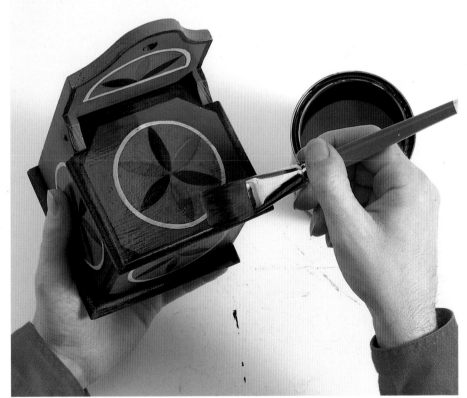

3 Use the compass to draw a circle ¼in (6mm) larger than the first, and fill this in with off white paint. Paint three sections of the motif with black paint.

4 Tint the water-based varnish with a small amount of raw and burnt umber and apply two coats to the outside of the box. Allow to dry, and follow with one coat of clear varnish.

WOODEN SHEEP DUMMYBOARD

Painted signs were a common sight outside shops and taverns in eighteenth-century towns. Recognizable symbols, such as the tailor's scissors, butcher's pig and optician's eyeglasses were designed to guide even the illiterate customer in the right direction. In early days in America most towns would have had just one shop representing each trade, but as business expanded the sign painter's art became more valued, as an attractive board was likely to draw trade away from the competitors.

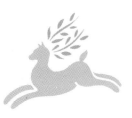

The tavern was the most popular meeting place, as well as being the stagecoach stop, and much prestige was attached to the signboard hanging on the bracket outside. The subject matter showed great variety, including portraits, landscapes, animals, ships and eagles.

This sheep dummyboard has been cut from a sheet of plywood and can either be hung on the wall from hooks, or made free-standing by adding a plank with a mitred end to the back of the sheep.

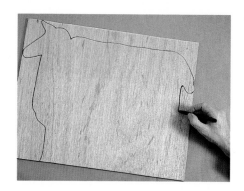

1 Follow the pattern on page 150 and draw the outline of the sheep on to the plywood. Cut this out by hand with a coping saw, or use an electric jigsaw (saber saw).

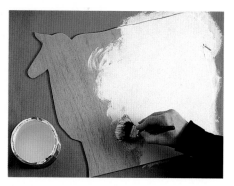

2 Paint the sheep off white. Use random "scruffy" brushstrokes in all directions.

You will need:
- A pencil
- A sheet of ¼in (6mm) plywood approximately 36in by 24in (90cm by 60cm)
- A coping saw or electric jigsaw (saber saw)
- Off white matt emulsion (flat latex) paint
- Two small household brushes, a fat stencilling brush and a fine-tipped artist's brush
- Artist's acrylics or stencil paints: black, burnt umber and deep grass green
- Coarse-grade sandpaper
- Clear matt (flat) water-based varnish
- Small tubes of raw umber and raw sienna artist's acrylic paints

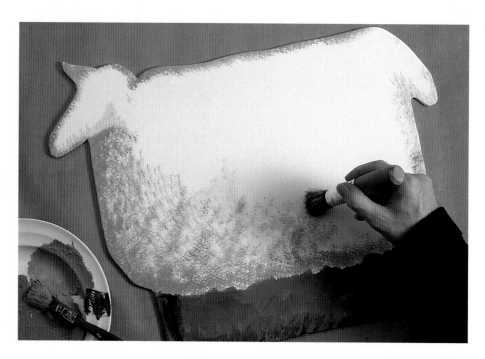

3 Mix the burnt umber into the off white paint to obtain two different shades of beige, one lighter and one darker, then apply these with the stencil brush. Shade the edges and under the chin first, and gradually build up the colour. Paint the grass and the black legs, adding highlights to the legs in dark beige.

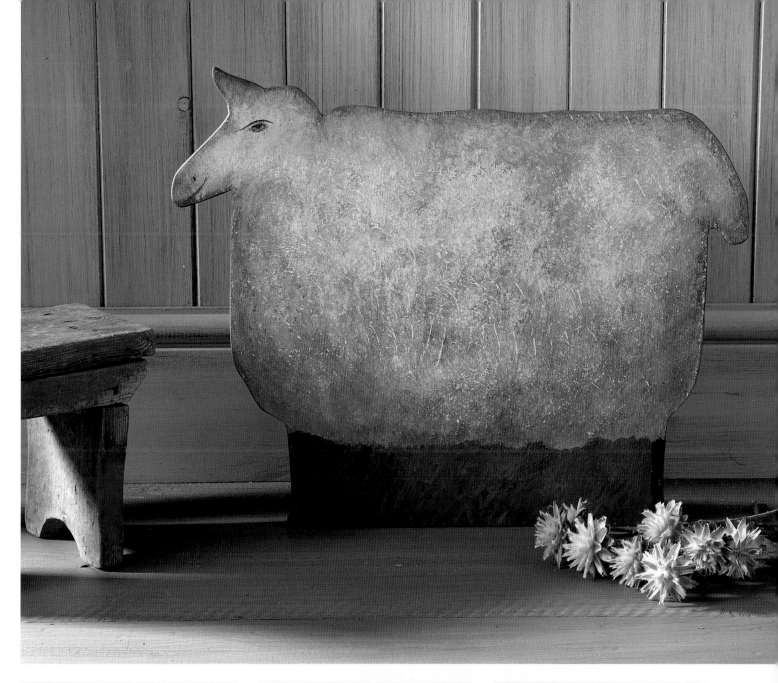

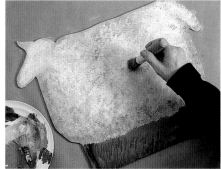

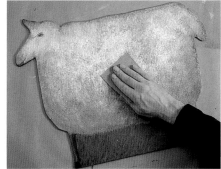

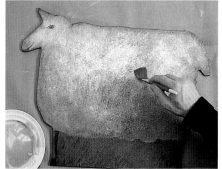

4 Use the darker shade of beige to create the textural effect of a fleece, applying the undiluted paint with a brush.

5 Rub the paint back with sandpaper in a patchy way to reveal the base coat below. Do not overdo this or you risk losing the woolly texture – use the sandpaper to add the highlights which will give the sheep more form.

6 Paint an eye and a happy mouth to give your sheep personality. Apply a coat of varnish, tinted with raw umber and raw sienna, and then a coat of clear matt (flat) varnish to finish.

TEXTILES

QUILTS • CUSHIONS • NEEDLEPOINT • RUGS

TEXTILES IN ALL THEIR FORMS ARE PART OF THE COUNTRY WAY OF LIFE. Worked by ladies and young girls, who were trained in the feminine arts at home, coverlets, cushions, the many varieties of the traditional quilt, intricate samplers and embroideries, together with braided and hooked rugs, are all an established part of the domestic folk tradition.

Often made out of scraps of materials, old folk textiles are unmistakable: they have distinctive patterns and definite personalities. They acquire character and dignity with the passage of time, and produce soft, faded colours that blend into any interior.

Sew old pieces of fabric, perhaps family favourites, into new in your folk quilt, or create an authentic-looking appliqué cushion for a less ambitious start. Rag rugs are also surprisingly easy to make, and another way of using up old bits of fabric.

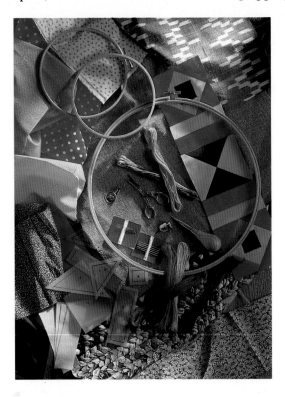

The joy of the projects in this chapter is in the range of materials you can use.

Opposite: For many women, patchwork and quilting, born of necessity, were often their only creative outlet. The combinations are endless – a rich kaleidoscope of pattern and form, colour and texture.

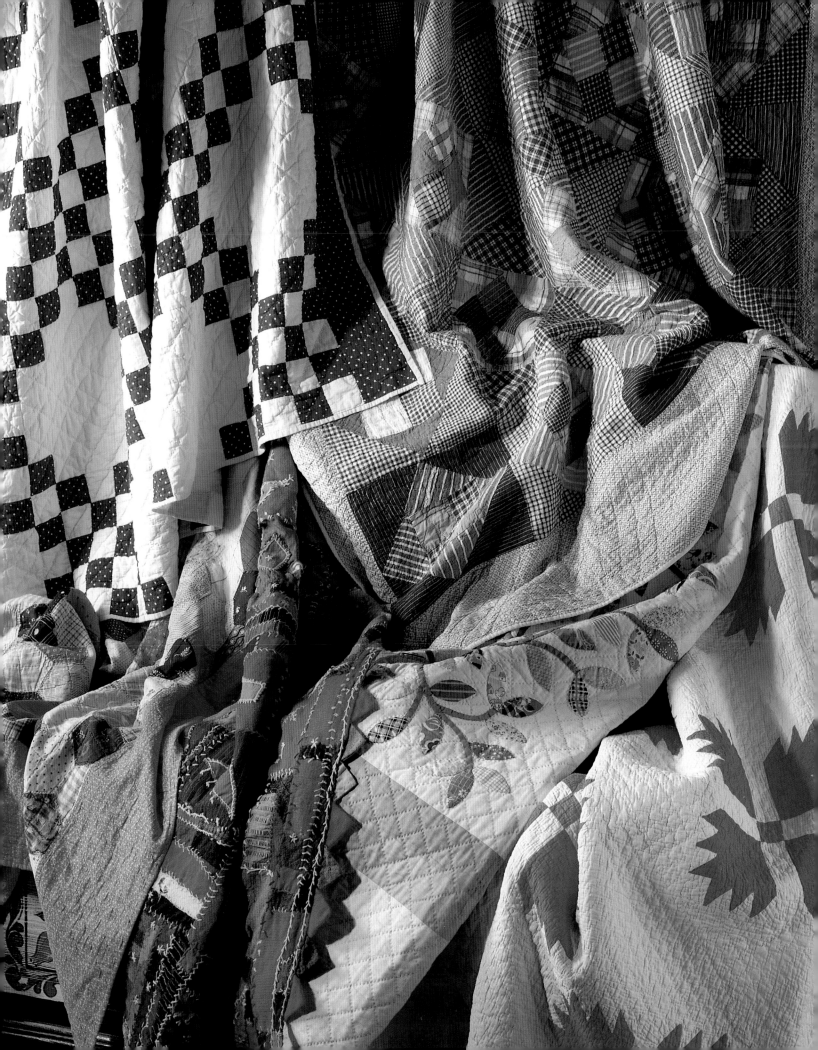

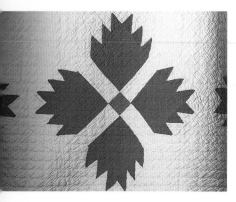

FOLK QUILTS

THE ANCIENT EGYPTIANS KNEW HOW TO QUILT, AS DID THE ANCIENT CHINESE ACCORDING TO OLD RECORDS. IN FACT, MANY CULTURES DEVELOPED THE TECHNIQUE, PROBABLY AT FIRST BECAUSE OF THE WARM, INSULATING PROPERTIES OF THE MATERIAL AND ONLY LATER BECAUSE OF ITS MARVELLOUS DECORATIVE POSSIBILITIES.

In seventeenth-century England, patchwork quilts became popular as a way of using up snippets of the sumptuous patterned silks and chintzes imported from the East Indies. And as the colonies expanded, women took their quilting arts with them to the new lands. Records reveal that each convict woman transported to Australia was issued with a bag of patchwork pieces to keep her busy on the sea voyage.

AMERICAN QUILTS

It was in colonial America that the quilt was elevated to an art form. Settlers grew flax to make linen fabric but it was laborious and time consuming to prepare, so prudent housewives saved every scrap of cloth and stitched the pieces together as patchwork. In pioneer spirit, women shared and exchanged their quilting and patchwork pat-

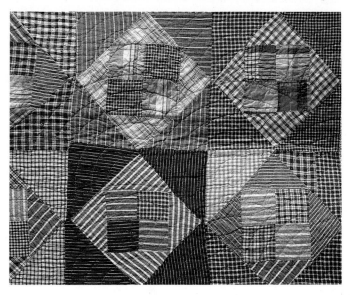

A twentieth-century denim quilt made from
workshirts and pyjama fabrics.

terns which were given picturesquely descriptive names such as Eight Hands Around, Jacob's Ladder, Steps to the Altar, Bear Tracks and Honeycomb. The beauty and complexity of these quilts is astonishing, especially when you consider the gruelling lives pioneer women led. The English quiltmaker took pride in sewing all her own stitches, but in America the loneliness of many homesteaders' lives gave rise to meetings known as quilting bees, where a dozen or so women regularly gathered around a quilting frame industriously sewing, while they exchanged stories, recipes and news.

There is an infinite variety of possible patterns, but basically quilting is constructed by stitching together three layers: a decorative top sheet; wadding or batting; and a plain backing sheet. Quilting can be divided into different categories depending upon the way it is put together. There is patchwork or pieced work, appliqué quilting, crazy quilting and stuffed work.

PATCHWORK OR PIECED WORK

Patchwork requires precision in cutting and stitching the geometric shapes, which must fit together exactly to produce a flat surface. The early examples were simple squares but as the art developed the designs became extremely intricate, often using colour, shape and tone to give a three-dimensional quality to the surface, as in the traditional Tumbling Blocks design where different coloured diamond shapes make up a "cube" and the illusion of depth is quite spectacular.

The most dramatic pieced quilts are those made by the Amish, whose lifestyle forbade the use of pattern or bright colours in their clothing. The fabric that the Amish settlers used for their quilts and clothing was plain

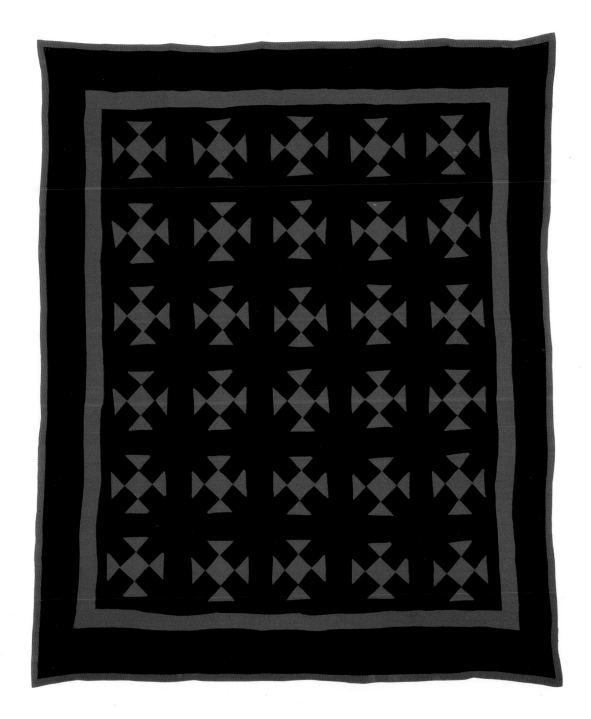

An Amish quilt made of plain coloured wools, showing their skilful use of
beautiful geometric patterns.

coloured wool, as printed pattern was considered too "fancy." By limiting their options the Amish created uniquely beautiful geometric patterns, often with a central diamond or square with another square within a wide border. There were many variations such as the Sawtooth Edge, or the Nine Patch Centre and all were elaborately quilted with feathers, ferns, roses or baskets. They also used colour contrasts to reinforce their designs and their superb quilting technique has seldom been equalled.

In contrast to the Amish quilts, sampler quilts used exuberant colours and patterns with a huge variety of different patterned blocks made up in different piecing styles, which were then stitched together with contrasting pattern borders.

APPLIQUÉ OR APPLIED PATCHWORK

The use of appliqué, or applied patchwork, for quilts became immensely popular in America during the mid-nineteenth century, when they were made more for display than warmth, and were often put away for "best". In this style of quilting shapes are cut and laid on a plain light background, either in medallion form, with a central motif surrounded by borders, or album style where individual pictorial blocks are displayed in a framework of contrasting fabric. The subject matter was often taken from the natural world and quaintly-named patterns evolved such as Turkey Tracks, Indiana Rose, Tulips and Ribbons, and Dresden Plate.

THE CRAZY QUILT

The crazy quilt is a wild and wonderful creation, the origins of which lie in the patched and mended bedcover. A patch would be sewn in place with feather-stitching and more would follow as they were needed. At some point an innovative quilter saw the potential for making a new quilt in this way and set the style for using silks, satins, brocades and velvets in irregular shapes joined together with a feather stitch of coloured silk. These voluptuous, tactile quilts were most popular during the Victorian era.

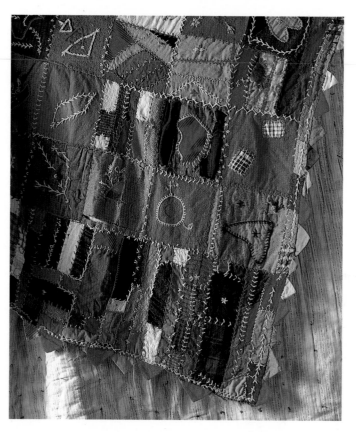

A naive and charming example of the decorative crazy-quilt that was popular in the latter third of the nineteenth century.

TRAPUNTO OR STUFFED WORK

Trapunto or stuffed work is by contrast the most controlled, disciplined and time-consuming of the quilter's arts. The style is Italian in origin and it involves only two layers of fabric sewn together with a design outlined in small running stitches. Loosely woven backing fabric was traditionally used, so that small amounts of stuffing could be pushed through; by this painstaking method a raised pattern appeared on the top sheet of the quilt, and the parted threads could be carefully moved back to their original position when the desired thickness was achieved. White cotton fabric was worked with white thread to produce subtle, complex work with all-over quilting as a background to the trapunto motifs.

Early American quiltmakers were proud of their work; they held competitions and exhibitions and the best quilts were seldom used as bedcovers in the way the early ones were, which accounts for the excellent state of preservation of many examples which can be seen in museums, private collections and shops around the world.

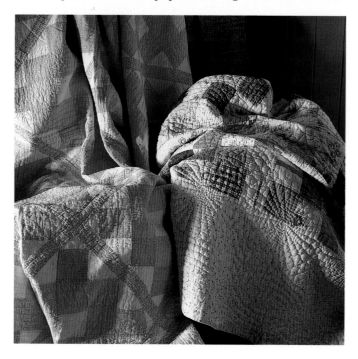

Examples of French (left) and English (right) quilting.

THE ALPHABET COT QUILT

The design for this quilt is taken from one made in Pennsylvania in about 1900. Most examples of early cot quilts are simply scaled-down versions of patterns used on full-size quilts, but the original that inspired this project was unmistakably designed for a child. The letter forms follow the quirks of the original, some of them being reversed, and the building in the bottom right hand corner represents a schoolhouse.

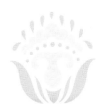

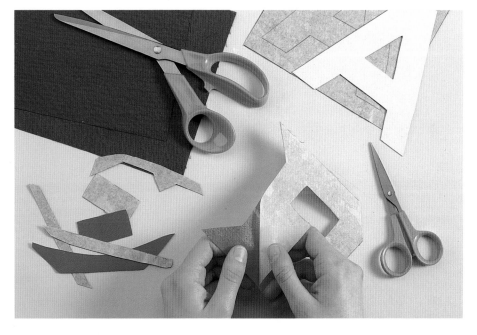

The colours of this quilt are strong compared with the pastel shades that are usually used for babies nowadays, but the quilt will brighten any nursery, and later make an attractive wall hanging for an older child's bedroom. It is best worked in fine cotton, which will not fray too much and will hold a firm crease well, which is important when sewing the pieces together. If you find the letters difficult to appliqué, try cutting actual-sized letters (without a seam allowance) from iron-on interfacing.

The choice of machine or hand sewing is a personal one; hand sewing will take longer to do and will not be as strong as machine sewing, but it is infinitely more controllable.

You will need:
- A pencil
- Thin cardboard and paper
- Bonding paper (iron-on interfacing)
- An iron
- 2½yd (2.3m) red fabric 45in (115cm) wide
- 1yd (90cm) of blue fabric 45in (115cm) wide
- A sewing machine
- Needles, pins, safety pins and scissors
- Thread to match and invisible nylon thread
- Wadding (batting) to fit
- A tape measure

These measurements include a ¼in (6mm) seam allowance.

Blue Fabric
28 6in (15cm) squares
2   28½in by 2½in (72cm by 6.5cm)
2   51in by 2½in (1.3m by 6.5cm)

Red Fabric
28 6in (15cm) squares
1   53in by 30½in (1.35m by 77cm)
2   24in by 2½in (60cm by 6.5cm)
2   46½in by 2½in (1.18m by 6.5cm)

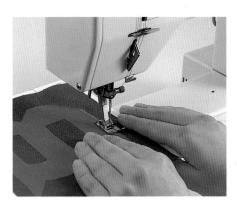

1 Enlarge the alphabet on page 151; draw up on cardboard. Each letter should fit in the squares allowing space around it. The alphabet should be in reverse at this stage. Trace it and the house on to bonding paper (iron-on interfacing) and cut them out. Use a steam iron to press each letter on to the reverse of the red fabric. Leave them to cool, then cut them all out. Peel off the paper and place each letter in the centre of a blue square. Press the work.

2 Fit an appliqué foot to your sewing machine if you have one and following your machine's instructions; set it to satin stitch and practise on a spare piece of material. Next, stitch the alphabet and house on to the squares, placing a piece of thin paper under each one as you work to stop puckers forming. Remove the paper after stitching. ▶

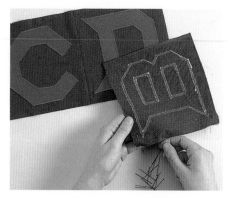

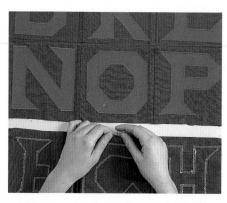

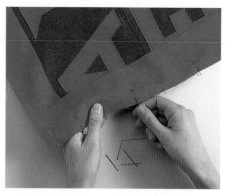

3 Lay out the quilt in the correct order and join the squares in pairs, pinning and tacking (basting) them first. Pass all the squares through the machine, running a short "chain" of thread between each pair. This speeds up production and saves thread.

4 Check and press the seams open, then lay out the squares and join them again to form rows. Join these rows together until the quilt is finished; press the work well.

5 Pin and tack (baste) the two shorter red strips to the top and bottom edges of the quilt, making sure the strip and quilt are right sides together. Sew and press, then join the remaining two red strips to the sides. Repeat, joining the blue borders to the red ones, then press the work well.

6 ▶ Lay the backing fabric on a flat surface, right side down and cover with wadding. The backing fabric is 2in (5cm) larger than the quilt; place it, centred over the wadding (batting), right side up. Tack (baste) using safety-pins, one in each letter and around the borders.

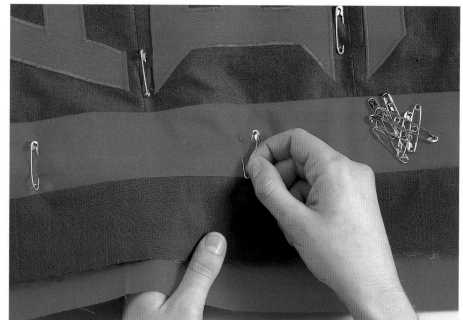

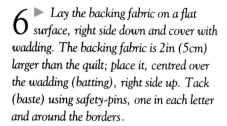

7 ▲ Machine-quilt, using a walking or a feed foot if you have one. For the quilt shown here, invisible nylon thread was used on the top with red thread in the bobbin and it was quilted "in the ditch" – stitched around each block along the valley that forms between the seams. Roll the quilt so that it will fit under the machine; you can use bicycle clips to hold it. When finished, pull the threads through to the back, knot the loose ends by sewing them into the back of the quilt.

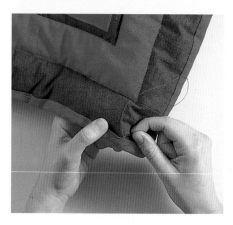

8 Fold the red backing fabric around to the front of the quilt to form the binding. Pin it and then slip stitch.

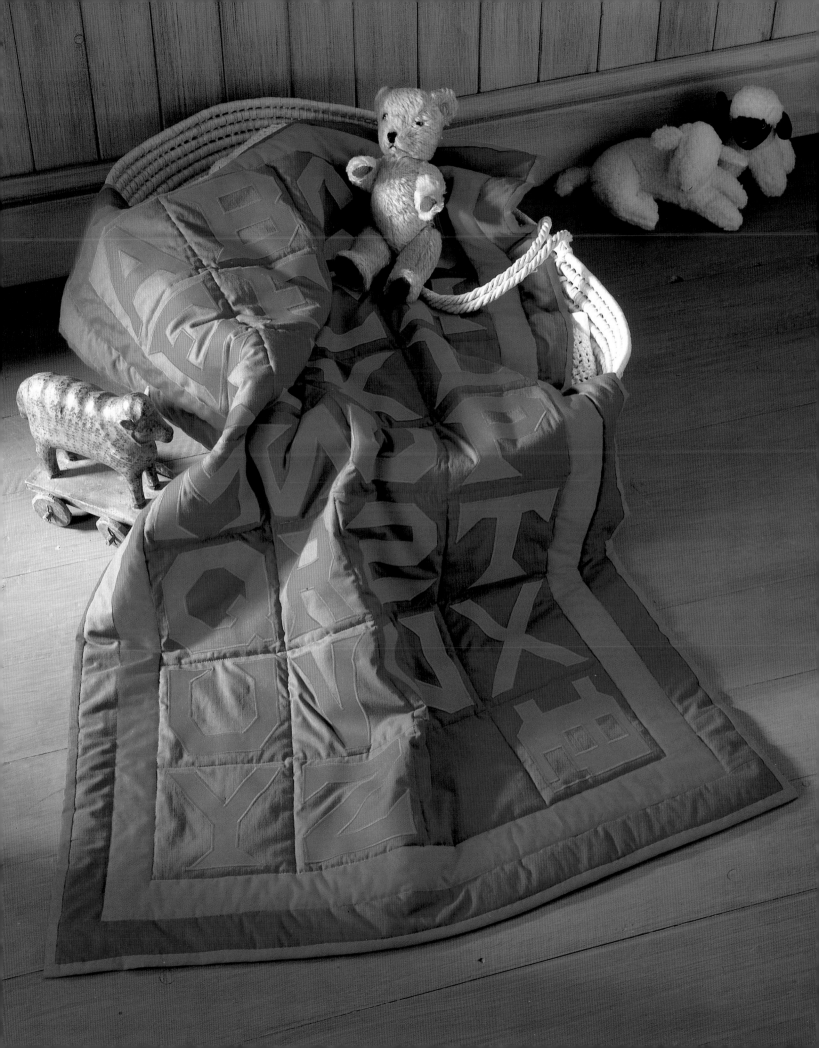

BEAR'S PAW QUILT

There was a time when almost every woman in America was engaged in making a quilt, such was the scale of the fashion for quilting in the late nineteenth century. The craft was more or less abandoned during and after the Second World War, but it resurfaced in the 1960s and there is now a huge revival of interest in it.

The quilt pattern used in this project is a traditional one called Bear's Paw. The pattern is made of squares, rectangles and triangles which require accurate cutting and stitching if the block is to lie flat. Use 100 per cent cotton fabric, pre-washed and ironed flat. The Bear's Paw works best with a simple two-tone colour contrast, which shows off the pattern well.

The choice of machine or hand sewing is a personal one; hand sewing will take longer to do and will not be as strong as machine sewing, but it is infinitely more controllable. This example has been made with the help of a sewing machine.

You will need:
- Template plastic
- A pencil and a ruler
- 4yd (3.5m) red fabric 45in (115cm) wide
- 5yd (4.6m) white fabric 45in (115cm) wide
- Needles, pins and scissors
- Thread to match and invisible polyester thread
- A sewing machine
- 5yd (4.6m) white backing fabric 45in (115cm) wide
- Wadding (batting) to fit
- 1½in (4cm) masking tape
- A tape measure

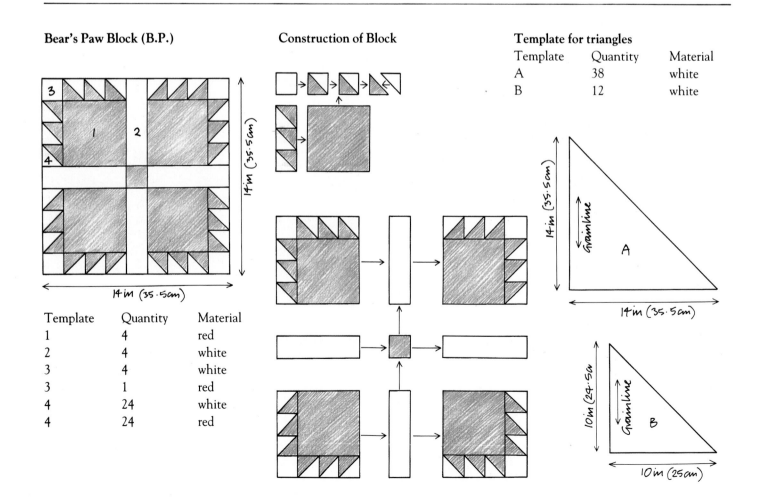

Bear's Paw Block (B.P.)

14in (35.5cm) × 14in (35.5cm)

Template	Quantity	Material
1	4	red
2	4	white
3	4	white
3	1	red
4	24	white
4	24	red

Construction of Block

Template for triangles

Template	Quantity	Material
A	38	white
B	12	white

A — 14in (35.5cm) × 14in (35.5cm), Grainline

B — 10in (24.5cm) × 10in (25cm), Grainline

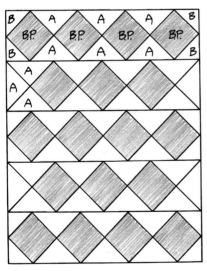

Backing fabric 100in by 80in
                (2.5m by 2m)

Binding strips 100in by 1½in
                (2.5m by 3.5cm)

                80in by 1½in

                (2m by 3.5cm)

1 Enlarge the Bear's Paw block to 14in (35.5cm) square and number each template as shown. Trace out the four shapes on to template plastic and add a ¼in (6mm) seam allowance on all sides. Mark in the straight grain line. Cut out the templates. You will need enough shapes to make 18 blocks.

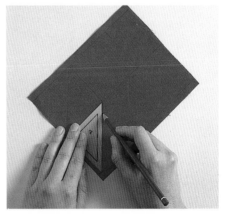

2 Lay out a block – start by joining the small triangles. Place the triangles right sides together, and pin and machine them one after the other, leaving a small "chain" of thread between. This will speed up production and save on thread. Check the seams, then press them open and join the block as shown in the diagram. ▶

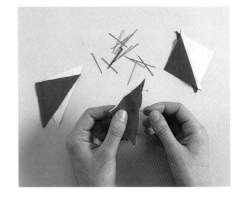

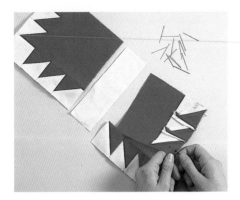

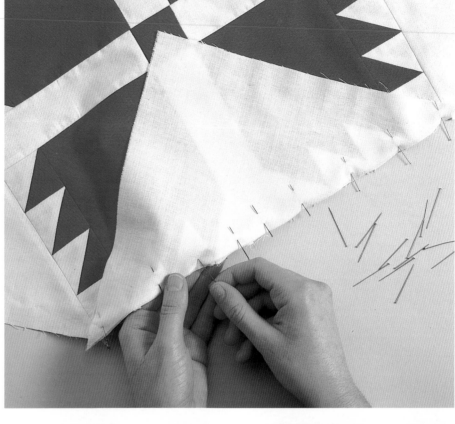

3 Work methodically, pressing between each step. When all the blocks are patched, check the measurements, and make corrections if necessary.

4 When all the blocks are patched, join the large triangles (A and B). Following the quilt plan, join the rows in the order shown. Press the work well. If you are quilting by hand, mark out guide lines with a straight-edge and a sharp pencil.

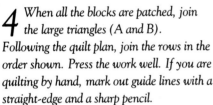

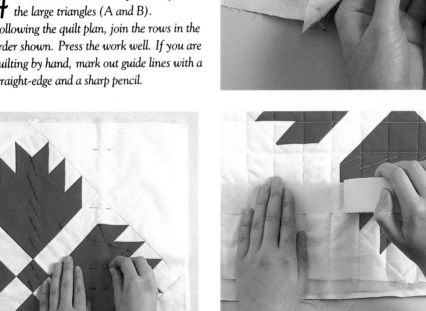

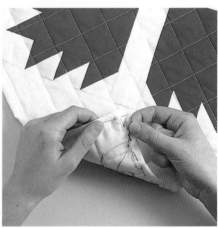

5 On a large flat surface, lay the backing fabric right side down. Carefully centre the wadding, and over this place the quilt top right side up. Check that all the sides match then, starting from the centre, pin then tack (baste) the layers together, smoothing any wrinkles towards the edge as you go. Work one side first, then the other starting from the centre again and tacking (basting) fairly closely so that the layers do not slip.

6 Quilt either by hand or machine. Starting from the centre, stick several lengths of masking tape as a guide, 1½in (4cm) apart. A walking or feed foot will help keep the stitches even on the machine. Use a polyester thread. You can re-use the masking tape several times. Quilt a 1½in (4cm) grid over the entire quilt.

7 When all the quilting is finished, trim the edges and put on the binding, right sides together and opposite sides first, then slip stitch to finish. Do not forget to put a label on the back with your name and date – your quilt may be a future heirloom.

QUILTED APPLIQUÉ CUSHION COVER

The album style of quiltmaking flourished in the state of Maryland in the mid-nineteenth century, and most particularly in the city of Baltimore, which gave its name to the style. These first appliqué album quilts were highly individual, depicting homes, families and pets as well as the usual folk motifs.

If you have never tried appliqué work before, it would be unwise to launch yourself straight into making a bedcover. Instead, begin by making just one square of an album quilt which can be framed as a picture, or made into a cushion cover.

This square was inspired by an intricate 25-block quilt known as the Baltimore Album, signed by Hannah Foote and dated 1850. Each block is different, depicting floral urns and baskets, wreaths, farm scenes, the eagle and flag and an anchor (the motif chosen for this project) which may represent a relative away or lost at sea.

You will need:
- Template plastic or paper
- Three squares of unbleached calico: 12in (30cm) square, 14in (35.5cm) square and 19in by 14in (48cm by 35.5cm)
- Scraps of material – finely woven pure cotton is best
- Cotton thread to match the scraps
- Cream cotton thread
- Wadding (batting) 13in (33cm) square
- Red print fabric, sufficient for four 12in by 2in (30cm by 5cm) strips
- Pins, needles and scissors
- ½in (1.5cm) ribbon (optional)
- An iron
- Cushion pad

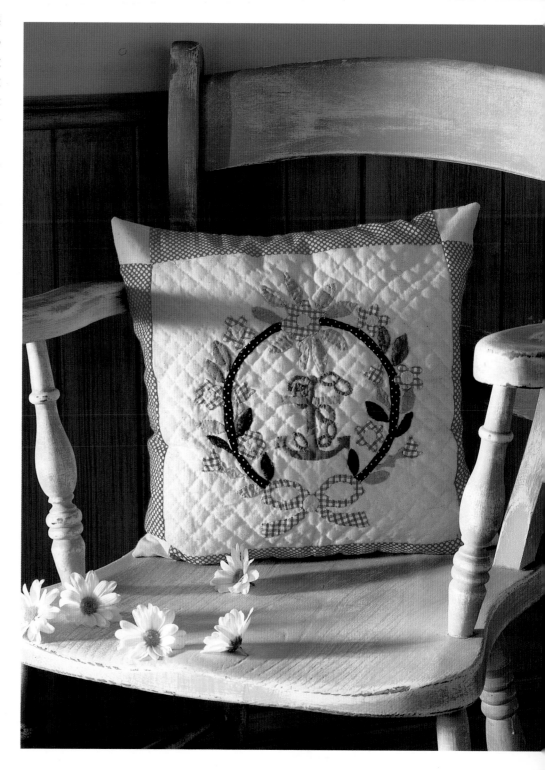

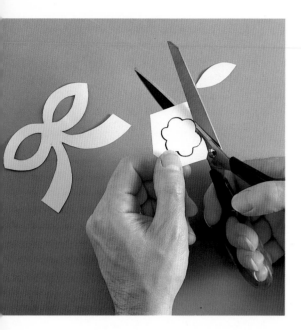

1 Enlarge the pattern elements and cut out the templates, and then the pieces from your scraps of material. Looking at the picture of the finished cushion, decide how busy you want your cushion to be, and therefore how many leaves to cut out.

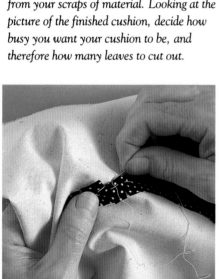

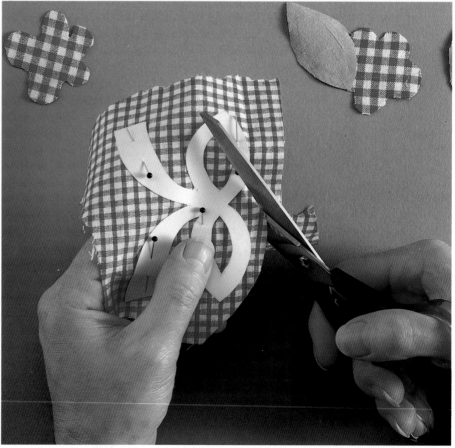

2 Working on to the smallest calico square, begin with the ring. Snip the edges at ¼in (6mm) intervals and position it centrally on the square. Tack (baste) down the centre of the ring and then begin sewing. Use a small slip stitch, and turn the seam under as you sew. Use this method for the other curved patterned pieces.

3 When cutting the bow, slit the fabric and snip around for the inside bow shapes, or the seam will rob your bow of body.

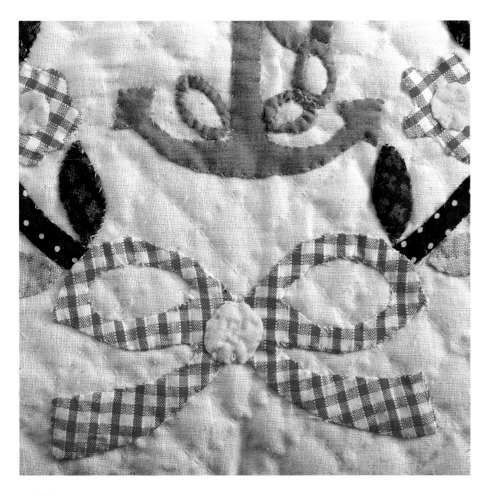

4 This picture shows the position of the bow. Then add the leaves and flowers, alternating between left and right to get an evenly matched wreath. You may find it easier to appliqué the flowers and leaves if you apply iron-on interfacing, without the seam allowance, to the backs of the pieces before you snip the edges.

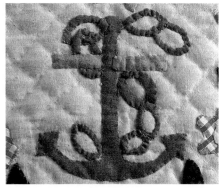

5 This picture shows the position of the anchor. It should be slip stitched into place. The chain is a challenge, but it can be worked in embroidery silk using chain stitch if you prefer. Embroidery was used for detailing on these squares.

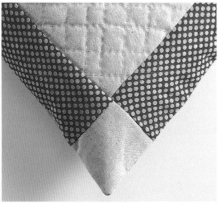

6 Attach the red border strips, adding a square connecting piece of plain calico at each corner. Then pin the wadding (batting) between your work and the backing square, which is the second calico square. Fold the appliquéd square over the edge of the wadding (batting), pin and sew around the edge using a running stitch.

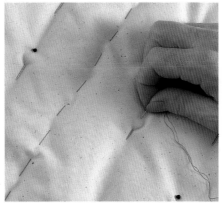

7 Tack (baste) the three layers together diagonally and crosswise using a contrasting colour.

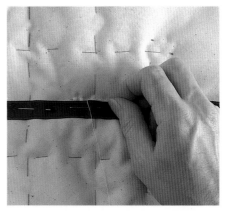

8 Sew through all three layers using a small running stitch. Keep the lines running up to the motifs and then beyond them in straight rows, first in one direction and then the other, until the background is quilted in a diamond pattern. Beginners will find it useful to pin a length of ribbon in a straight line, and stitch along either side of it. To make the back of the cushion see step 7, page 92.

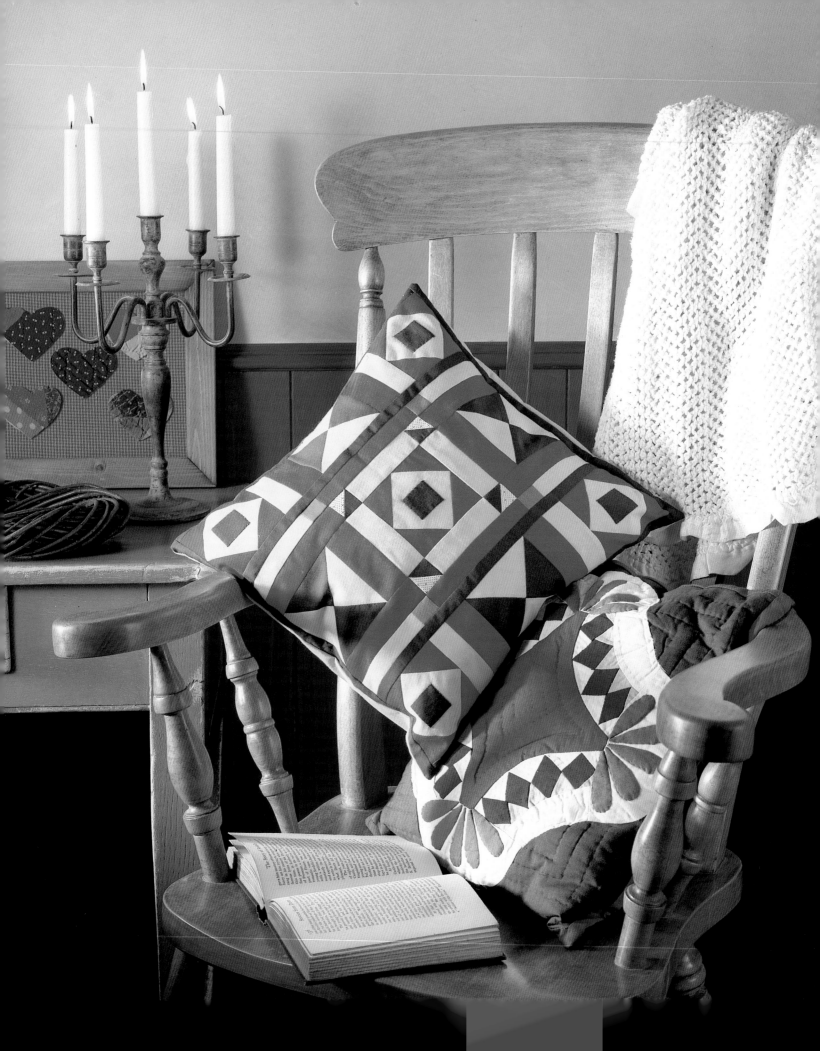

PIECED CUSHION COVER

The pattern for this cushion comes from a single block on a very large sampler quilt made in Lancaster County, Pennsylvania, in about 1870. The original quilt is a masterpiece of 85 different patchwork squares, 28 triangular edging patchworks and a green and red zig-zagged frame within a patterned border. The squares are made to a mixture of traditional and original patterns and the quilt is signed 'Salinda W Rupp.'

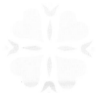

This project is worked in the original quilt colours; you can use another combination, but it is important to keep to the design by using darker and lighter colour tones.

Accuracy is vital when cutting and sewing geometric patchwork and pure cotton fabrics are most suitable; they fold well and do not fray much. The finished cushion is 16in (40cm) square, but can be drafted to any size. The quantities of material given are for this size.

You will need:
- Graph paper and a pencil
- Template plastic
- 10in (25cm) red fabric 45in (115cm) wide
- 18in (45cm) green fabric 45in (115cm) wide
- 18in (45cm) yellow fabric 45in (115cm) wide
- Scraps of bright green and red spotted fabric
- Scissors
- A sewing machine and an iron
- Needles, pins and thread to match
- Cushion pad

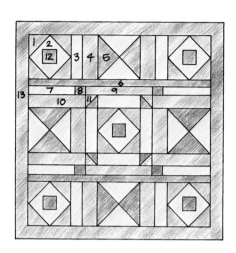

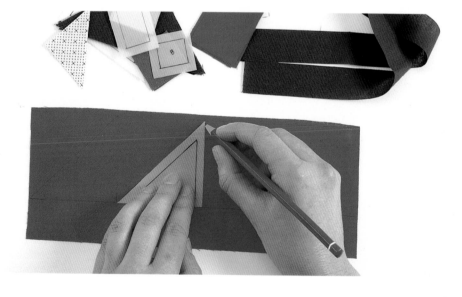

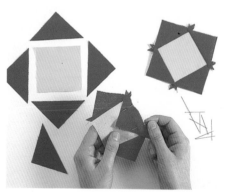

1 Enlarge the design to the size you want. Number the templates as shown, then trace them out on to template plastic, leaving enough room for a ¼in (6mm) seam allowance to be added on all sides. Follow the chart for the number of each template shape. Cut out the shapes. Lay out the whole block to check that you have all the pieces.

Red:	20 of no. 1; 6 of no. 4; 2 of no. 9; 4 of no. 10
Green:	8 of no. 5; 4 of no. 11; 2 of no. 6; 5 of no. 12; 4 of no. 13
Yellow:	5 of no. 2; 6 of no. 3; 8 of no. 5; 4 of no. 7
Bright Green:	4 of no. 8
Red Spotted:	4 of no. 11

2 Start to join the pieces, working in rows. Take a yellow square, then pin and sew two red triangles on opposite sides of it, with the right sides together. Press the work, with the seam allowance under the darker fabric. Join the two remaining red triangles on opposite sides. Press the fabric. ▶

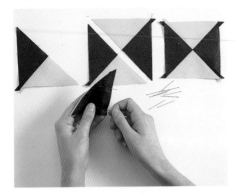
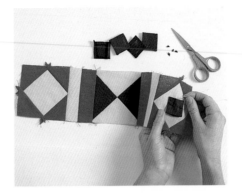
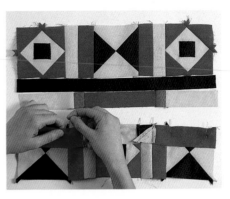

3 Pin together and sew one yellow triangle and one green triangle. Press and repeat with the remaining triangles. Join them diagonally to make a square, then press the work.

4 Sew the yellow and red stripes together, then join all the pieces for the top strip, and press the work. Press in a ¼in (6mm) seam allowance on the five green squares and hand appliqué them using yellow thread and tiny stitches.

5 Continue patching each row, then join them, pressing between each step until the cushion is finished.

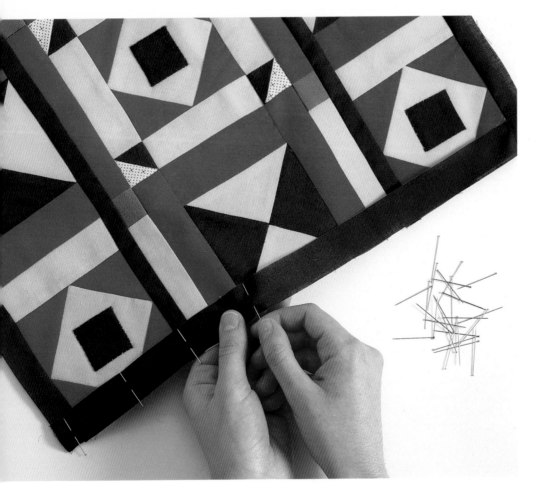

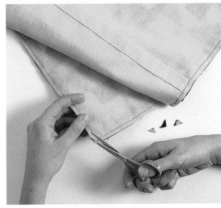

7 To make the back of the cushion cover, cut a piece of fabric the same width but about 5in (13cm) longer. Cut this fabric in half and turn in a hem at one end of each piece. Lay the two pieces on the cushion cover, right sides together, with the hemmed edges overlapping. Pin all the way around the edge, then sew it. Trim off the corners diagonally, within the seam allowance. Turn the cushion cover through, press it and insert a cushion pad.

6 Cut out 1in (2.5cm) borders from the green fabric to fit two opposite sides of the piece. Pin, then sew and press the fabric. Cut two more borders to fit the remaining sides and repeat, then press the work.

STENCILLED QUILT

Stencilled quilts made in the early nineteenth century featured complicated arrangements of fruit or flowers with wide borders and central motifs reminiscent of those used in theorem paintings. This was a style where individual stencilled elements were combined to make a picture. The painted images did not wear well and unfortunately few examples survive.

This project is not a traditional one, although it was inspired by an appliquéd quilt made in about 1840, the Willow Oak quilt. This quilt is unusual because it was executed in only two colours, a dark blue spotted fabric for the motifs and a plain cream linen background. It features twelve framed medallions with a border of willows and flower shapes, and its dramatic contrasts make it very suitable for a stencilled version.

This project is ideal for someone who wants a quick result; the most time-consuming part is cutting and positioning the stencils. Once this is done, the quilt grows quickly.

You will need:
- Two single cotton bed sheets. Dip them in tea, then dry and iron flat
- An enlargement of the stencil on page 150 and 151
- Acetate sheet or waxy stencil card
- Scissors
- Spray adhesive
- Navy or black spray, or fabric paint (which takes longer and is harder to use)
- Two long straight-edges and a set-square
- Needles and pins
- Pale pencil or crayon
- Wadding (batting) to fit
- Masking tape and tape measure
- Cream thread
- A sewing machine

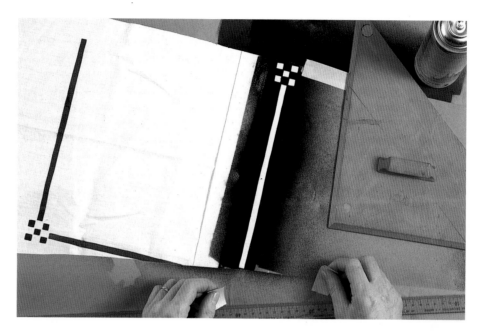

1 Lay out flat one of the sheets, in a well-ventilated room. Cut the stencils out of acetate or stencil card (see page 147). Work out roughly how much of the sheet the pattern will cover. Lightly fold the sheet in half and half again, and then unfold it leaving a slight crease as a guide. Begin by laying your grid along the centre fold and then work in blocks above and below it,

2 When you have completed the central grid, stencil the medallions within the squares and add the corner motifs. Stencil the border, completing one side at a time. Press the quilt top. With right side uppermost decide how far beyond the motifs you want the quilting to extend. Mark a line on all four sides of the quilt. Measure and mark a second line 1¼in (3cm) outside the first one all round the quilt, keeping the corners as square as possible. Trim away excess fabric leaving 2in (5cm) "insurance" around the outer line. ▶

according to the pattern. Spray the back of the stencil lightly with spray adhesive and press it firmly on to the fabric. If you are using spray paint, mask the edge of the stencil with newspaper to protect the fabric from drifting colour. Apply fabric paint according to the manufacturer's instructions. Use the set-square to get an accurate 90-degree angle for the grid.

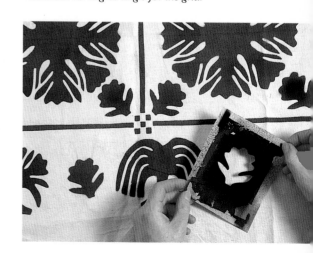

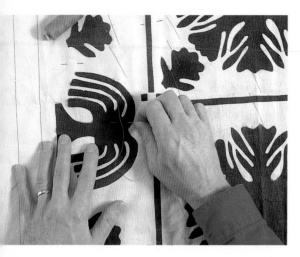

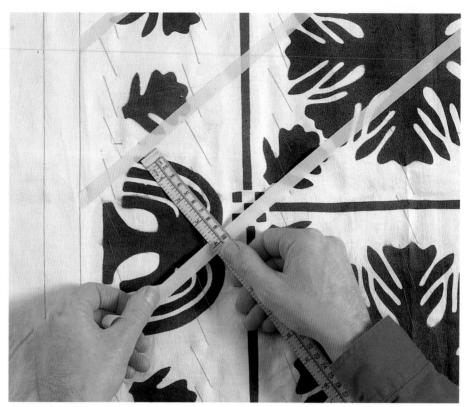

3 Use the trimmed top as a guide to cut a
piece of wadding (batting) and the
second sheet (backing fabric) slightly larger.
Assemble the quilt by putting the backing
fabric right side down on a large flat surface.
Next, place the wadding (batting) on top,
checking that it is central. Then place the
stencilled quilt top, right side up. Starting in
the centre, pin then tack (baste) the layers
together, smoothing the way towards the
edges as you go. Tack (baste) one side from
the centre outwards, then the other.

4 Place a strip of masking tape diagonally
across the centre of the quilt and then a
second, about 4in (10cm) away. Use them
as your quilting guide, then remove and
re-use them. If you want to quilt by hand,
mark your lines using a straight-edge and a
sharp pencil. You may want to emphasize
the motifs by quilting around their shape.
Roll the quilt diagonally, so that it will fit
under the machine. If you have a walking or
a feed foot it will help to feed the fabric
through evenly. Machine-quilt the grid then
the perimeter line, using a stitch length of
around ¹⁄₁₀in (2.5mm) and slightly less top
tension than for dressmaking. Finish off the
ends of the machining on the back of the
quilt, either by sewing them in or by tying off
the threads and trimming.

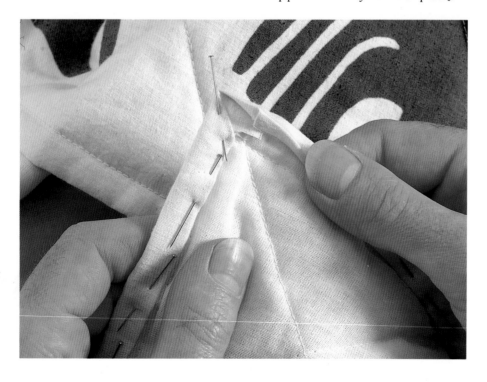

5 From the back, mark a line 1¼in
(3cm) out from the perimeter
machining. Trim the wadding (batting) and
backing back to this line. Turn the quilt over
and check that the 1¾in (4.5cm) line is
straight then trim along this line. Turn the
edge of the trimmed quilt over to the back,
fold in 1½in (4cm), fold again, pin and
slip-stitch. At the corners fold in a triangle
first, then fold the side turnings to create a
neat mitre.

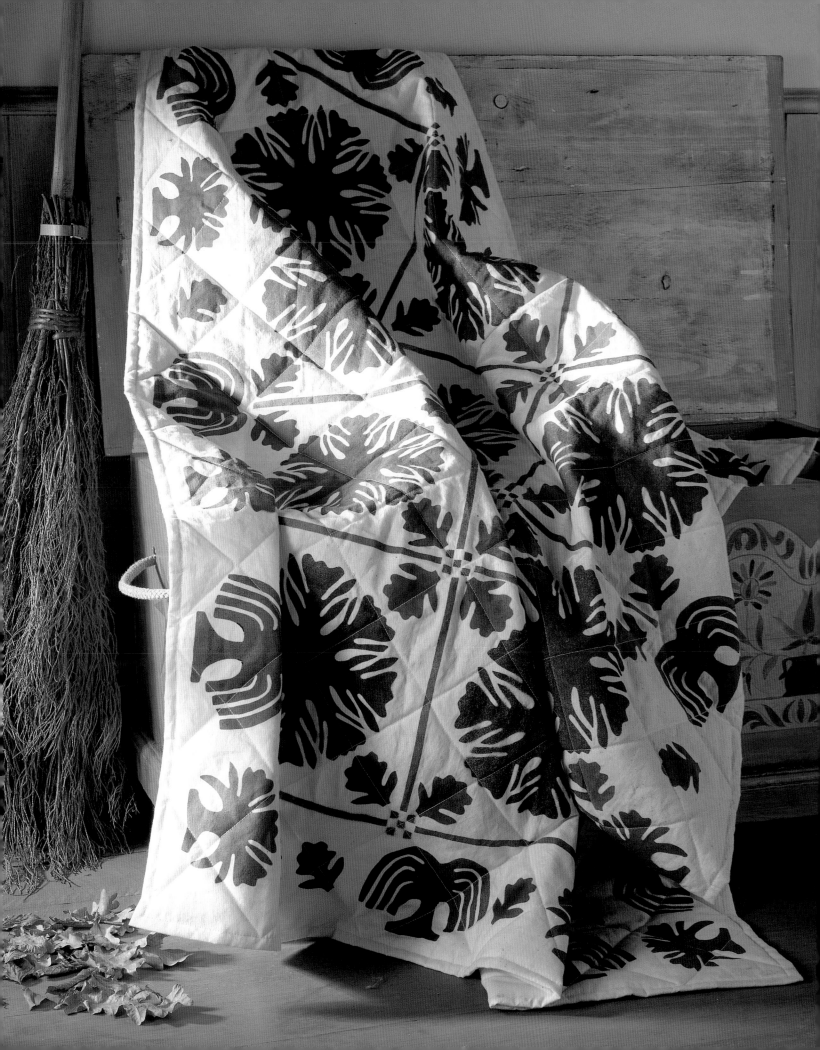

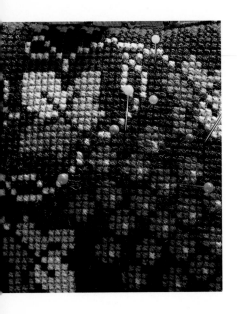

CROSS STITCH
AND NEEDLEPOINT

NEEDLEPOINT WAS TAUGHT TO GIRLS FROM AN EARLY AGE, AND WHEN YOU CONSIDER THE AMOUNT OF SEWING THAT WAS NEEDED IN A HOME, WITH NO SEWING MACHINE OR FACTORY-PRODUCED LINEN AND CLOTHING, THE IMPORTANCE OF TEACHING A GIRL STITCHCRAFT IS OBVIOUS. THE ART OF EMBROIDERY WAS NOT ONLY CONFINED TO YOUNG GIRLS; IT WAS CONSIDERED A HIGHLY SOPHISTICATED AND REFINED ACTIVITY – EVEN AMONG THE LADIES AT THE COURT OF QUEEN ELIZABETH I. A SAMPLER DATED 1634, EMBROIDERED WITH THE QUEEN'S COAT OF ARMS, CAN BE SEEN IN THE MUSEUM OF LONDON.

SAMPLERS

One of the most popular forms of needlepoint was the making of samplers. Samplers have been made by many cultures over hundreds of years. They were originally made and kept as personal records, so many have survived and are fascinating social documents, revealing much about the lives of their makers. They were begun as a means of recording border patterns, alphabets and "spot" motifs such as animals, birds or flowers, and as young girls learnt their stitches, they added more over the years until the work was considered finished. Some beautifully intricate examples survive.

The first books of printed embroidery patterns began to appear around this time, and it is interesting to note that they are all accredited to men. The original books were from Germany, but soon Italian, French and English versions were widely available and the sampler ceased to be an important record but became more of a practice piece for the refining and showing off of stitchwork. Families framed and exhibited their daughters' work to advertise their suitability as wives. In England, orphans and poorhouse children were taught to stitch alphabets and letters, and their services were advertised for the marking of linens with the owner's initials worked in coloured cotton and cross stitch.

Wealthy women, for whom needlepoint was a pleasant pastime, embroidered with many colours of fine silk, usually on to a cream linen background. In Italy, cross

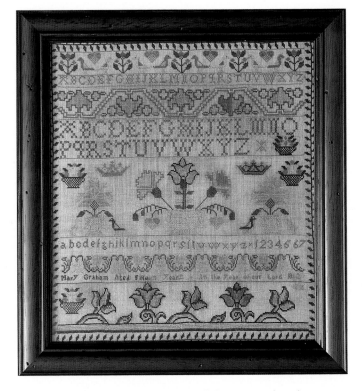

Samplers were originally made by young girls and kept as personal records.

stitch was less popular than satin, chain and feather stitches; Spanish and Mexican samplers are purely satin stitch; Danish work is renowned for its fine stitching and delicate colouring; French samplers for their border patterns, while Dutch and German styles are similar, often

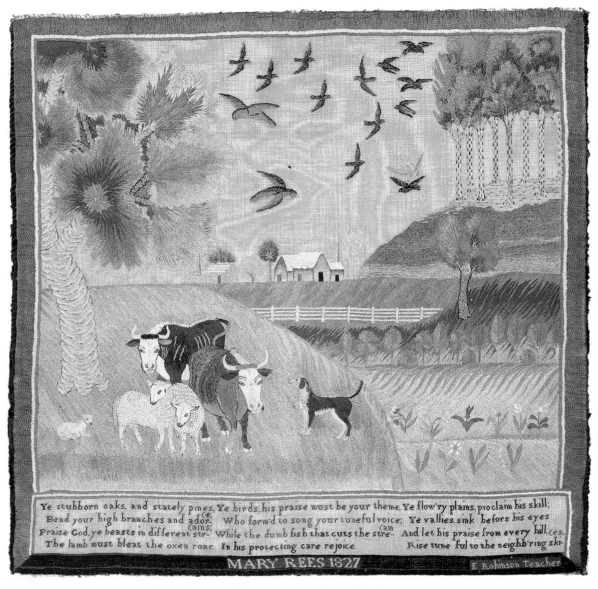

Ye stubborn oaks, and stately pines, Ye birds, his praise must be your theme, Ye flow'ry plains, proclaim his skill;
Bend your high branches and ador- Who form'd to song your tuneful voice; Ye vallies, sink before his eyes
Praise God, ye beasts in different str- While the dumb fish that cuts the stre- And let his praise from every hill,
The lamb must bleat the oxen roar. In his protecting care rejoice. Rise tune ful to the neighb'ring ski-

MARY REES 1827   E. Robinson Teacher

Barnyard scene by Mary Rees, c. 1827. The careful selection of colour and the
direction and type of stitching make the scene both naturalistic and decorative.

using heraldic devices. American samplers show a strong English influence until the end of the eighteenth century, after which time the natural exuberance of the settlers began to assert itself and their subject matter became more domestic and patriotic.

BERLIN WOOLWORK

A great change took place in the early nineteenth century when a new form of coloured squared pattern appeared in Berlin. This was the forerunner of needlepoint, set to become the embroidery craze of the century. Worked on canvas with coloured wools according to an accurate,

easily counted stitch plan, it was both simple and quick to do. The arrival of this new style more or less coincided with the decline of the traditional sampler, although Berlin work samplers did become popular.

Because needlepoint uses strong wool sewn on canvas, it is extremely durable and it became immensely popular during the Victorian era as a covering for chairs, stools and firescreens – many 100-year-old examples are still in use. There has been a resurgence of interest today in both sampler making and needlepoint, and although samplers usually still follow the traditional format, contemporary designers are creating interesting new styles.

CROSS STITCH PINCUSHION

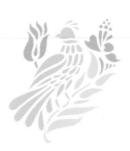

A pincushion was an invaluable sewing aid for women who spent hours stitching for their families; pins could be plucked effortlessly from, or returned to, the pincushion without interrupting the sewing rhythm. Wool was used as a filling because its natural greases helped the pins glide in and out and protected them from rust.

Amish women had a particular need for pincushions as their strict dress code forbade the use of buttons and all their clothing was fastened with straight pins. Because they were practical objects, Amish pincushions were allowed some decoration – some were made from patchwork, others were embroidered and lace-trimmed and some, like the one in this project, were worked in needlepoint. Most had a loop at one corner so that they could hang from the wrist when working, and from a shelf hook when not in use.

You will need:
- Needlepoint canvas 8in (20cm) square, 10 or 11 mesh double-thread
- A soft-leaded pencil and a ruler
- Tacking (basting) thread in contrasting colour
- A tapestry needle, size 24, and a sewing needle
- Persian yarn: one skein each of light green, mid green, deep green, gold, grape, red and bottle green
- Two pieces of dark green corduroy fabric 4½in by 8in (11cm by 20cm)
- Matching sewing thread and matching top-stitching thread
- A sewing machine
- Scissors
- Polyester toy stuffing
- A knitting needle
- Small beads

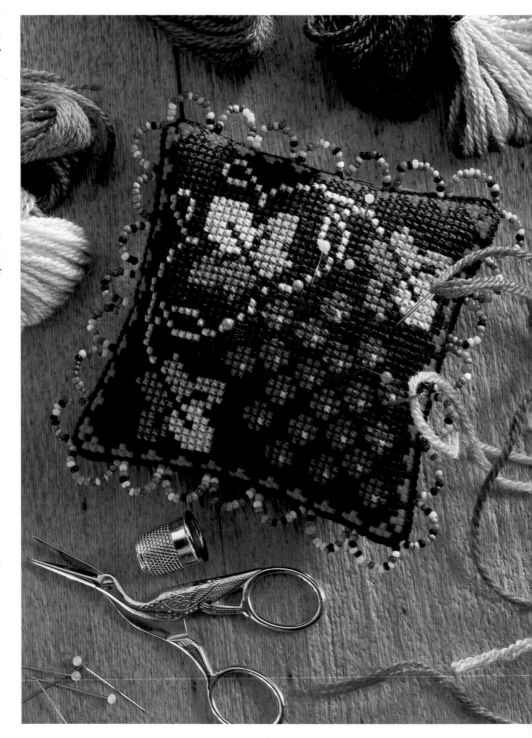

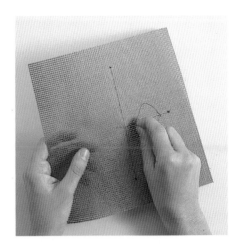

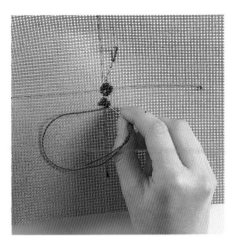

 light green

mid green

deep green

gold

grape

red

bottle green

1 Rule vertical and horizontal lines on the design to mark the centre, using a soft pencil which can be erased. Work vertical and horizontal rows of tacking (basting) in a contrasting colour thread to mark the centre of the canvas.

2 Embroider the design in cross stitch from the chart, using one strand of thread and working outwards from the centre of the design. Note that each coloured square on the chart represents one complete cross stitch worked over one canvas intersection. Work each cross stitch horizontally in individual rows.

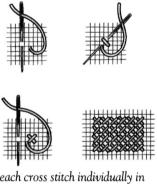

Work each cross stitch individually in horizontal rows, as shown above.

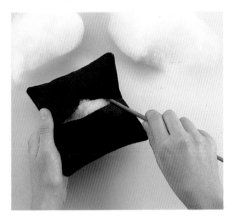

3 Place the corduroy pieces right sides together and make a seam along one edge, leaving an opening of about 4in (10cm) at the centre. Making sure the seam is in the centre, place the back and the finished embroidery right sides together and pin round the edge. Machine-stitch close to the last row of embroidery. Trim the seams, clip the corners and turn the work right side out through the opening. Stuff it firmly with polyester stuffing, using the knitting needle to press the stuffing into each corner, then stitch up the opening.

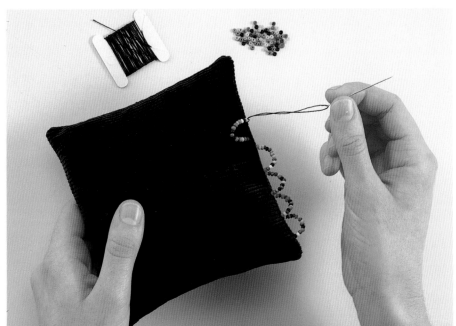

4 Using the top-stitching thread, stitch groups of beads around the edge to make a looped fringe. You will need about 15 beads for each loop. Work from the back of the pincushion and tighten the thread after each loop, securing it by making two or three small stitches into the fabric. Make sure you secure the beginning and the end of the thread carefully to prevent the beads from working loose.

SAMPLER

There was a time when every little girl began her first sampler at about the age of five. She would work alphabets, numbers, motifs and a variety of stitches neatly in many different colours on a strip of linen. The final addition was her name, age and the date of her work's completion. There are some remarkably detailed pieces of work surviving which declare the maker to be just six years old.

Old samplers from England, Denmark, Germany, Greece, America and other countries are strikingly similar not only in the regularity of the cross stitch pattern, but also in their arrangement and the subjects they depict.

The project sampler takes some of the elements from an old Danish family tree sampler featuring hearts and birds, both symbols of love. Match the colours, or make up your own colour scheme, but do buy all your silks at the same time to be sure that they are harmonious.

You will need:
- Graph paper 10 squares to 1in (2.5cm)
- Coloured pencils or pens
- 20in (50cm) square of 11 count cross-stitch fabric in cream
- Tacking (basting) thread in a contrasting colour
- Tapestry needle, size 26, and a sewing needle
- Stranded cotton: one skein each of light pink, deep red, purple, light blue, mid blue, orange, light green and deep green, and two skeins of mid green
- A stiff piece of card (cardboard)
- Scissors
- Pins and button thread
- A picture frame

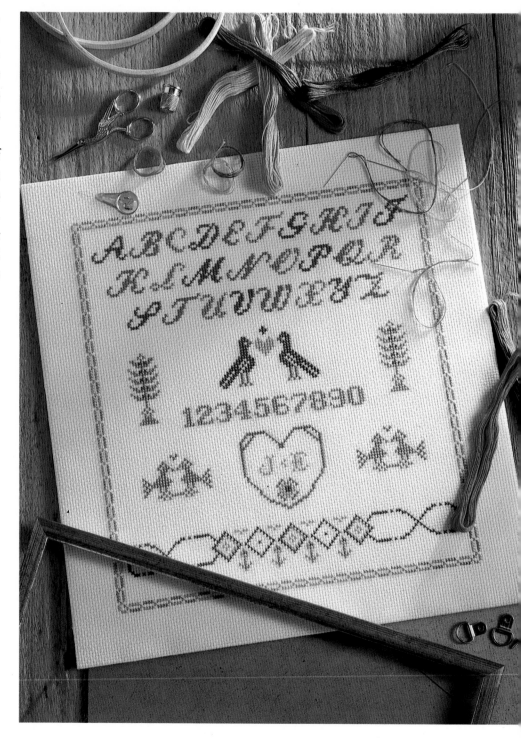

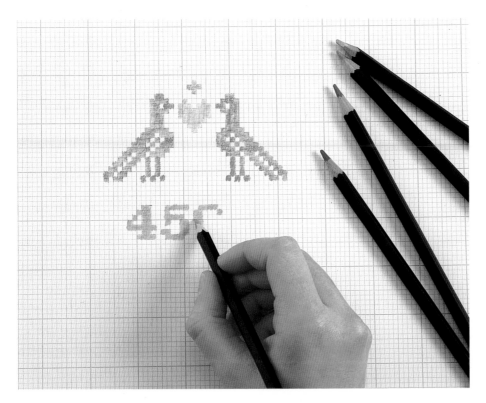

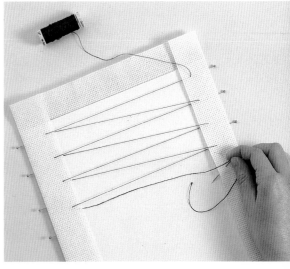

2 Mark the centre of the canvas with coloured thread.

1 Using the motifs and alphabets on page 152, sketch out your own design on graph paper using coloured pencils or pens, reversing the bird motifs as necessary.

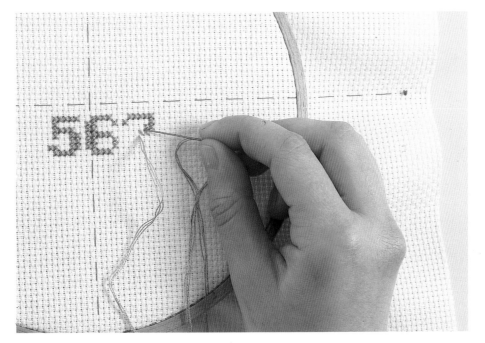

3 Work the sampler design in cross stitch using the method shown on page 99, but remember that the top diagonal stitches of each cross should always slant in the same direction, usually from bottom left to top right.

4 ▶ Centre the piece of card over the wrong side of the finished embroidery. Cut away the surplus fabric leaving a margin of about 2in (5cm) all round. Fold over the fabric at the top and bottom of the card, secure with pins, then take long

stitches between the two fabric edges using the button thread. Knot the thread at one end, tighten the stitches and secure the other thread end. Repeat along the other two sides. Mount in the picture frame.

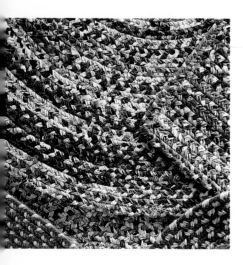

RAG RUGS

THE CRAFT OF RAG RUGMAKING MAY HAVE COME TO THE AMERICAN COLONIES FROM SCANDINAVIA, BUT ITS DEVELOPMENT INTO AN ART FORM TOOK PLACE ENTIRELY IN AMERICA IN THE EIGHTEENTH CENTURY. THE FIRST RUGS WERE BRAIDED FROM TORN STRIPS OF WORN-OUT CLOTHING. THREE STRIPS WERE PINNED TOGETHER AT ONE END, THEN TIGHTLY BRAIDED WITH THE FRAYING EDGES TURNED IN DURING THE PROCESS. THE FINISHED BRAIDS WERE THEN COILED AND STITCHED TO MAKE A FLAT CIRCULAR FLOOR RUG.

The early rugs were not hardwearing, but must have provided some relief from the hard floors; and being relatively quick and easy to make, new rugs would soon replace worn ones. In time, some housewives took to dyeing batches of rag strips in different colours to produce more ordered patterns, but the circular shape did not alter much because of the construction method.

Like braided rugs, hooked rugs were fashioned from

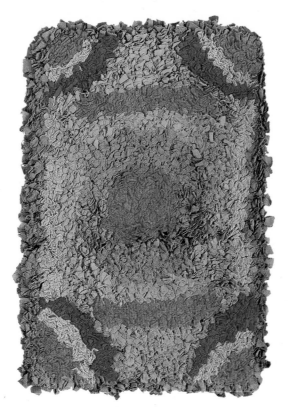

An early twentieth-century rag rug from the Welsh border.

torn strips of cloth, but they were made entirely differently. To make a hooked rug, a backing of burlap or loosely woven canvas was used sometimes stretched on a wooden frame. The rug maker traced or drew a design on to the canvas, then used an instrument resembling a large crochet hook to punch a hole in the backing and pull up a loop of cloth from below. This action was repeated, with colour changes as the pattern required, and as it took some skill to produce even-sized loops, these were often cut to give a tufted texture to the finished rug.

MOTIFS

The making of hooked rugs became tremendously popular and soon patterns progressed from the basic geometric shapes to those of a far more pictorial content. The subject matter varied from county to county: in Maine in the early 1800s fully rigged schooners were a popular subject; and further inland, farmers' wives often choose to immortalize a favourite farm or domestic animal on a rug. There are marvellous naive renderings of dogs, roosters and bulls, which give little thought to proportion, but are loaded with character.

Floral motifs and borders suited the medium well and were particularly popular during the Victorian era, when dark backgrounds with floral borders would be used to frame a suitably serious religious text. Amish women made many exquisite hooked rugs and their favoured subjects were garden flowers such as forget-me-nots and pansies as well as horses and birds. As with all Amish fabric crafts, it is rare to find any patterned materials used

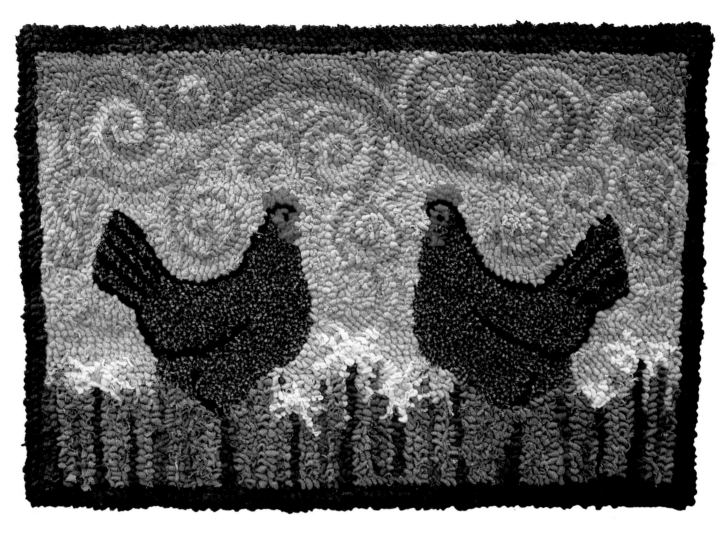

A modern hooked rug from Scotland.

in a rug, so the solid areas of colour make their designs very strong.

E.S. FROST

In the 1850s a travelling tin merchant called E.S. Frost saw so many housewives busy making rugs that he realized a market existed for printed patterns and began stencilling directly on to burlap and selling his designs. He became immensely successful and the craft spread like wildfire across America. Unfortunately, the availability of these ready-printed patterns had the effect of popularizing rug making while robbing the craft of much of its spontaneity and character.

Another style of rug made by early American women, which was never meant to go on the floor, was a table rug made of woollen felt. Known as a penny rug, it would be made up of circles of felt, blanket stitched at the edges, usually in contrasting thread with the pattern made by layering three graduated sizes of contrasting felt on top of each other. Penny rugs sometimes had teardrop edging pieces sewn in the same way, and dark earthy colours were the most popular. In New England pictorial designs were most common, with appliquéd and embroidered animals framed by a border of felt shapes. It was possible to buy pre-cut lozenge-shaped pieces of felt called pen-wipers, originally intended for wiping excess ink from a nib, which the ingenious rug makers use as borders for their rugs. Fortunately, some women were so proud of their finished rugs that they could not bear to see them being walked on and they put them away carefully for best, which is why so many fine examples of both hooked and penny rugs survive to be admired today.

THE BRAIDED RUG

The settler housewives made these rugs from plaited strips of worn clothing, with no more equipment than pins to hold the three strips together at one end and a needle and thread to sew the coil of braids together. This is the easiest sort of rug you can make and it can be made as small or large as you need. The most time-consuming part is cutting the strips; after that it grows like Jack's beanstalk.

The simple construction method does not mean that all braided rugs have to look alike; you can achieve a variety of different effects by the controlled use of colour and pattern. Plaits made up from a single colour make broad stripes which can then be contrasted with another plain colour. If you use two coils of a colour, you get a broader stripe, and by introducing a patterned fabric you add another dimension.

The combinations are limitless and you can use any sort of fabric, so long as it is recycled. This rug can be made to any size – simply keep adding more plaits. If the rug is going to receive a lot of wear back it with some backing fabric.

You will need:
- Cast-off clothes, sheets or tablecloths
- Scissors
- Needle and button thread
- Pins
- A strong safety pin
- Wallcup or hook

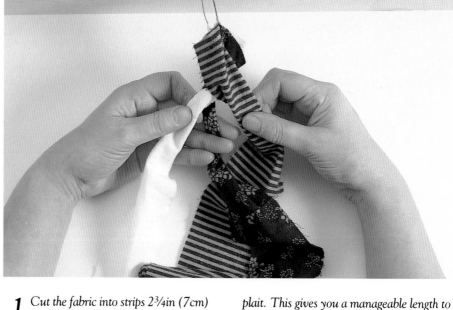

1 Cut the fabric into strips 2¾in (7cm) wide and sew the strips end to end into lengths of about 90in (2m). To start the plait, roll three strips and secure each one with a pin, leaving about 36in (90cm) to

plait. This gives you a manageable length to work with. Using the safety pin, secure the three fabric ends together and place the pin over the hook which should be screwed into some wood.

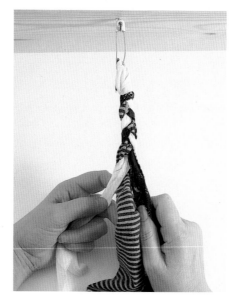

2 Turn the raw edges away from you (to the back and into the middle) as you work, and start braiding next to the pin with the rolled ends dangling down. Form a firm plait, gradually unrolling the steps as the plait gets longer.

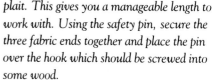
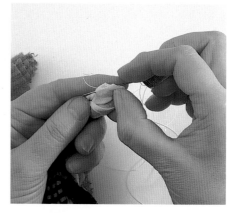

3 Begin making your oval spiral by carefully neatening off the braid end, trimming and hand stitching as necessary making it pointed.

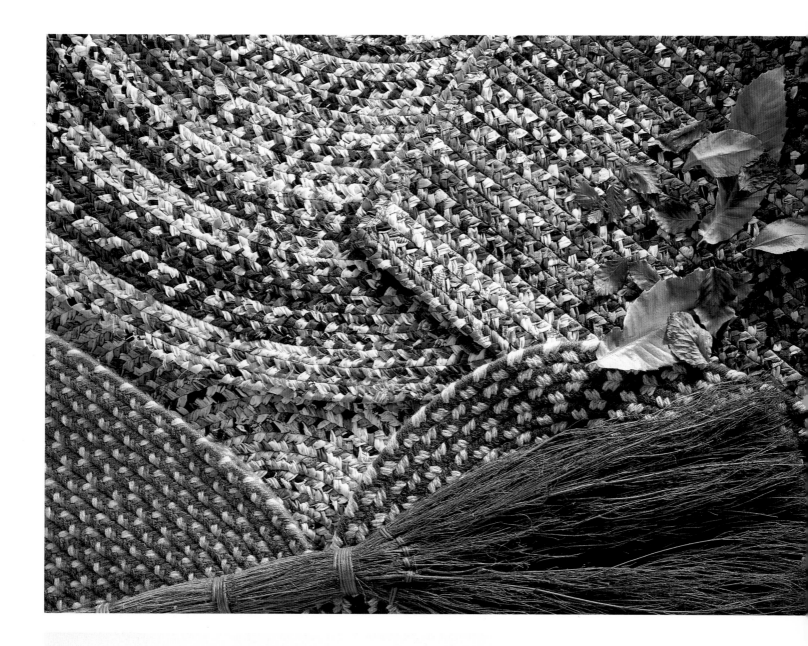

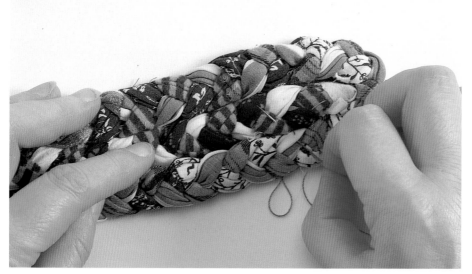

4 Bend the braid around and sew two adjacent sides together using button thread and "ladder" stitch so the stitches are concealed within the plait. Either pass the needle right through the plait or catch a small section of it, whichever is easier. Add more and more braided fabric strips as you go along, turning it around and around so you build up the oval shape. When the rug is large enough, neaten off the end as before. Sew the tapered end to the rug, making as smooth a curve as you can.

THE BALTIMORE BEAUTY HOOKED RUG

Most American settlers homes had just bare floors until hooked and braided rugs were discovered. Rag rugmaking first became popular in America and was then taken up in Europe and England in particular, where it found great favour during the "Make do and Mend" campaign of the Second World War, when all the national wealth was turned towards the war effort and parsimony was considered one of the finest of female qualities.

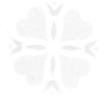

The rug in this project was made by Ann Davies, whose inspiration came from a wonderful appliquéd album quilt made in Baltimore in about 1850.

Using a transfer pen trace your selected pattern on to transfer paper. Transfer it on to the hessian by reversing the transfer paper and ironing over the design. You will need to work on a frame for this project and the hessian must be large enough to cover the frame to the outside edge. Attach the hessian using staples or drawing pins, and stretch it tight, making sure the threads are kept as straight as possible. Then mark out the area you are going to work within, allowing a border of ¾in (2cm) inside from the edge of the frame.

You will need:
- Transfer paper
- Transfer pen
- Hessian/burlap
- An iron
- An artist's stretchers for frame
- Staples and drawing pins
- A medium black felt-tip pen
- A tape measure
- Old blanket and a variety of woollen materials
- Scissors or rotary cutter and a mat
- A hook
- Carpet binding tape (wash before use)
- Needle and thread

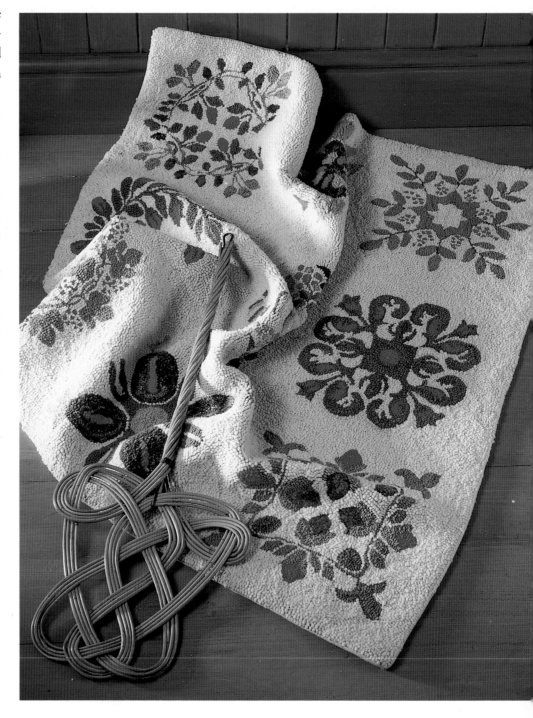

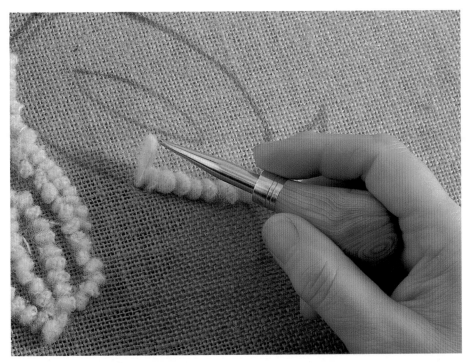

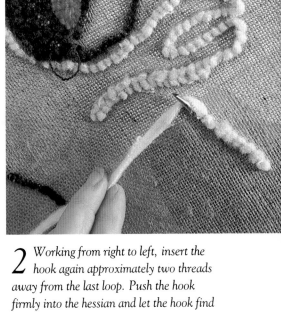

1 Cut the material on the straight and bias, into strips not less than 6in (15cm) long. Hold the hook facing upwards in one hand, as though using it for writing. In the other hand, hold the material between your thumb and forefinger underneath the hessian. Insert the hook firmly into the hessian from the front and let the hook find the material. Bring one end of the material up to the front and leave about 1in (2.5cm).

2 Working from right to left, insert the hook again approximately two threads away from the last loop. Push the hook firmly into the hessian and let the hook find the material. Do not feed the material on to the hook, let the material run loosely between your thumb and forefinger. If you hold it tightly you will pull the previous loop out. Pull up, from the back to the front making a loop. Remove the hook from the loop and repeat.

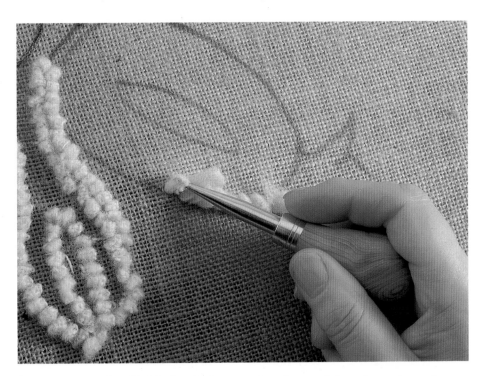

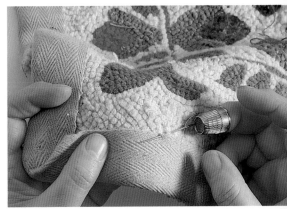

3 Continue to the end of the length of your material or colour. Bring up the ends to the front and cut level with the loop, and continue with a new strip going back into the same hole as the previous strip. Don't work in a straight line unless the pattern calls for it; it is better to work in a random fashion.

4 When you have finished your design take the rug off the frame. With the front of the rug facing you, sew the binding closely to the last row of hooking. Continue all round, easing it round the corners; do not mitre them at this stage. Turn in the two ends so they look neat and tidy the hessian so it is just covered by the binding. Turn down to the reverse side and hem all around, easing the corners into a mitre. When completed, place face down on a large towel and with a damp cloth press the reverse side.

WOOD, PLASTER AND PAPER CRAFTS

WOODCARVING • LOVE TOKENS • CHALKWARE

FOLK ARTISTS AND CRAFTSPEOPLE WORKED IN A WIDE VARIETY OF materials – wood, tin, plaster and paper – creating and decorating signboards, trade figures, pottery, decoys and ornaments for the home. The combination of these crafts displays the intuitive and instinctive style of folk artists, with these objects often showing an overriding sense of imagination and design ability.

The projects in this chapter may sound daunting at the outset, but with only the simplest of materials, for example, a sheet of paper and a scalpel, it is easy to make a delicate love token or decorate a lampshade. Alternatively, with the help of one or two specialist tools, try the woodcarving or burning projects.

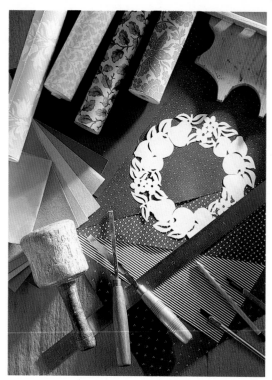

A wide variety of materials are used in the chapter, some of which you may need to purchase specially, but others, such as the paper projects, are a good way of making use of ends of rolls of wallpapers.

Opposite: Three hand-carved and painted decoys made in the second half of the nineteenth century. The two birds in the background are probably avocets, and the one in the foreground a wood pigeon.

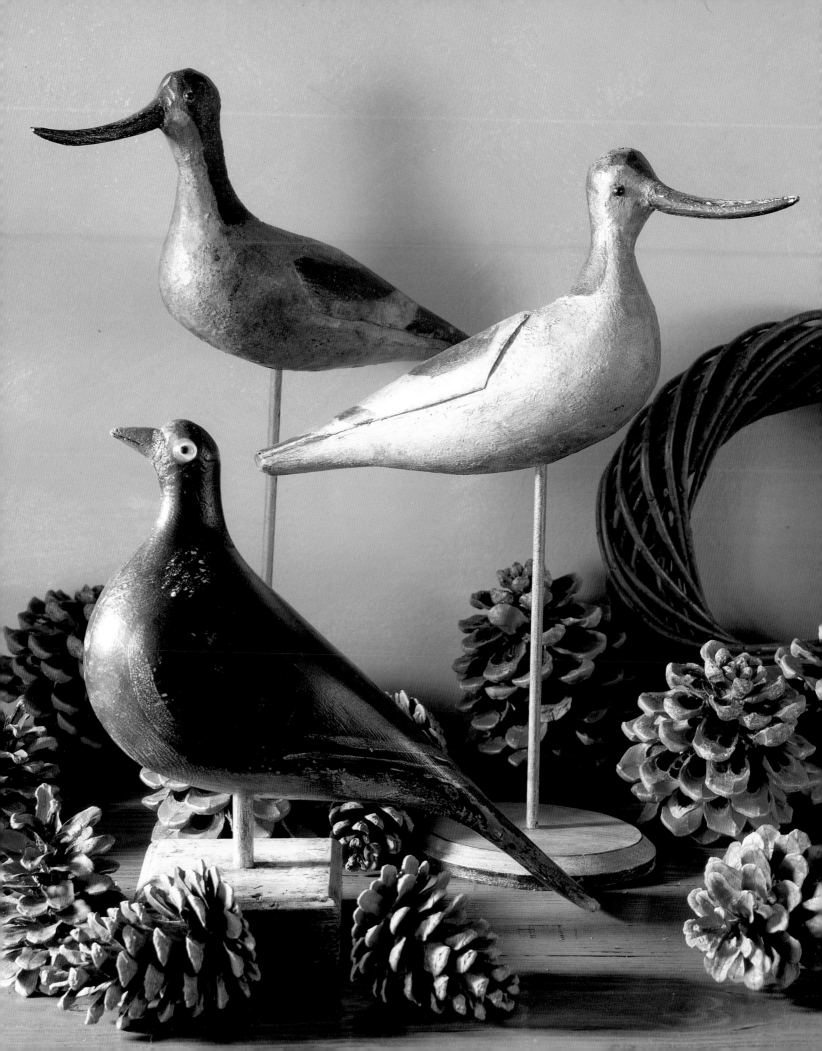

WOOD AND PLASTER CRAFTS

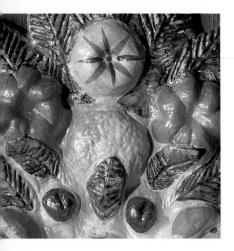

AMERICAN FOLK WOODCARVING SHOWS THE INFLUENCES OF CENTURIES OF TRADITIONAL EUROPEAN CARVING SKILLS THAT WERE PASSED DOWN THROUGH THE GENERATIONS IN SCANDINAVIA, BAVARIA AND SWITZERLAND. WHEN THE SETTLERS FROM EUROPE ARRIVED IN THE NEW WORLD THEY BROUGHT CHESTS AND BOXES, POSSIBLY BOWLS AND MUGS TOO, DECORATED WITH THE TECHNIQUES AND MOTIFS OF THEIR OWN CULTURAL TRADITIONS.

EUROPEAN WOODCARVING

In European interiors, carved decoration was not confined just to objects; in the Telemark region of Norway, for example, borders of intertwined vines were carved on the outside surfaces of a house. In the Alpine regions of Switzerland and Germany farmers traditionally lived in wooden chalet homes, and among these people woodcarving became a highly developed art form.

The countries of southern Europe were not without their woodcarvers, but most of the traditional objects tended to be smaller pieces, such as spoons carved by herdsmen on hillsides with many hours to fill. Carved spoons appear in many folk cultures; Wales, for example, has a tradition of carved love spoons, the handles of which were carved into a free-flowing chain from a single piece of wood. Also in Scandinavian folk culture a man showed his good intentions towards his chosen bride by placing a highly carved spoon protruding from his jacket pocket. Spoons for daily use were generally made of metal but they were displayed in spoonracks which were often very elaborately carved. There are some especially intricate Dutch examples.

Among the many other carved household objects, one of the most individual was the buttermould, which was a chip-carved wooden mould used by farmers to decorate and identify their product. Buttermoulds were popular in England, Scandinavia, Switzerland and the Low Countries but it is the early American moulds that show the most exuberant, rustic charm. The patterns featured magical hex signs to protect the milk from going sour, dairy scenes, cockerels, tulips, stars, eagles, acorns and many others besides. Each buttermould had to be unique, acting as it did as the farmer's trademark.

The cake and biscuit (cookie) moulds that originated in Bavaria were carved to a far higher level of sophistication. The woods had to be very hard in order to withstand the high oven temperatures, so they used close-grained walnut and oak and were able to make finely detailed carvings on the moulds. Some of the finest moulds were *Springerle* boards, which were divided into 24 squares, each carved with a different motif, usually naturalistically portrayed animals, birds or flowers.

AMERICAN WOODCARVING

Not all woodcarving was done on practical objects; some was purely decorative, as in the work of the travelling woodcarvers of nineteenth-century Pennsylvania and New England who moved around the country peddling their carving talents door to door.

Wilhelm Schimmel, who was working in New England in the second half of the nineteenth century, is the most famous of the itinerant woodcarvers. His favourite subject was the eagle, and he made many representations of them which are highly sought after by folk art collectors today. He coated the finished pieces with gesso – a paste used to prepare wood for paint or gilding, which was made out of a combination of powdered whiting and rabbit skin glue – and then painted them in bright colours which were often dictated by what the commissioning farmer happened to have in the shed at the time.

Domestic fowl, especially the rooster, were favourite subjects of the travelling woodcarvers. The eagle was also

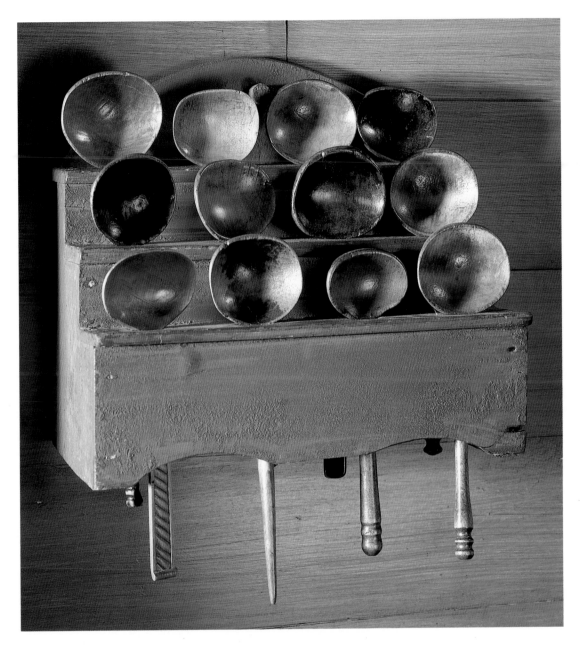

A Welsh spoon rack (c. 1870), containing a collection of hand-carved sycamore
"cawl" or soup spoons (1780–1840).

popular, but rooster carvings were always more successful, probably because there was more opportunity for close-range observation of the birds. Woodcarvers also turned their hands to making spoonracks, mirror frames, gate-posts, ladles, weathercocks, toys and ornaments.

CHALKWARE

Another ornamental item that was peddled from door to door was plasterware, a cheap and cheerful substitute for the much admired Staffordshire pottery in the nineteenth century. The trade was started by Italian immigrants who began casting from moulds they had brought with them to America. These usually took the form of religious subjects, pastoral scenes, arrangements of fruit, or peasant couples. As demand grew and the old moulds wore out, a whole new variety of images was made including deer, lovebirds, Staffordshire dogs and cats, and American heroes. Although these figures were mass produced out of plaster of Paris, each one was hand-painted in vivid colours by the Italian peasant folk artists.

CHALKWARE COMPOTE

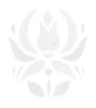

When nineteenth-century Italian immigrants first cast ornaments in plaster of Paris they found that demand for their products was huge. The timing was perfect because life had just begun to be easier for settlers, who had reached a stage of relative comfort and were ripe for new ideas of a purely ornamental nature for decorating their homes. Chalkware was cheap and cheerful and a variety of ornaments made a vivid display on a dresser.

This project was inspired by a pair of ornaments made in the late nineteenth century, now in the Museum of American Folk Art, New York. The chalkware compote is in fact made from self-hardening clay which is available from any hobby shop. It provides an accessible short cut for anyone who does not want to bother with the more authentic mass-production technique. Later, you may want to use the results of this project to press a vinyl mould from which you could cast in plaster. Ask about vinyl moulding at your local hobby shop.

You will need:
- Self-hardening modelling material
- Clay modelling tools and knife
- White acrylic primer or matt emulsion (flat latex) paint (primer gives a better base coat)
- Two small household paintbrushes and a selection of artist's brushes
- Artist's acrylic or stencil paints: red, yellow, green, orange and black
- A cake rack
- Clear water-based varnish
- Small tubes of burnt sienna and raw umber artist's acrylic paint

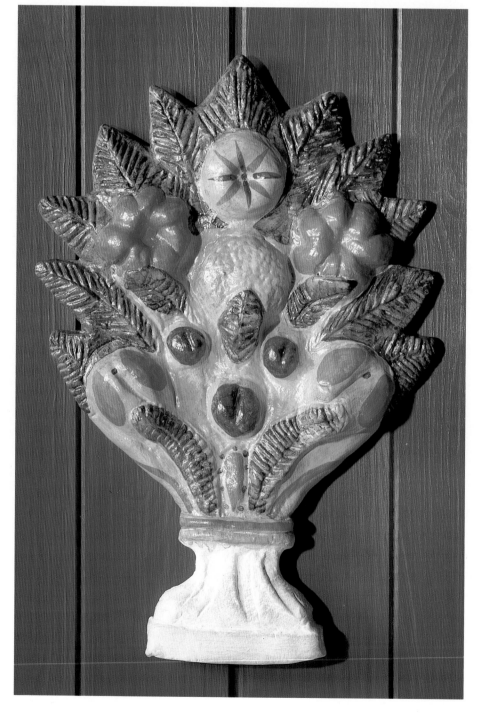

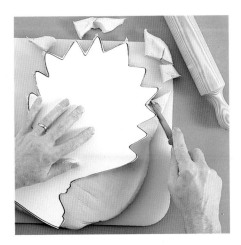

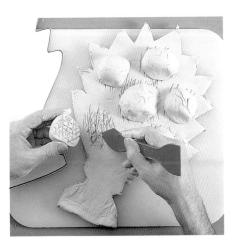

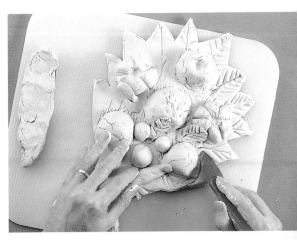

1 Enlarge the base pattern on page 152 to be 14in by 9½in (36cm by 24cm) at its widest. Roll out a piece of clay to an even 1in (2.5cm) thickness on a flat surface and, using the pattern as a template, cut out the shape.

2 Roll three balls of clay, each about 1½in (4cm) in diameter and cut them in half to make the six large fruit. Roughen the underside of each and do the same to the base before pressing them firmly into position. Roll a medium-sized ball and two smaller ones for the plums, and rough sausage shapes for the leaves. Press them into place in the same way.

3 Use the modelling tools to smooth, form and decorate the surface of the fruit and leaves. Leave the plaque to harden for at least 24 hours in a warm, dry room, then transfer it to a raised ventilated tray; a cake rack is ideal. You can put the plaque in an oven at the lowest possible temperature to speed the drying process – follow the instructions on the clay packet.

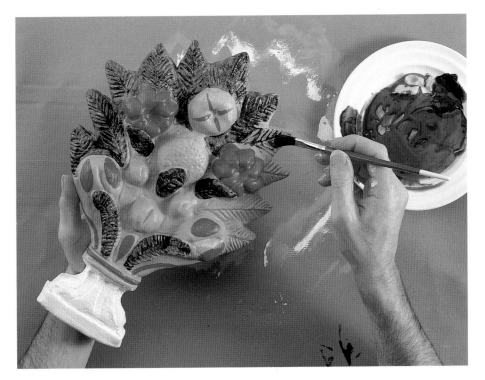

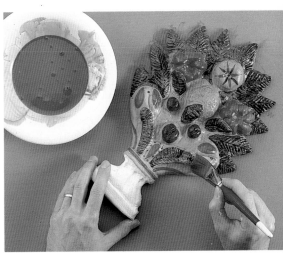

4 Paint the plaque white and then decorate it with the other colours. Allow your brushstrokes to follow the surface direction rather than being faithful to the pattern. The painting should look fresh and spontaneous.

5 Finally, apply a coat of varnish tinted with a small squeeze of raw umber and burnt sienna, allow to dry and then give both sides a coat of clear water-based varnish.

Woodburning

The burning of patterns into wooden objects is most common in the folk art of Scandinavia, where for centuries ancient patterns were pressed into wooden objects using shaped hot irons. Folk artists used rows of repeat patterns to circle drinking vessels and kitchen containers with crosses, circles, zig-zags and squiggles, all of which held folkloric meaning. More refined objects were burnt with more naturalistic decoration, featuring leaves and flowers, produced with a single pointed hot iron. Woodburning was only used to decorate small objects, in particular kitchenware because the pattern withstood vigorous scrubbing.

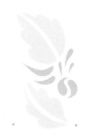

The specialist tool used for woodburning today is very easily manipulated, and allows far greater room for artistic interpretation than the old heated-iron technique. For this project, a pyrographic tool, which comes with three different shaped ends, was used.

The box is made from old pine. Any plain wooden box would suit the design, which is borrowed from an old painted candle box of Pennsylvanian Dutch origin.

You will need:
- An enlargement of the pattern on page 153 drawn on tracing paper
- Chalky-backed transfer paper
- A soft pencil
- Low-tack masking tape
- A woodburning kit with different-shaped ends – chisel-ended and flat
- Clear satin water-based varnish
- A small tube of burnt sienna artist's acrylic paint
- A small household paintbrush

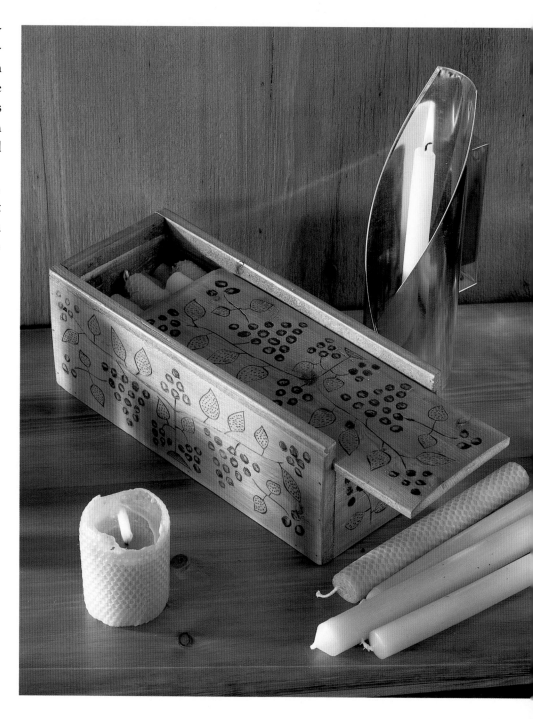

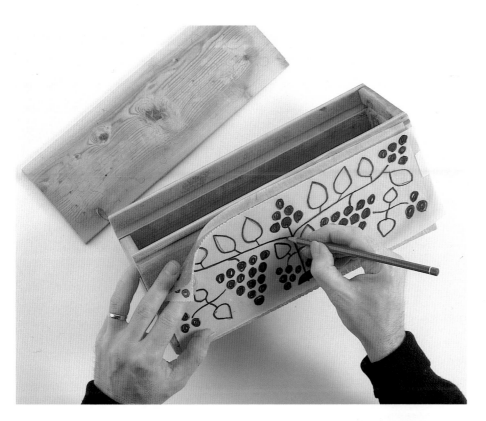

1 Place the transfer paper between the pattern and the box and trace it on to the box using the soft pencil. Secure with masking tape if necessary.

2 Set the woodburner at a medium heat and follow the pattern lines for the stems and outlines of the leaves. Use the chisel-ended tool and keep it moving or lift it off the surface, as it will burn a deeper hole if held static.

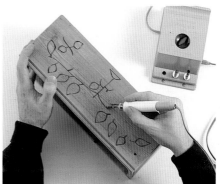

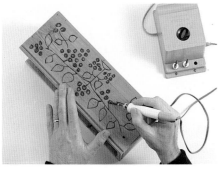

3 Outline the fruit with the flat tool, and remember that this is a rustic craft, so irregular shapes will contribute to its charm.

4 Fill the leaf outlines with a pattern of dots, using the chisel-ended tool with a prodding movement.

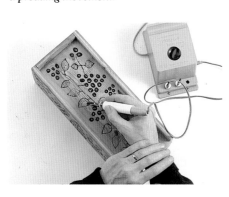

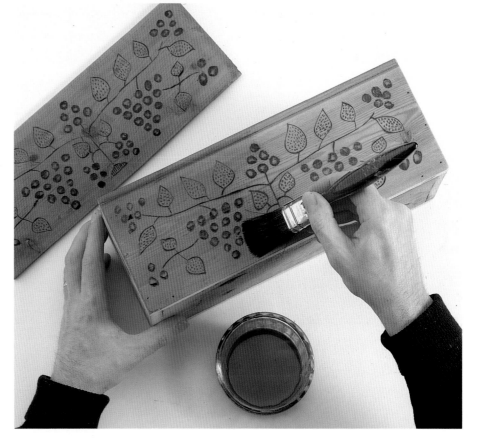

5 Finally, apply two coats of water-based satin varnish tinted with a squeeze of burnt sienna acrylic paint, followed by one coat of clear varnish.

CARVED WOOD SPOON RACK

Kitchen fashions change over the years, and recently utensils and cookware which had been kept hidden have come out on display. The European influence has spread to include a more friendly style in kitchen design, with pots and pans hanging on the walls, comfortable chairs around the table and interesting receptacles, such as this spoon rack, adding to the convivial style.

This spoon rack is similar to many that appeared in farm kitchens all over Europe between the sixteenth and eighteenth centuries. The shape is an old-English pattern called "chicks" and the motifs are similar to those found on any chip-carved household object in European folk art. Spoon racks were usually chip-carved and given as presents from husbands to wives, and were displayed with pride. Designs varied from region to region, with some of the most intricately carved examples coming from Scandinavia.

The wood is old oak, a hardwood with a dense grain that is most suitable for carving. Although a knife is trad-itionally used for chip-carving, this does require a considerable amount of practice and skill. Use a small, sharp chisel and a gouge instead.

You will need:
- A piece of hardwood approximately 10in by 20in (26cm by 50cm)
- An enlargement of the pattern on page 152 drawn on tracing paper
- A coping saw or electric bandsaw
- Chalky-backed transfer paper
- A soft pencil
- Low-tack masking tape
- A small sharp chisel and a sharp gouge
- A wooden mallet
- Three pieces of hardwood 3in by 10in (8cm by 26cm)
- Medium-grade sandpaper
- Wood glue and paintbrush

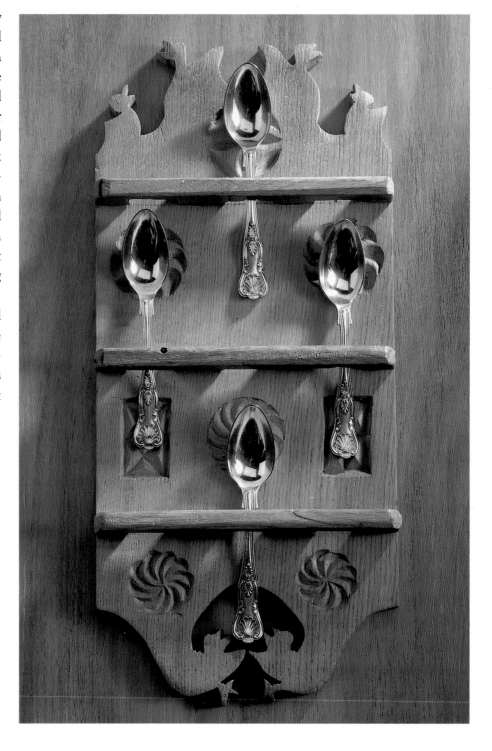

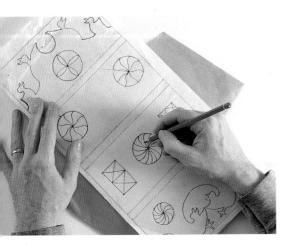

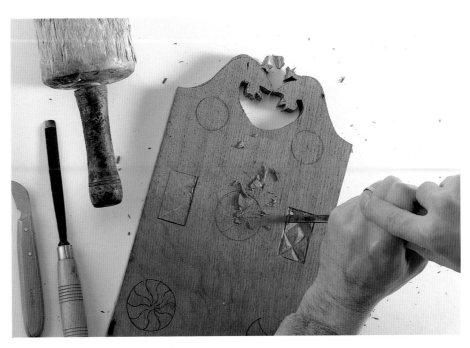

1 Cut the outer shape of the rack using the saw. Place the transfer paper between the pattern and the wood and trace it on to the rack using the soft pencil. Secure with masking tape if necessary.

2 Use the very sharp chisel with a wooden mallet to outline the shape first, holding the chisel almost vertically. Try to keep the carving free of small shavings, as this will make it easier to achieve a consistent depth. Always work with the chisel going away from your body. Alter the angle to 45 degrees and chip away the pattern to a depth of approximately ¼in (6mm). You may find that you can work without the mallet if your chisel or gouge is sharp enough. Apply pressure with one hand over the other – this will guide the tool.

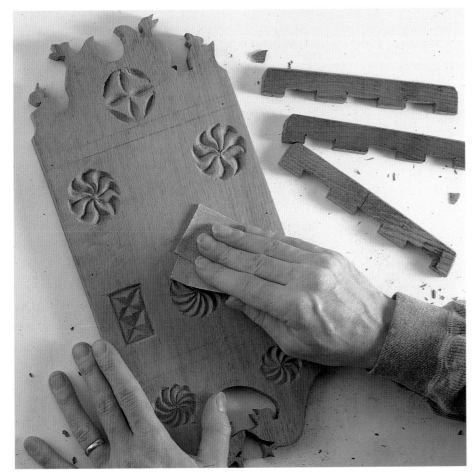

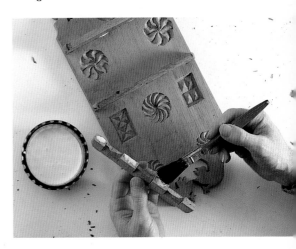

3 Cut three strips of wood to fit widthways across the carved board and use a chisel to cut three evenly spaced indents for the spoon handles. Make sure they are deep enough to fit a spoon through them. Round off the edges with sandpaper and sand the whole piece. Mark the position of the racks with pencil lines.

4 Use strong wood glue to attach the racks and leave to dry overnight.

PAPER CRAFTS

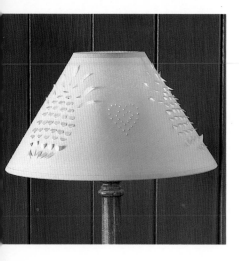

NTIL THE MIDDLE OF THE SEVENTEENTH CENTURY PAPER WAS A LUXURY ITEM. MAYBE ITS VERY RARITY WAS RESPONSIBLE FOR THE INTRICACY OF THE LOVE TOKENS OF THE TIME, CUT FROM A SINGLE PRECIOUS SHEET OF PAPER. THE PRACTICE OF MAKING PAPER VALENTINES CAME FROM GERMANY, WHICH ACCOUNTS FOR THEIR NAME, *SCHERENSCHNITTE*, WHICH MEANS SCISSOR CUTTINGS. SEVENTEENTH-CENTURY LOVERS DID NOT LIMIT THEMSELVES TO THE EXCHANGE OF HEART MOTIFS JUST ON ST. VALENTINE'S DAY, BUT GAVE THEM AT ANY TIME OF YEAR.

To make a *Scherenschnitt* a piece of paper was folded in half twice and the remaining quarter was cut into with small, very sharp scissors. The detail of some examples is stunning, especially considering that these were often cut by sailors at sea, whose hands were used for the roughest tasks. Popular patterns included hearts, turtle doves and flowers, as well as geometric borders and lacy edges.

Pierced decoration was a variation on cut paper work. Possibly it grew out of pierced quilting patterns, in which a design was pierced on to paper and then placed over the fabric and transferred by "pouncing" chalk powder through the holes. The pastime of piercing paper was very popular with young ladies in the mid-eighteenth century and was done by making holes in the form of a pattern, using a variety of different sized pins.

SILHOUETTES

Silhouette-making was a craft that was left to the professionals. The silhouettes were portraits in profile cut out of small pieces of paper. They were originally known as "shadow likenesses" but began to be called silhouettes in France during the sixteenth century, as a derisory term for a skill that was not highly thought of, like their namesake Etienne de Silhouette, a much hated aristocrat.

At first the silhouettes were cheap versions of painted portraits. The subject sat in profile in front of a candle and his or her shadow was cast on to a wall. The artist placed a sheet of paper on the wall and outlined the shadow. This was then filled in with black ink for contrast. It was not long before the idea of cutting silhouettes from black paper developed and they became immensely popular, with most homes displaying a framed silhouette.

FRAKTUR

Another highly skilled papercraft was *Fraktur*, a form of illuminated manuscript which had its origins in Germany, and took its name from a sixteenth-century German

Hanna Elizabeth Clodfelder's certificate, c. 1810.

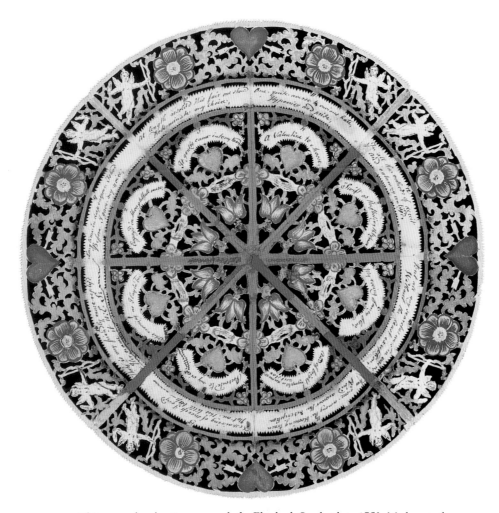

This cutwork valentine was made for Elizabeth Sandwith in 1753. Made out of
watercolour and ink on laid paper, it is an exceptional example of scissor-cutting.

typeface. It was the direct descendant of the medieval
monks' craft of decorating written script with watercolour
and goldleaf designs. *Fraktur* was mostly done by school-
masters or church ministers for family records and birth or
marriage certificates. The family records were the most
static designs, with columns listing names, dates of births,
marriages and deaths, each of which had symbolic decorative elements of suitable gravity. The calligraphic *Fraktur*
was more celebratory, with sweeping penstrokes and birds
with rolling plumage. Stencilled motifs were widely used
to illustrate childrens' *Fraktur* work which was taught to
them at school.

BANDBOXES

Making and decorating bandboxes was a three-
dimensional papercraft. These boxes had been used in
Europe to hold wigs, hats, lace collars and other finery,

but they were commonly made out of thin wood. In
America they were made from pasteboard, lined with
newspaper and covered with printed paper. The newspapers allow accurate dating and it seems that the boxes were
highly fashionable until rail and boat travel superseded
the stagecoach. The arrival of these new methods of travel
meant that passengers were separated from their luggage
during their journey for the first time and were therefore
unable to supervize its handling, so stronger leather boxes
and cases began to replace bandboxes.

Originally the printed paper for covering bandboxes
was imported from England and France, but demand was
so great that soon printing began in America. The
patterns were mostly classical and romantic, reminiscent
of seventeenth-century French wallpapers, but as travel
became a feature of American life, designers began to
illustrate sailing ships, paddle steamers and stagecoaches.

LOVE TOKENS OR SCHERENSCHNITTE

Intricate cut paper designs existed for many centuries in the Middle and Far East before they became popular in Europe and America. The cut and folded paper love token originated in Switzerland and Germany, where men such as Johann Hauswirth elevated a pastime into a skilled craft, creating beautiful symmetrical compositions. The fashion for paper cutting was soon taken up by young ladies who used their sharp embroidery scissors to cut complicated valentines for their loved ones.

The *Scherenschnitte* were cut from rag paper and sometimes pierced and tinted with watercolour for further decoration before being mounted on a contrasting colour, usually black.

Folding and cutting a heart shape is much more effective than drawing one freehand, because the result is symmetrical. The symmetry of folding and cutting also suits flowers, trees and ornamental borders, and a bird or animal will have its mirror image facing it when unfolded.

You will need:
- A sheet of paper
- A sharp pencil and ruler
- Thin black paper
- A sharp craft knife
- Spray adhesive
- Mounting paper

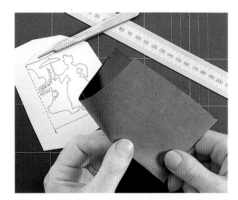

1 *Enlarge the pattern on page 153 to the size you require and draw it on paper. Fold the black paper in half.*

2 *Cut along the centre edge of the design, using the craft knife and a ruler.*

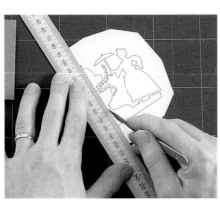

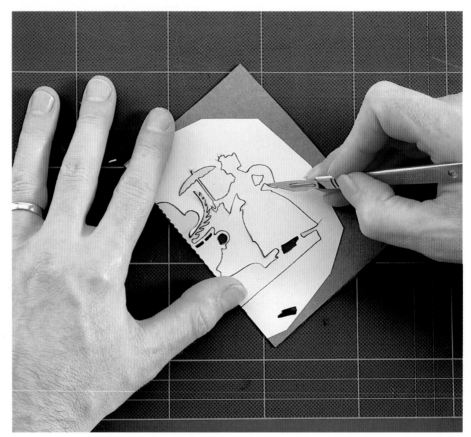

3 *Give the reverse side of the tracing the lightest coating of spray adhesive and stick it to the back of the black paper. Cut out the shapes very carefully, using just the* sharp tip of the craft knife. Move the paper around when you cut, so that you are always cutting at the easiest angle.

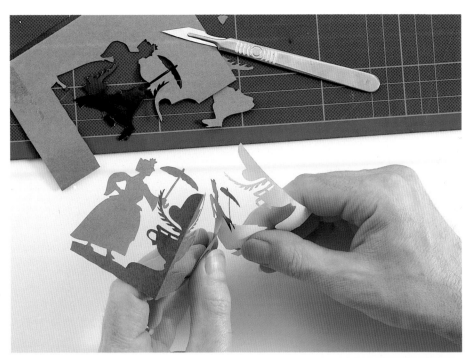

4 Separate the black paper from the tracing. Take great care when you do this, for although the spray adhesive allows surfaces to be parted after sticking, a Scherenschnitt *is fragile and easily torn.*

5 Unfold your Scherenschnitt *and display it on paper.*

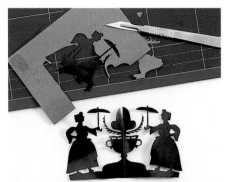

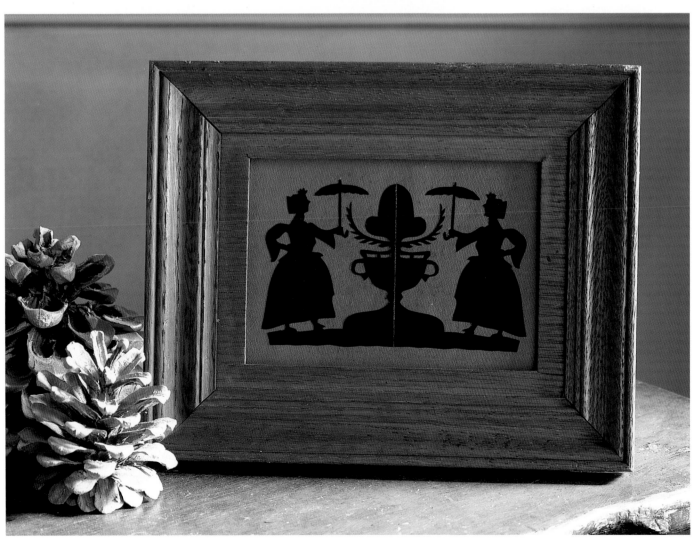

SILHOUETTES

The first silhouette likenesses were drawn life-size by illuminating the model's profile using candlelight. A shadow was projected on to paper, traced around, coloured black, cut out and mounted on white paper. Fine details such as ringlets were often added afterwards. In the nineteenth-century a machine was invented which shrank the shadow to allow miniature portraits to be cut, and itinerants travelled around with these machines making and selling silhouette likenesses door to door.

This project uses modern technology by starting with a photograph, but the end result has the authentic look of an old silhouette portrait. To take the photograph pose your subject with a bright light behind them, either by a sunlit window, or a back-lit sheet of white paper. This should eliminate foreground detail and give a dark silhouette shape. You may find that your camera is "fool-proofed" so that it will not take a photograph this way. In that case, just try for a plain white background and sharp focus.

A child also makes a good model for a life-sized silhouette. Simply pin a sheet of paper to the wall, sit the model in front of it with a reading lamp behind, and trace the shadow on to the paper. Colour it black, cut it out and mount on white paper.

You will need:
- A photograph
- Low-tack masking tape
- Tracing paper
- Thin black paper
- A hard, sharp pencil
- A sharp craft knife
- Mounting paper and glue

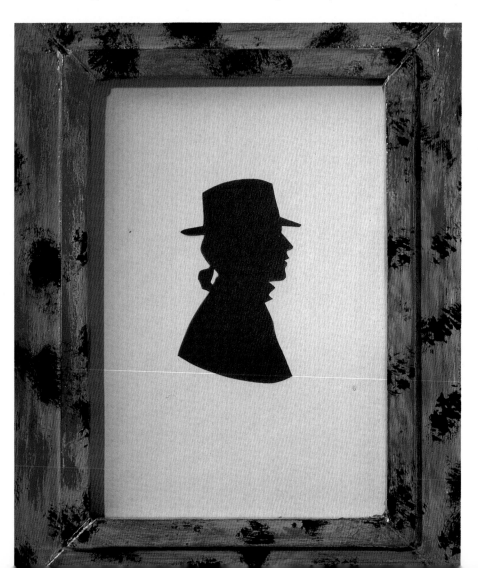

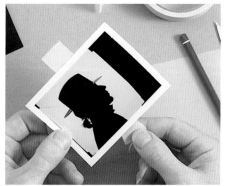

1 Stick a strip of masking tape across the back of the photograph, so that it overlaps each side.

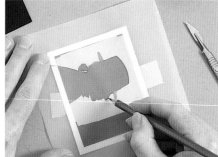

2 Place a sheet of tracing paper over the top. The tape will hold the tracing paper still while you draw around the profile.

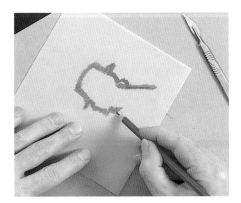

3 *Rub the reverse side of the tracing with a pencil.*

4 *Secure the tracing on black paper using masking tape, and use a hard, sharp pencil to go over your traced lines.*

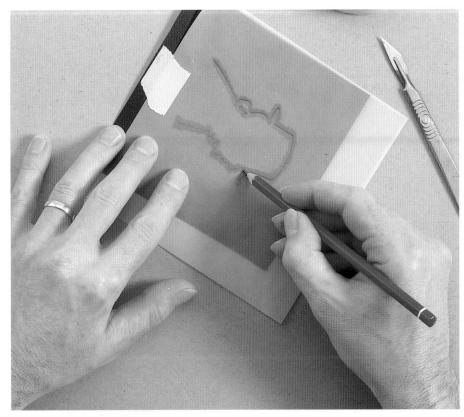

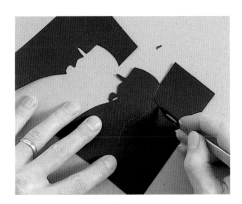

5 *Cut out the silhouette with a sharp craft knife, beginning at the back of the head. Move the paper to help you get clean lines, and hold the knife upright so that you only cut with the point. If you are nervous of a craft knife, use small, very sharp needlework scissors to cut the silhouette, moving the paper as you cut.*

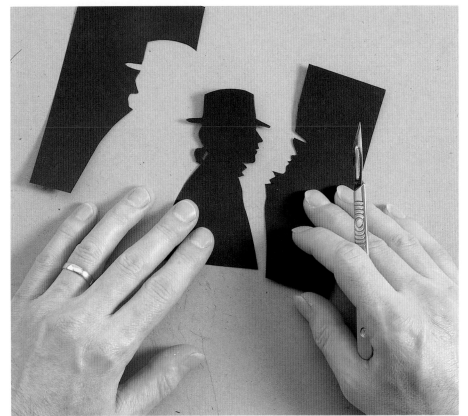

6 *Cut out the facial features and separate the image from the background. Stick the black silhouette on to a sheet of paper and display it in a frame.*

BANDBOXES

These brightly coloured oval pasteboard boxes were the early nineteenth-century equivalent of modern hand luggage. The hats, wigs, collars and ruffs that a lady needed when travelling were safely held in these rigid containers which, it is said, were never entrusted to the coachman, but kept safely on the lady's lap, being accessories in their own right.

During the 1830s the mills were established and young women began working and earning a wage, and they created a new market with their spending power. Bandboxes were manufactured in factories to meet the upsurge in demand, and papermakers printed woodblocked designs for decorating them. Some adapted patterns from wallpapers while others produced complete pastoral or commemorative scenes. Classical mythology and romantic subjects were especially popular.

A bandbox is easy to create, and much more satisfying to make than to buy. Look for decorator's sample books of wallpapers, or try printing your own paper using stencils.

You will need:

- Two sheets of corrugated cardboard 15in by 15in (40cm by 40cm)
- Drawing pins and a paperclip
- A ruler
- Cotton thread
- A pen
- A craft knife
- A sheet of thin card (cardboard) 15in by 15in (40 cm by 40cm)
- Strong matt (flat) finish sticking tape
- Glue and paste
- Wallpaper
- Scissors
- Clothes pegs (pins)
- Braid (trim)
- Wrapping paper

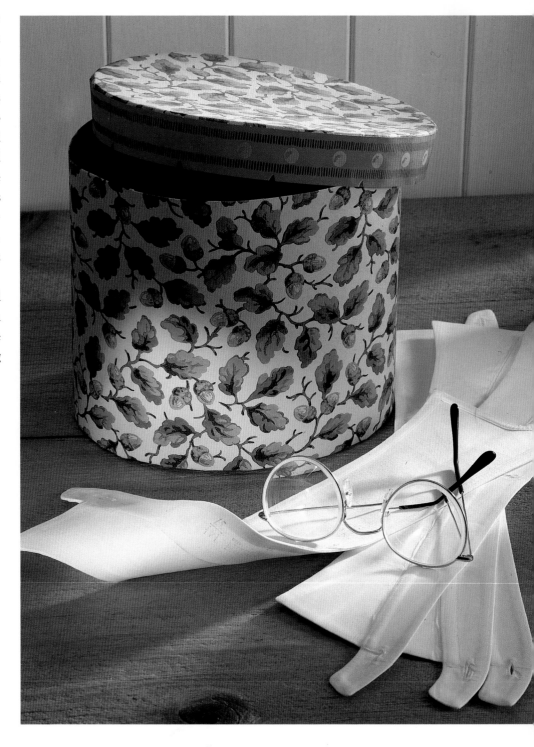

1 There is a useful technique for drawing oval shapes. First, draw a central line along your sheet of corrugated cardboard. Place the drawing pins 4in (10cm) apart along the middle section of the line. Measure a 12in (30cm) length of cotton and join the ends. Loop this around both the pins and hold the cotton taut to one side by placing a pen within the loop. Draw with the pen, clockwise, holding the cotton taut all the time. This will produce an oval shape to cut with the craft knife.

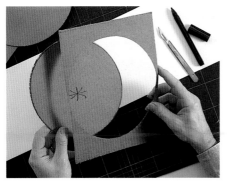

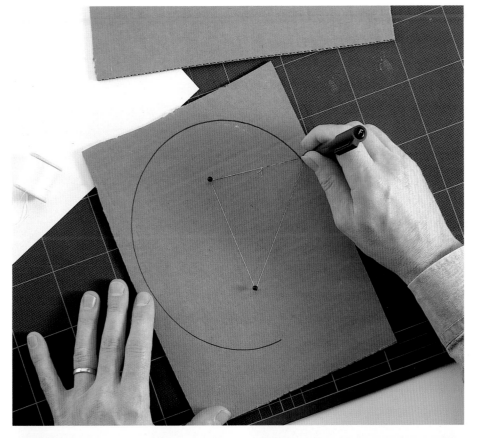

2 Place the base on to the other corrugated sheet and draw around it. Cut around the outside of the line, making a slightly bigger oval for the lid.

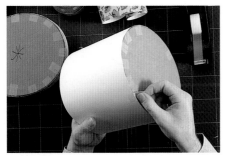

3 Wrap the thin board around the base to form the oval box and secure the shape with a paper clip. Begin sticking strips of tape around the base, to join the two sections. Make each strip at least 3in (8cm) long and space them around the base to give a firm join. Glue down the side seam.

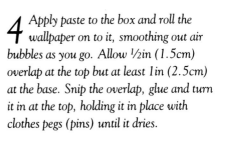

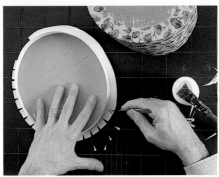

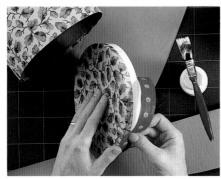

4 Apply paste to the box and roll the wallpaper on to it, smoothing out air bubbles as you go. Allow ½in (1.5cm) overlap at the top but at least 1in (2.5cm) at the base. Snip the overlap, glue and turn it in at the top, holding it in place with clothes pegs (pins) until it dries.

5 Place the lid on the paper and cut around it allowing a 1in (2.5cm) overlap. Make the lid as you made the box, but use a strip of card 1½in (4cm) deep, secured to the top with strips of tape. Glue the side seam, then paste the wallpaper to the lid. Snip wedges out of the overlapping paper and glue the edges. Repeat for the base.

6 Glue the trimming to the edge of the sides of the lid and secure it with a clothes peg (pin) until it dries. If you prefer, you can cut another strip of matching paper for this. The box can then be lined. Parcel wrapping paper was used in this example, measured and stuck in the same way as the outer paper.

PIERCED AND CUT LAMPSHADE

Victorian young ladies spent a great deal of time sitting demurely in the parlour attending to their needlework, and pierced and cut paperwork was an extension of this kind of work. The same pins, needles and small sharp scissors were used to cut intricate patterns and pictures out of paper, which were then displayed in frames. At some point the idea was developed further, and the designs were cut into vellum and illuminated as lampshades.

This project uses a ready-made stiff paper lampshade suitable for a table lamp, and although it is not difficult to cut the pattern, you should be extremely careful when using the sharp-bladed craft knife. Never be tempted to place your fingers behind the paper as you cut.

The pineapple is a symbol of hospitality and was a great favourite with folk artists and decorators. Here, it is interspersed with a pierced heart motif.

You will need:
- An enlargement of the pattern on page 153
- Tracing paper
- A pencil
- Low-tack masking tape
- A hatpin (or similar) and a sharp-pointed thick needle
- A sharp craft knife and spare blades

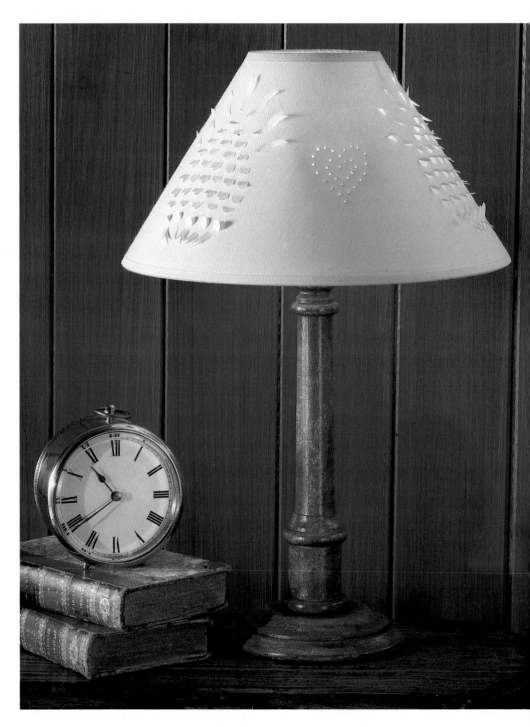

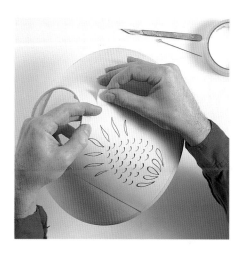

1 Trace the pineapple motif and stick the tracing to the lampshade, using masking tape to hold it taut.

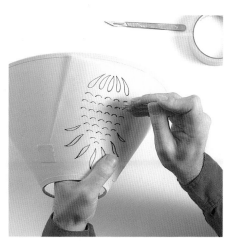

2 Prick out the design with the hatpin, marking the edges of the scallop shapes and the leaves.

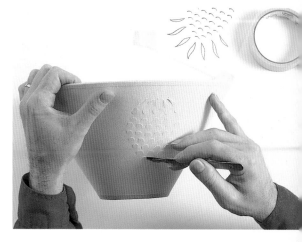

3 Cut the scallops using your pinpricks as a guide. Insert the blade at one pinprick and form an arc to the next. Hold the lampshade steady with your spare hand, and keep your fingers clear of the blade.

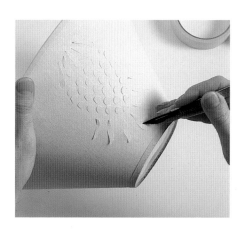

4 Cut each end of the leaf shapes, leaving a "bridge" in the middle. Take your time when cutting because the bridge is vital to the design, and a slip of the knife will spoil the effect.

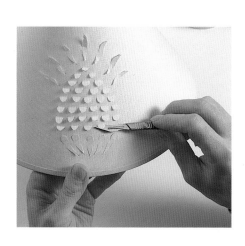

5 Use the blunt edge of the craft knife to ease the shapes away from the background to roughly 45 degrees, which will allow them to settle at 30 degrees. Do not despair if the first pineapple is not perfect – let that be the one that faces the wall.

6 Cut two more pineapples around the lampshade, and then tape a tracing of the hearts in the spaces between them. Use the thick needle to prick out the hearts. Hold the lampshade firmly, but keep your fingers away from the point of the needle.

TINWARE
AND TOYS

WEATHERVANES • DOLLS • CHEQUERBOARDS

FOLK ARTISTS AND CRAFTS PEOPLE WERE OFTEN ABLE TO TURN THEIR hands to anything. Painters might have painted portraits as well as stencilled walls, skilled carvers crafted everything from the smallest toys up to elaborate architectural ornaments, and metalsmiths produced weathervanes, whirligigs and locks. Whatever the object that was commissioned it was usually decorated, either painted with brightly coloured motifs or, with tinware, punched or pierced.

This chapter includes a range of techniques – metalwork, needlecraft and painting. The pierced metal project embodies the thrifty principles of folk art and the modern recycling movement at the same time, for it is made out of an old cookie tin. Based on a very simple idea of punching holes through the tin, this is a classic, easy-to-make object that will liven up your home and encourage the creative spirit.

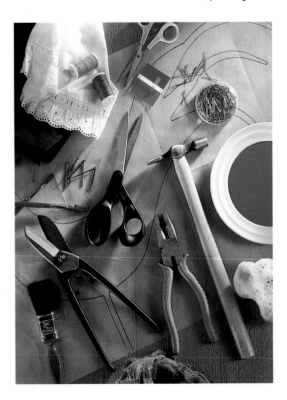

The projects in this chapter include sewing, painting and metalwork. If you are not used to working with metal it may be a good idea to wear a pair of protective gloves.

Opposite: French tinware cheese strainer, decorated with geometric patterned punched holes that serve to draw away water in the drying of soft cheese such as brie. Two earthenware jugs; the primitive spotty decoration is typical of robust domestic pottery from eastern France.

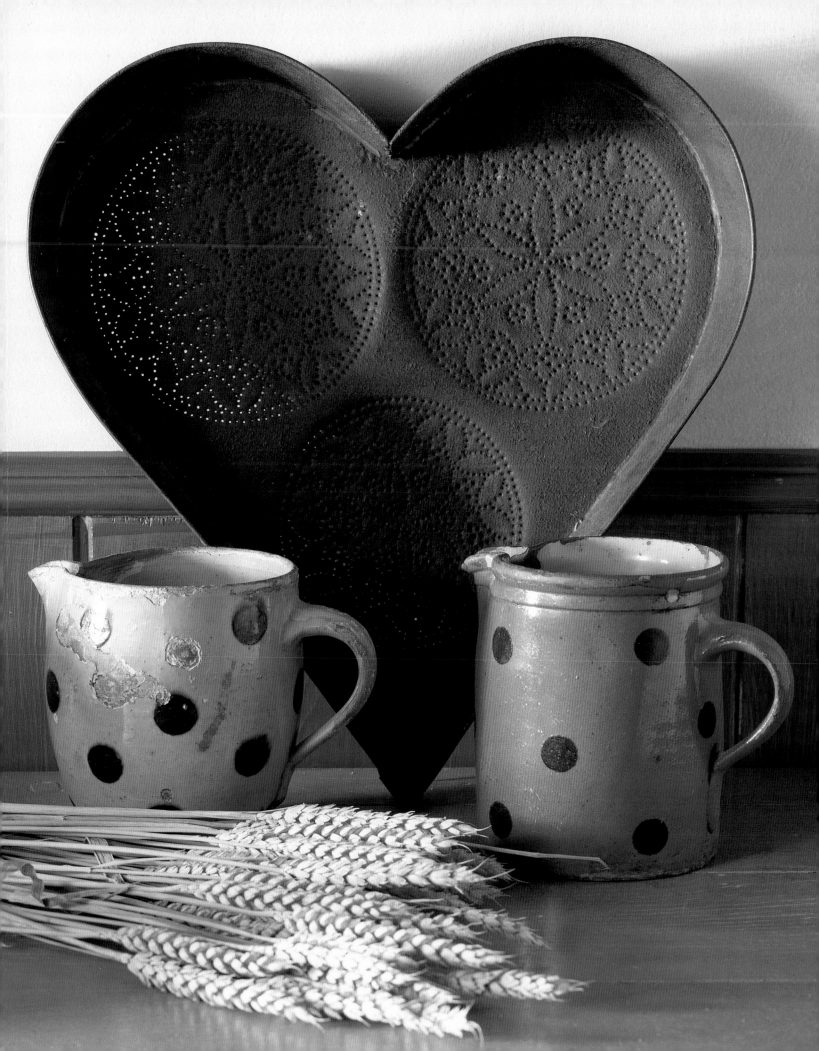

CUT AND PIERCED METALWORK

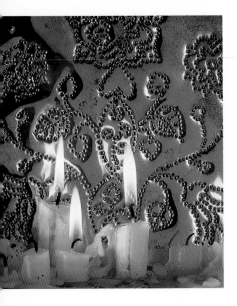

FOR 3000 YEARS STRONG, LONG-LASTING UTENSILS HAVE BEEN MADE OUT OF IRON, AND MOST FOLK COMMUNITIES WOULD HAVE HAD A BLACKSMITH OR METALWORKER AMONG THEM. THE SCANDINAVIANS WERE PARTICULARLY SKILLED, HAVING A TRADITION OF LOCK-MAKING DATING BACK TO THE NINTH CENTURY. THEY ALSO USED VERY ORNATE WROUGHT IRON MARKERS ON THEIR GRAVES WHICH TOOK THE FORM OF CROSSES WITH HANGING AND TURNING FLAGS, HEARTS AND FINE METAL SWIRLS. THEIR SKILLS EXTENDED TO MAKING CHANDELIERS AND WROUGHT IRON GATES.

WEATHERVANES

Weathervanes were among the most popular metalwork items among country communities, and farmers would often make these for themselves, cutting a simple shape from metal or wood to sit on top of a barn and keep bad luck at bay. The rooster had been traditionally used on weathervanes in Europe since the time when a ninth-century Pope decreed that every church should display one on its rooftops as a symbol of Christian faith.

But the rooster was by no means the only creature used on weathervanes – sheep, cows, pigs, pheasants, dogs, eagles and galloping horses were all quite common. Tradesmen also soon saw the weathervane's potential as an advertising medium – the butcher displaying a pig or a sheep, the blacksmith a horse and the tobacconist an Indian Brave with his bow drawn.

CANDLEHOLDERS

Before the advent of improved oil lamps, candlelight was the usual after-dark illumination, and even when these lamps were introduced they were unreliable and smoky, so candles remained popular.

Candles needed candleholders and the tinsmiths used their ingenuity to create many different kinds. Apart from the freestanding holder there was also the wall sconce which consisted of a circular tin backing plate and a protruding candleholder below. The unpainted metal reflected the light and heat from the burning candle into the room, but it was decorative as well as functional. Patterns were crimped or punched into the tinplate, to produce a raised design. Tulips, stars, the sun, hearts, eagles or radiating rays were the commonest patterns. Enclosed candleholders, such as the famous Paul Revere lantern, were made by piercing a fretwork pattern in a sheet of tin and forming it into a cylinder with a conical top. The candle stood in a holder on the base and the light shone through the pierced holes. In fact it shed its light inefficiently, but as a decorative item it is now prized by folk art enthusiasts.

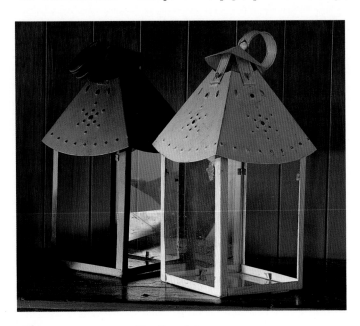

Two French lanterns.

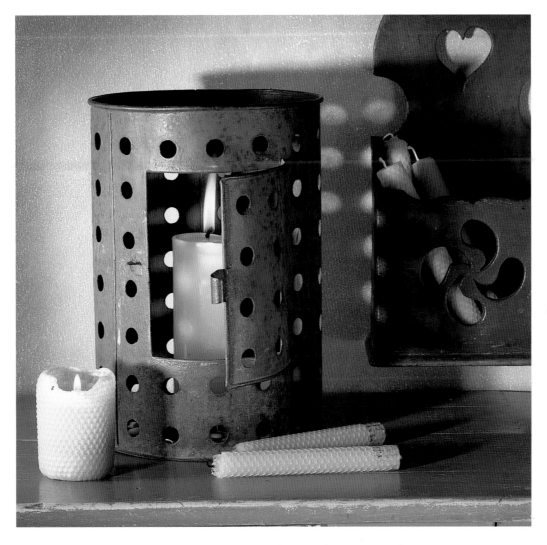

A lantern of 1000 eyes; when a candle burns inside it a mass of light spots appear
in the room. c.1830.

Pierced tin was also used in footwarmers, where a hot brick was encased in a wooden-framed tin box and put at the end of the bed. The piercing which allowed the warmth to pass through took the form of a decorative motif. Another use for this type of metalwork was the pie safe, a cupboard which needed ventilation while remaining secure against flies, scavenging children and pets.

KITCHENWARE

Apart from locks and hinges and farm implements, the most common use for metalwork among folk communities was in the kitchen. In the seventeenth century all cooking was done over an open fire, either by boiling, roasting or baking, and each one of these activities required a special set of utensils. There were pot hooks for suspending pots over the fire, kettles, baking pots and toasters to sit on the fire and a variety of ladles, forks and strainers for dealing with the food as it cooked.

Most of these were undecorated, having a purely utilitarian character, even among the Pennsylvania Dutch whose love of ornament was far-reaching.

One of the few cooking utensils that proved the exception was the trivet – a three or four-legged stand for kettles and pots that was often very decorative. The early trivets were made of wrought iron, and twisted into well-loved folk motifs such as hearts, flowers, stars and sunbursts. The later ones were made of cast iron and adopted a more Victorian style, of naturalistic leaf and floral forms, sometimes including words like "Good Luck" or religious texts.

WEATHERVANE

Early weathervanes were introduced as religious symbols. The most significant of these was the rooster which has long stood proudly on rooftops warding off evil and changing its direction according to the wind. In time weathervanes developed a more secular nature and all kinds of birds and beasts became popular. Before long everything from large grasshoppers to a locomotive was visible on the skyline.

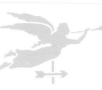

The design chosen for this project was taken from one of the older farm-made weathervanes which often features in studies of folk art. It typifies the spirit of an age, being simple, beautiful and practical. The shape of the pheasant is distinctive and easy to cut.

Metal cutting is beyond the bounds of most domestic tool boxes, but a local blacksmith or metalworker will have no difficulty in cutting the shape in his workshop if you provide a template. Take his advice on the most suitable metal; this one is cut from sheet steel. The method you use to attach the weathervane will depend on the surface on which you are erecting it, and the blacksmith will be able to provide suitable fixtures for your requirements.

You will need:
- Tongs (optional)
- A cotton cloth
- Machine oil
- Emery paper

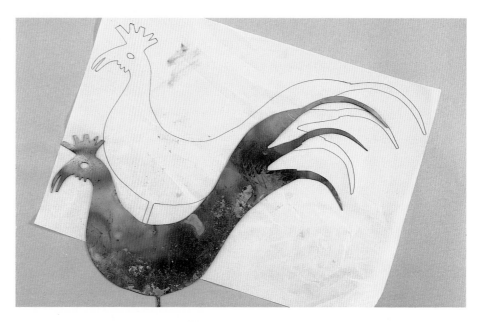

1 *Enlarge the pheasant pattern on page 153 – it will need to be at least 2ft (60cm) from beak to tail to be effective. Take the pattern to a blacksmith or metal-working shop. If you wish to "distress" the metal to give the appearance of natural* ageing, this can be done over a fire. Use tongs to hold the pheasant over the flames, so that the smoke blackens the metal, giving a mottled effect. Leave it to cool before attempting to rub it back.*

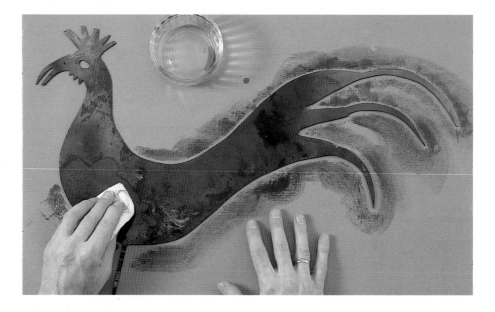

2 *Sand down with emery paper to smooth any jagged edges. Lay the weathervane on a protected flat surface and use a cotton cloth to rub machine oil on to the surface. Some of the soot will come off, but continue to rub with the same oiled section of cloth until the whole surface has been covered. The oil will protect the metal from rust.*

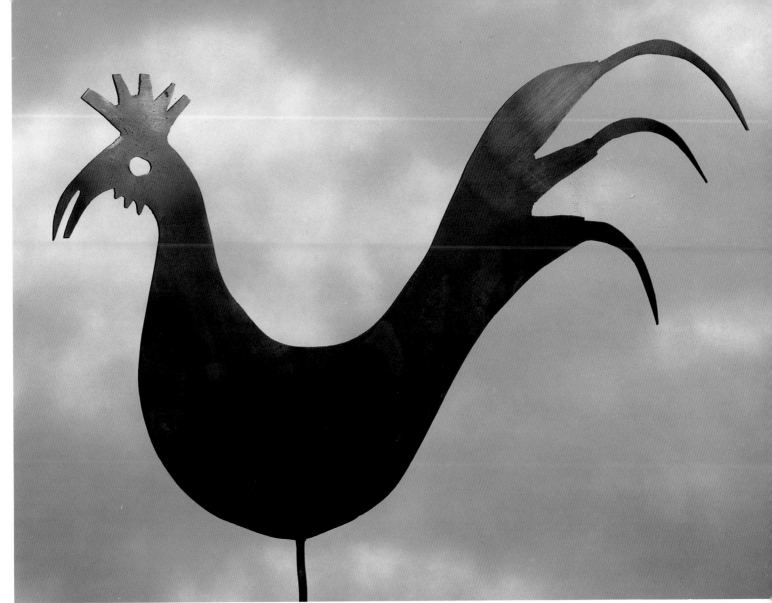

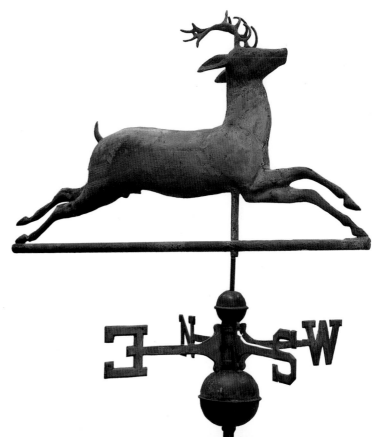

Right: A stage weathervane
made out of moulded copper
and manufactured by J. Fiske
& Co., New York, c.1890.
It measures 17in by 30in
(43cm by 76cm).

PIERCED TIN SHELF

Tin piercing is a wonderfully cheap and effective form of decoration, but with the Industrial Revolution it became possible to produce decorated mass-produced tinware at a very low cost and so hand-pierced work disappeared. The folk art revival has, however, brought new interpretations of tin piercing from countries such as Mexico and India, where artefacts are made solely for export to shops in Europe and America.

This project borrows from the ingenuity of new folk artists and mixes it with a traditional quilting pattern from eighteenth-century America, to make a small shelf from a recycled cake tin. Old baking tins are a good source of material, and their residual greasy coating will pro-tect them from rust. Be extremely careful when handling the raw edges of freshly cut tin, as it is very sharp. It is therefore important that the folding and crimping of the edges is done immediately after the cutting out: in this way you will protect yourself and others from harm.

You will need:
- A sheet of paper
- Scissors
- A pair of tin snippers
- A pair of pliers
- A marker pen
- A small tacking hammer
- Several fine sharp nails
- Protective gloves (optional)

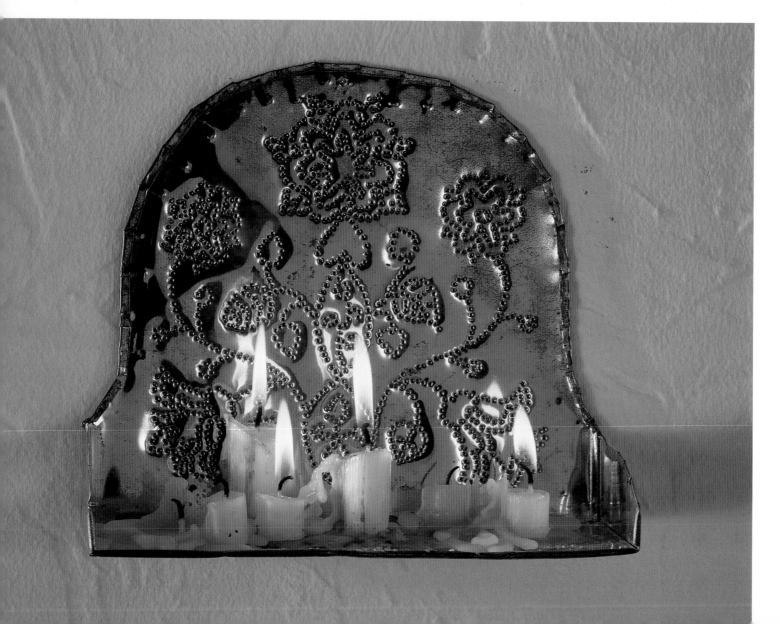

1 Make a pattern for the arch by folding a
sheet of paper, the size of the base of the
tin, in half, and cut a curve out of one half.
The actual shelf will consist of one of the
tin's sides, so select one and using the paper
as a guide, draw the arch above it. A small
section of the sides adjoining the shelf
remains intact to form retaining shelf-ends,
but the rest of the tin is cut away, leaving the
arched backing plate attached to the shelf.

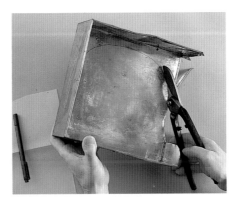 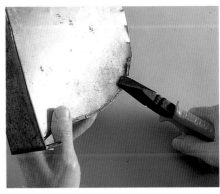

2 Proceed immediately with this step.
Snip ¼in (6mm) into the raw edges at
1in (2.5cm) intervals and use pliers to
firmly fold and crimp until no sharp edges
remain exposed.

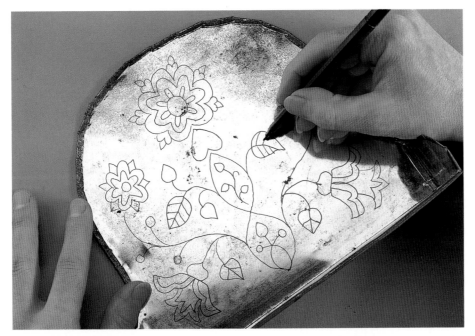

3 Draw your pattern on to the backing
plate using a marker pen. This is an old
quilting pattern, but a folk style embroidery
pattern would also be suitable.

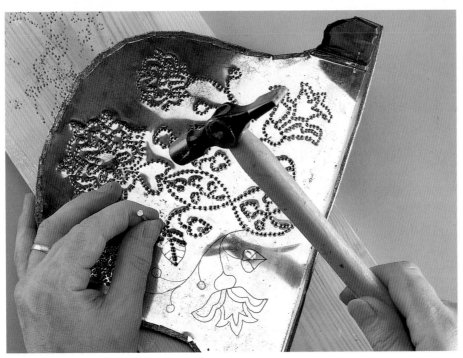

4 Place the tin on a flat piece of scrap
wood and use the hammer to tap the
nail through the tin along the pattern lines.
The perforations should be quite close to
each other without causing the holes to join.
A few mistakes look fine; this is a charming
hand-made shelf which will benefit from a
few irregularities.

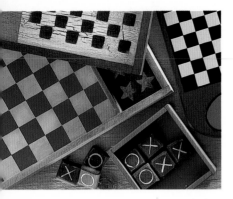

TOYS AND GAMES

Childhood has not always seen the indulgence that exists today, with fortunes being spent by the toy industry on creating new fashions in playthings. Children's toys used to be scaled-down versions of the adult world – a boy would play with carved wooden animals and farm equipment and a girl would have her doll and small cooking pots.

WOODEN TOYS

Like the doll, examples of which survive from classical times, the cup and ball is another simple toy that has been played with throughout the ages to the present day. This is a whittled wooden ball which is tossed into the air and caught in the cup; often the two are attached by a length of hide or string to limit the distance the ball can travel.

Many of the earliest European toys were very simple and made out of wood, such as the spinning top, which was a particular favourite with small boys. Hoops and skittles became popular during the early nineteenth century, as well as pull-along farm animals which were cut out of wood and mounted on wheels. Older children played with the diabolo, a wooden reel which was set in motion to spin in the air on a length of string which was held between each hand. This was the forerunner of the single-handed yoyo that was invented in the 1930s.

AMERICAN TOYS

The Native Americans taught settler families to make dolls from corn husks, carved wood or buckskin, and there are some very well-preserved examples of their own dolls dressed in tribal garments. Dolls' heads were sometimes made from apples, left in the sun to ripen; the features were pinched into the apple's loose skin which would tighten as the fruit dried, producing a wizened but realistic head whose body would be a simple stick with rag clothes.

Early American rag dolls were made from salt bags and feed sacks, stuffed with rags and dressed in the style of the day. In the Amish community, dolls were forbidden from having facial features because of the Biblical prohibition on making graven images, but the dolls are very distinctive with attached limbs and Amish costume, either a child's dress with a front pleat or a woman's plain dress and black half-apron and bonnet.

The American Raggedy Ann doll with woollen hair in bunches and button eyes did not appear until about 1910, when Johnny Gruelle added features to a doll his daughter had found among her grandmother's possessions. He immortalized his present to her by writing popular children's stories based on the doll's adventures.

Rocking horses and hobby horses were made by fathers to amuse their children, and many examples remain. Rocking horses either had flat plank bodies which needed a small chair for the rider, or more realistic carved shapes, reminiscent of the fairground carousel horses. There were many variations in style but they were all made to look as much like the real thing as their maker could manage, and to withstand many hours of rocking.

On a smaller scale, carved animals were made for children and the more prolific carvers undertook the making of Noah's Ark with its many inhabitants – a toy much loved by both boys and girls. Toys that were made for boys alone were often transportation-based, starting with carts, then stagecoaches, sailing boats, trains and paddle steamers as new modes of travel appeared.

THE WHIRLIGIG

The whirligig was a favourite home-made toy and it was made in many forms, although the principle remained the same – an animated wind-driven figure with propellers to catch the wind and turn moveable parts. These could be as simple as a man, often Uncle Sam, with paddle arms, one up and one down, that turned with the wind. Some very complicated whirligigs were made with all kinds of connecting rods that worked gears to turn different parts;

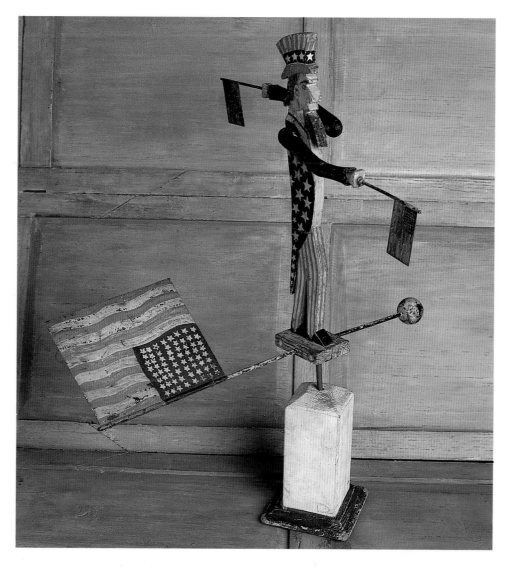

An American whirligig. The wind catches "the propellors" and turns the
moveable parts.

one example featured a farmer sawing wood while a hen
pecked corn and the blades of a windmill turned, all at the
same time in different rhythms. The whirligig is probably
the most famous American folk art toy because many
different patriotic versions were made.

BOARD GAMES

Adults had their own toys, or rather board games, to play
and draughts (checkers) was a favourite. The boards were
marked up with squares for the game with a keeping
division at either end for accumulating the opponent's
pieces. It was at these end sections that the folk artist had
an opportunity to express himself. The decoration was
sometimes a familiar stencilled motif such as a bird but

some featured country scenes, sunrises and stars and
moons. The game appears to have been a masculine
pastime and the colours and decoration reflect this.

Gameboards were also made for Parchisi and Chinese
chequers, and they would have hung from a peg on the
wall as decoration when not in use. Parchisi is an
ancient game from India which was first taken to England, and from there it travelled to America, where it has
remained popular for many generations.

The children's toys that have survived many years of
use are a testament to the softer side of the hard lives that
these people led, where a father's exhaustion gave way to
enthusiasm in making playthings for his children, and
mothers took time to make rag dolls for their daughters.

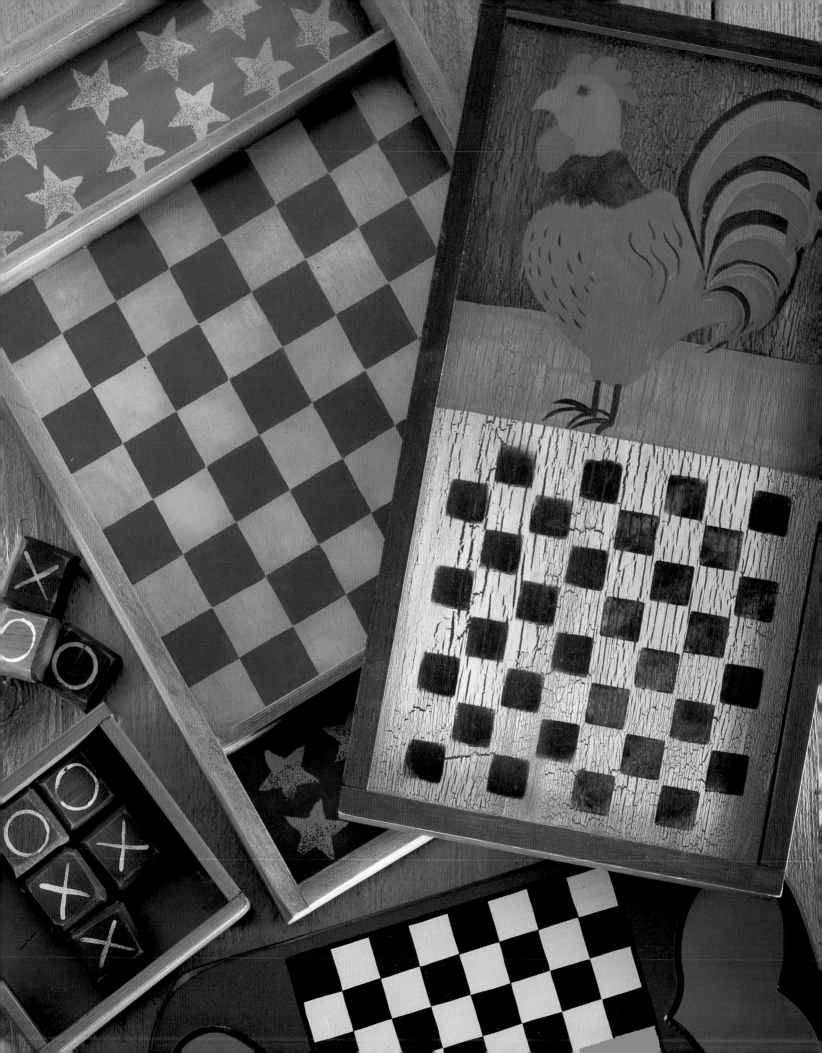

THE DRAUGHTBOARD (CHECKERBOARD)

In the days before radio and television people spent a lot of time playing games, and draughts (checkers) was a favourite. Men would sit out on the porch with the board between them, smoking their pipes and playing the game. Draughts (checkers) is a familiar game, simple enough for very young children to enjoy, though when played by two determined adults, it can be very competitive.

This board follows the pattern of old draughtboards (checkerboards), which were often made by sign painters, and which came in a variety of different decorative designs. They always included divisions for the opponent's winnings, and these sections also had painted decoration.

To make the board, simply measure a rectangular piece of plywood and cut narrow wooden strips with mitred corners as a surround. Use panel pins to nail these in place and then glue and pin two narrower strips crossways, to form a square in the centre of two narrow rectangles. The draughts (checkers) can be bought, or cut from a broom handle and painted black and white.

The stars and stripes are a popular folk pattern and even though the stripes have become checks, they still "read" as a patriotic flag design.

You will need:

- A no. 5 soft artist's brush, a ½in (1.5cm) square-tipped brush and a small household paintbrush
- Matt emulsion (flat latex): pumpkin yellow, off white and brick red
- Artist's acrylics or stencil paints: jade green and cobalt blue
- A cloth, ruler and a pencil
- A small square of foam, cut into the shape of a five-pointed star
- Clear water-based varnish
- A small tube of burnt umber artist's acrylic paint

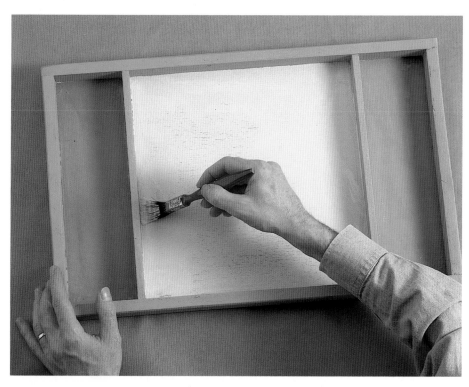

1 Paint the base, sides and dividing strips pumpkin yellow, the rectangular ends jade green and the centre square off white.

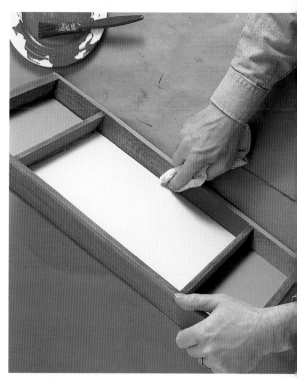

2 Paint brick red over the pumpkin yellow and then rub it off with a cloth while it is still wet. ▶

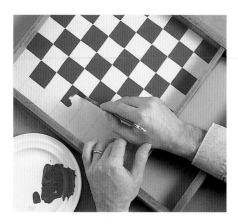

3 Rule up a grid by dividing the sides into eight parts both ways. Carefully fill in alternate squares using brick red and the no. 5 brush.

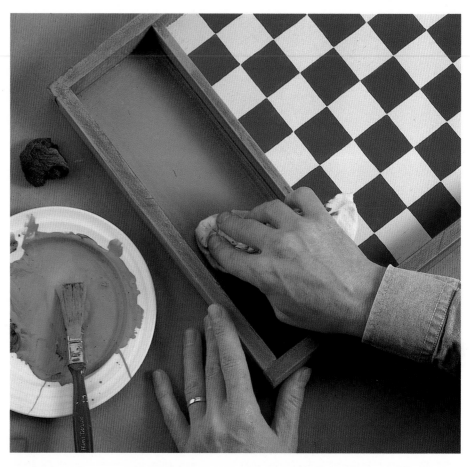

4 Brush on a thinned coat of cobalt blue and then wipe it back while still wet.

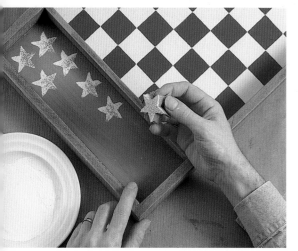

5 Use the off white paint on the star sponge to print the stars on to the blue end sections. Blot the paint from the star before printing to avoid blobs.

6 Finally, give the whole board a coat of varnish tinted with burnt umber, working it well into the corners to give a slightly darker tone there.

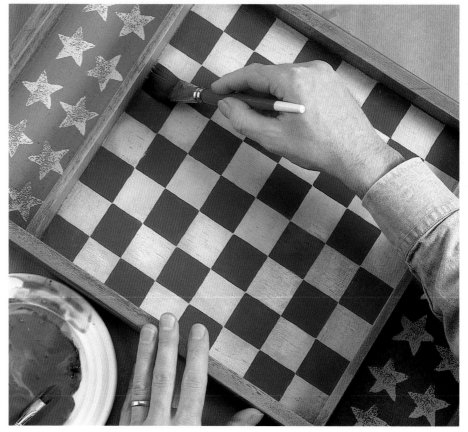

AMISH-STYLE RAG DOLL

The Amish dolls are distinctive for their lack of facial features and their clothing, which is a scaled-down version of their strict dress code. The dolls were passed down through families and if no young girl was born then the dolls would pass to another child who shared the owner's Christian name. In some cases, dolls are the only evidence of the slight alterations that have been made in Amish women's clothing styles over two centuries.

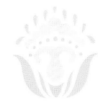

The original dolls would have been made from salt or feed bags. In the absence of these materials, unbleached calico is used here which is an acceptable substitute, being coarsely woven and a natural colour. A doll that is purely for display can become very lonely and look too precious, so make her as resilient as you can and let her be played with and loved.

Try to make her clothes from cast-offs – the Amish wore only plain, dark fabric for outer garments, although their petticoats were sometimes brighter colours with braid trims. The petticoat can be trimmed with braid or cotton lace. The dolls were always firmly stuffed so do not be mean with the filling.

You will need:
- The pattern pieces on page 142 enlarged to size, allowing ¼in (6mm) for a seam allowance
- 1¼yd (1m) unbleached calico
- Scissors
- Needles, pins and thread to match
- 1 bag of wadding (batting)
- A wooden spoon
- 20in (50cm) dark, plain fabric
- A square of black felt
- Scraps of white cotton and lace
- Velvet ribbon
- Iron-on interfacing

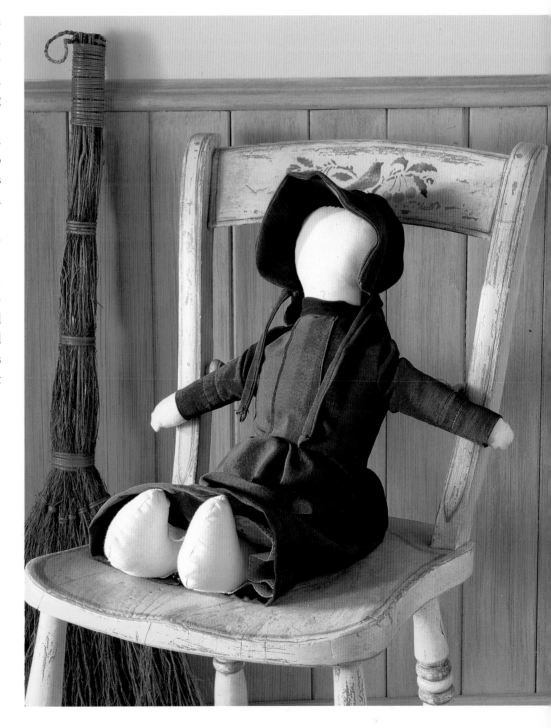

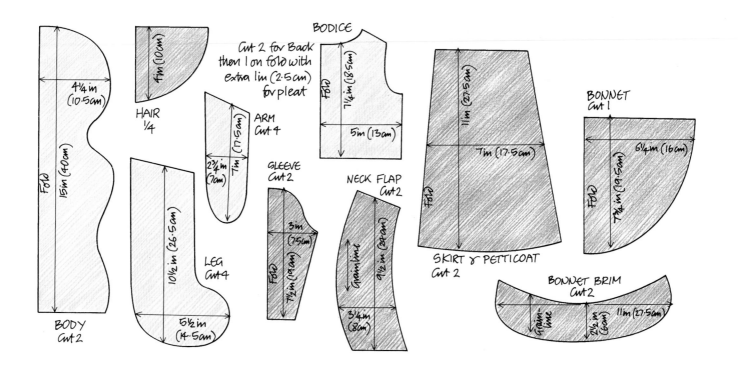

HAIR
1/4

4in (10cm)

BODY
Cut 2

Fold
15in (40cm)

4¼in
(10.5cm)

ARM
Cut 4

2¾in
(7cm)

7in (17.5cm)

LEG
Cut 4

10½in (26.5cm)

5½in
(14.5cm)

BODICE

Cut 2 for Back
then 1 on fold with
extra 1in (2.5cm)
for pleat

Fold
7¼in (18.5cm)

5in (13cm)

SLEEVE
Cut 2

3in
(7.5cm)

Fold
7¼in (10cm)

NECK FLAP
Cut 2

Grainline

3¼in (8cm)

9½in (24cm)

SKIRT & PETTICOAT
Cut 2

Fold

11in (27.5cm)

7in (17.5cm)

BONNET
Cut 1

Fold
7½in (19.5cm)

6¼in (16cm)

BONNET BRIM
Cut 2

Grainline

2½in (6cm)

11in (27.5cm)

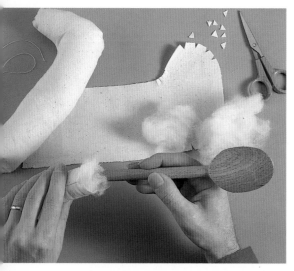

1 Cut the pattern pieces for the body out of the unbleached calico. Sew each section together leaving one straight edge open for filling. Two rows of small stitches are needed to prevent the seams opening. Snip all the curves and turn the pieces the right way out. Fill the pieces well, pushing the wadding (batting) in with a wooden spoon. Sew up the openings, closing the legs so that the feet splay outwards. Sew the arms and legs in place and close the seams around them.

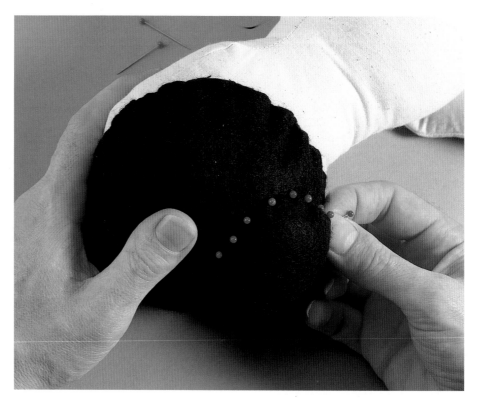

2 Cut the circle for the hair out of black felt. Run a gathering stitch around the circle. Gather it up to fit the head. Turning the gathered edge under, pin it in place and slip stitch. Before closing the seam, insert some wadding (batting) to add shape to the hair. The bun is made in the same way, using a smaller felt circle.

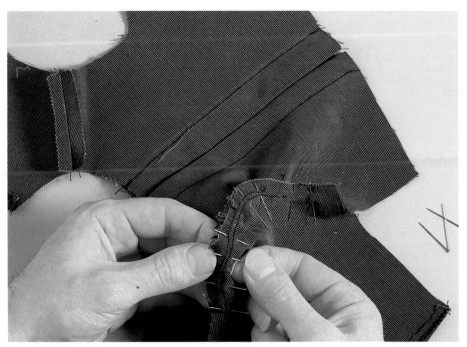

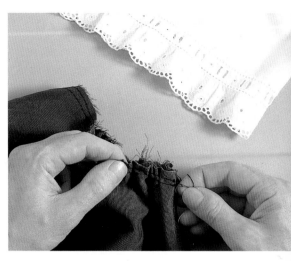

3 Cut the dress pattern out of the dark material. In the front, the bodice has a centre pleat, so allow 1in (2.5cm) at the centre fold to allow for this. Fold in the pleat and sew it in place, then stitch the shoulder seams together. Hem the sleeves and run a

gathering stitch around the shoulder ends. Pull up the gathering threads and fit the sleeves into the shoulders. Sew the sleeves into the bodice, then stitch a seam from the waist, up under the arm to the sleeve end. Turn the bodice the right way around.

4 Join the skirt panels at the sides, then hem the bottom edge and run a gathering stitch around the waist. Repeat for the petticoat. Draw up the gathers to fit the bodice. Turn both pieces over the bodice so that the right sides face and the waist edges meet. Sew through the three layers. Finish off the neck edge by attaching velvet ribbon, sewn along the neck edge and folded over to cover the rough seam. Fit the dress onto the doll and sew up the back seam.

5 Cut out the bonnet pieces and iron-on interfacing to line the brim. Iron the interfacing on to both brim pieces and then sew around the shaped edge, leaving the straighter edge open. Turn the work through and press it. Sew the neck flap in the same way and then turn and press it. Gather the curved edge and back of the bonnet to fit inside the two sections of the brim and neck flap; the seams should be hidden within the two parts, so that no edges are exposed.

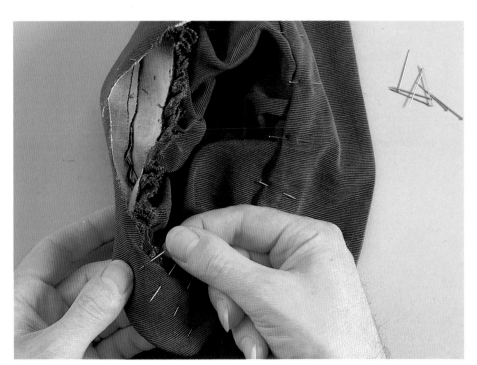

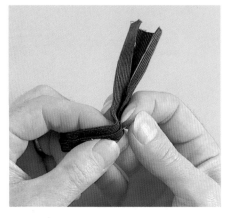

6 Sew one edge of the brim to the bonnet, then fold the outer brim over the seam, sewing it down to conceal it. Do the same with the neck flap.

Fold and sew a long strip of fabric for the ribbon tie, or use ribbon. Sew across the neckflap seam, leaving the ends free to act as bonnet ties.

R E F E R E N C E

TIPS • TEMPLATES • COLLECTING

EARLY FOLK ARTISTS NEVER THREW AWAY ANYTHING THAT COULD BE restored or regenerated, and their philosophy has been adopted for this book. The patterns and techniques shown in the projects can be adapted to be used on a wide range of objects; equally, alternative designs from sourcebooks can be substituted for those suggested. With this in mind, search around attics, market stalls and thrift shops for useful materials before buying them new, and the results will often look more authentic.

Many of the methods and materials recommended for the projects are not true to the originals, but they are modern-day substitutes which are easier to work with. The paints and varnishes, for example, are almost all water-based because they give a high degree of durability and are much quicker and less messy to work with. This book is not about making fakes, but a guide to making folk art that has a satisfying visual authenticity.

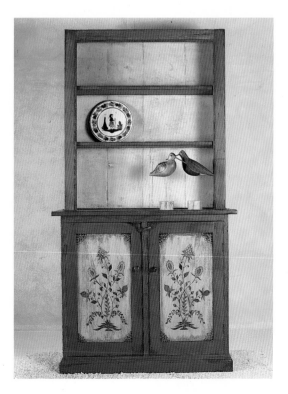

A modern half-dresser with painted decoration inspired by the old Pennsylvania Dutch furniture.

Opposite: A detail of a Swedish room which was used for festive occasions.

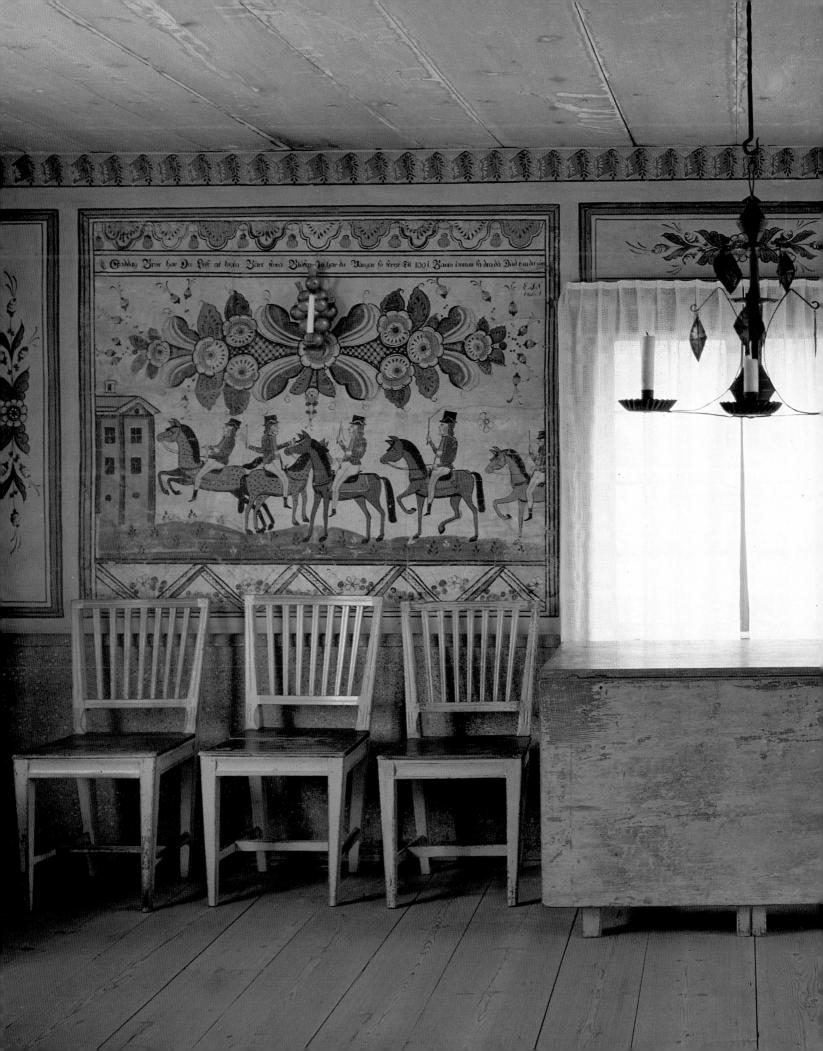

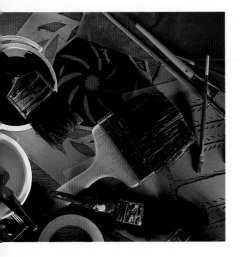

BASIC TECHNIQUES

THERE ARE TWO MAIN TYPES OF PAINT, WATER-BASED (EMULSION OR LATEX), AND OIL-BASED. WHEREVER POSSIBLE WATER-BASED PAINTS (EMULSION OR LATEX), HAVE BEEN SPECIFIED FOR THE PROJECTS. THESE PAINTS CAN BE THINNED WITH WATER. YOU MAY, HOWEVER, PREFER TO USE OIL-BASED PAINTS; THESE CAN BE THINNED WITH WHITE SPIRIT (RUBBING ALCOHOL). OIL-BASED AND WATER-BASED PAINTS ARE NOT COMPATIBLE AND SHOULD NOT BE MIXED. WITH ALL PAINTS ALLOW EACH COAT TO DRY THOROUGHLY BEFORE APPLYING SUCCESSIVE COATS.

STENCIL PAINTS

Artist's acrylics and stencil paints have been recommended for use in the projects. Stencil paints are sold in both oil and water-based varieties. The water-based variety resemble thick emulsion (latex) paint, and are very fast drying. The advantage of using these over artist's acrylics is that they have been made specifically for stencilling and can be used directly from the pot. Artist's acrylics may need to be thinned very slightly with water. If you do use oil-based stencil paints you must use an oil-based varnish as well.

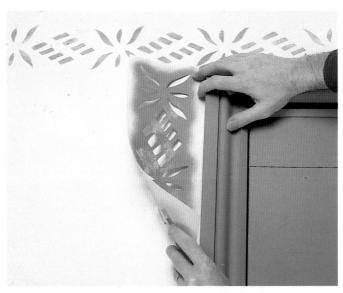

Spray the back of the stencil with the lightest coating of adhesive – just enough to hold it in place, and to peel off easily.

COLOURS

Colours have been suggested for each project, but these shades vary when made by different manufacturers, so be sure to check that the paints are the shade you want before you buy them. The specified colours can be replaced with others more suited to your home.

You can also mix paints to obtain different tones and shades. When tinting, always add colours together gradually, and try to anticipate how much paint you will need before you start – if you run out it will be difficult to mix the exact shade again.

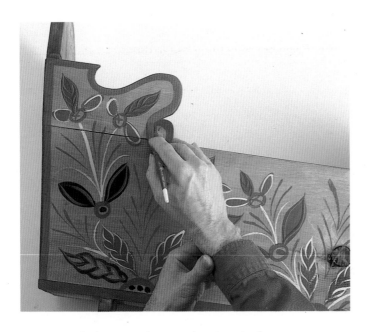

The key to good paintwork is choosing the correct brush. Here a 1in (2.5cm) square-tipped brush is being used to draw a 1in (2.5cm) line.

VARNISHES

Varnishes are used to protect paintwork from general wear and tear. As with paints, varnishes come in both oil and water-based varieties and matt (flat), satin or gloss finishes. Oil-based varnishes must only be tinted with oil-based colours, and water-based with water-based colours. When applying the varnish always use a clean brush that has not been used for the paintwork.

BRUSHES

The key to good paintwork is choosing the correct brush. The three main types of brushes recommended in the projects are household, artist's and stencil brushes, and they come in a huge variety of shapes and sizes. Household brushes should be used for the basecoats and varnishes, and the artist's brushes for the fine paintwork. You can buy specialist varnishing brushes, however, household ones are adequate. Always ensure a different brush is used for the varnish and the paintwork, otherwise the varnish will have flecks of paint in it.

Brushes are either coarse-bristled, or made from natural or synthetic soft hair. The synthetic ones are less expensive and are quite adequate for craft work. Brushes must always be cleaned immediately after use. Oil-based paint should be cleaned off with white spirit (rubbing alcohol), and water-based paint with water.

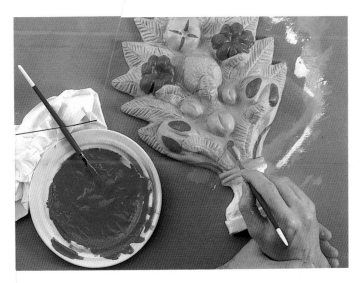

Always clean your paintbrushes thoroughly if you
are changing colour.

STENCILS

Stencils can be cut either from waxy stencil card or acetate sheet. Card is slightly easier to control when cutting, but the advantage of acetate is that it is washable and that you can see through it when aligning design motifs. If you are using card the stencil patterns can be traced on to it, but if you are using acetate the tracing should be coated with spray adhesive and stuck to the back of the sheet. Cut out the stencil with either a craft knife, or small sharp scissors, securing it firmly to the cutting surface with tape.

When you are stencilling, spray the back of the stencil lightly with low-tack spray adhesive, such as mounting spray. The glue should be just strong enough to hold the stencil in place, but weak enough for it to peel off easily. Do not use a strong adhesive.

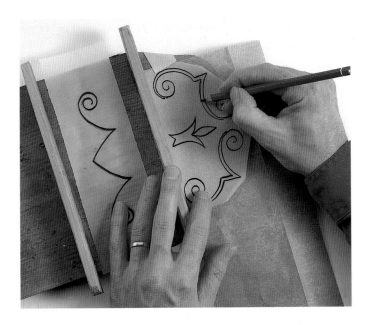

Place the transfer paper between the tracing paper
and the surface to be decorated.

TEMPLATES

Templates are guides which can be traced around in order to transfer a design on to the object to be decorated. In order to enlarge the templates to the size that you require, draw a grid of equal-sized squares over your tracing. Measure the space where the shape is to go and then draw a grid to these proportions, with an equal number of squares as appear on your tracing. Take each square individually and draw the relevant parts of the pattern in the larger square. Alternatively, you can enlarge your tracing on a photocopier.

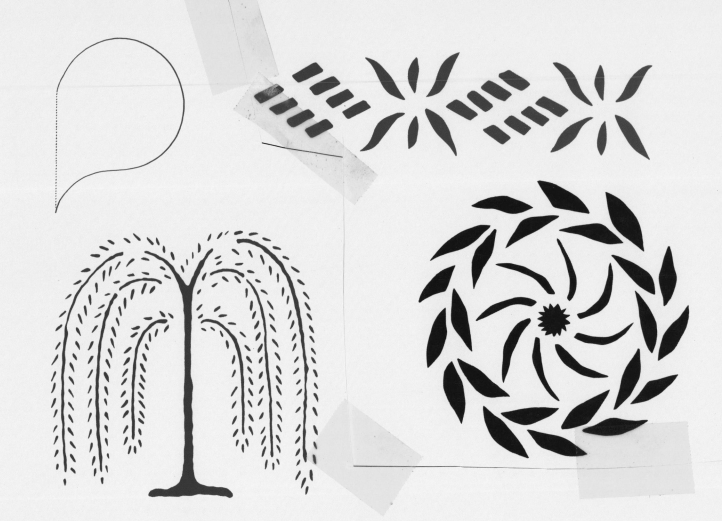

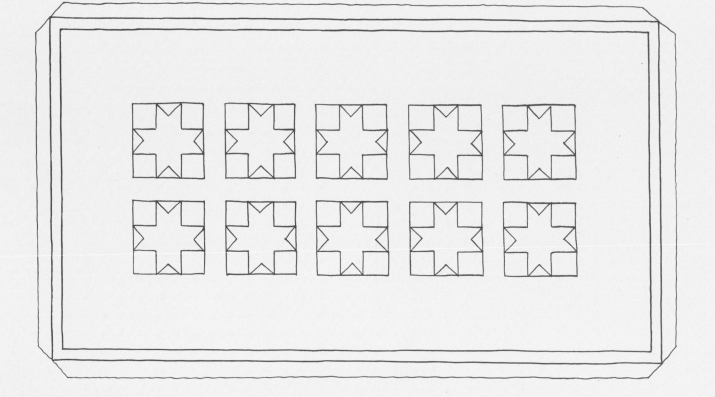

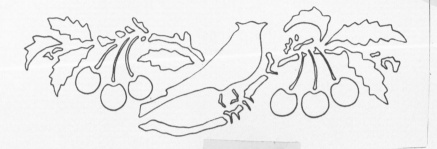

Scanned

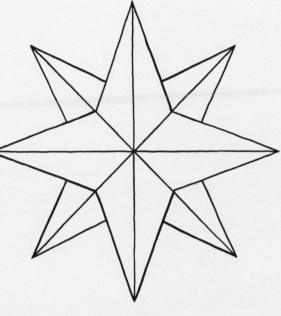

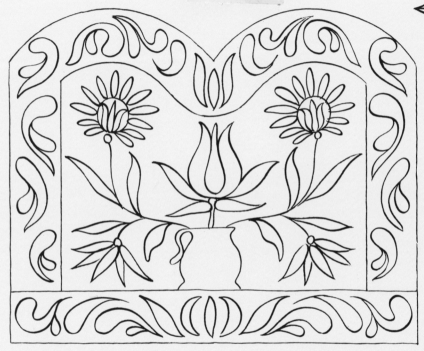

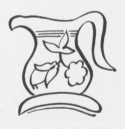

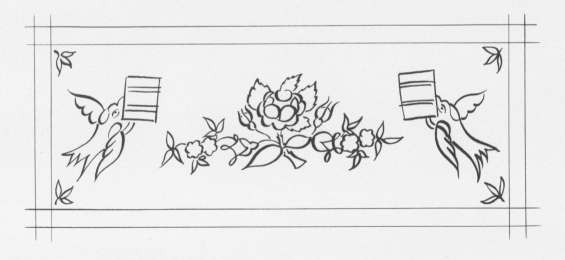

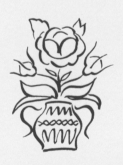

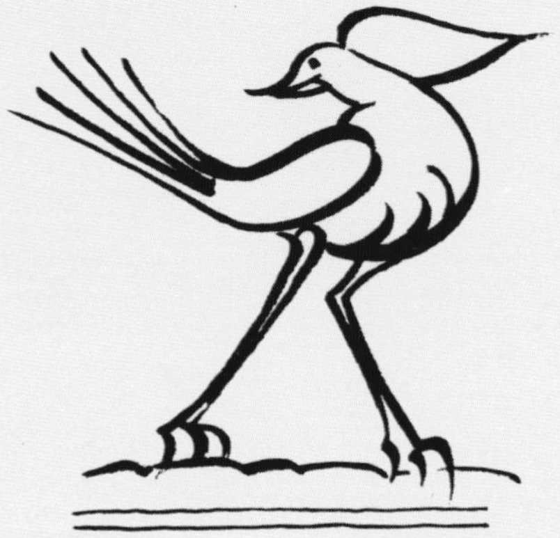

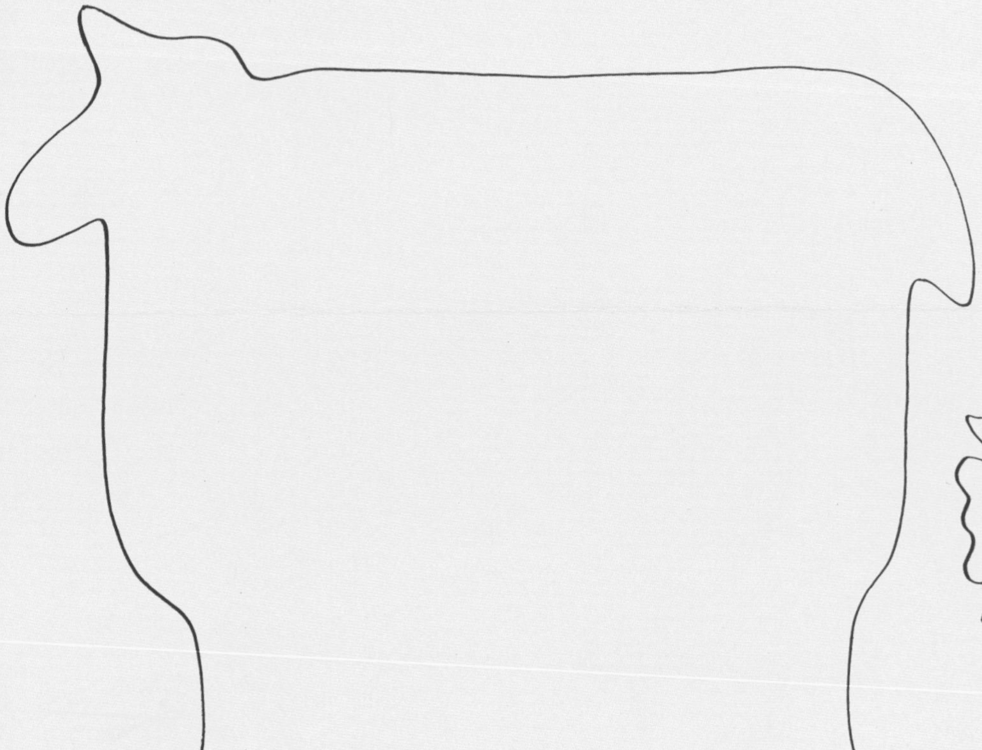

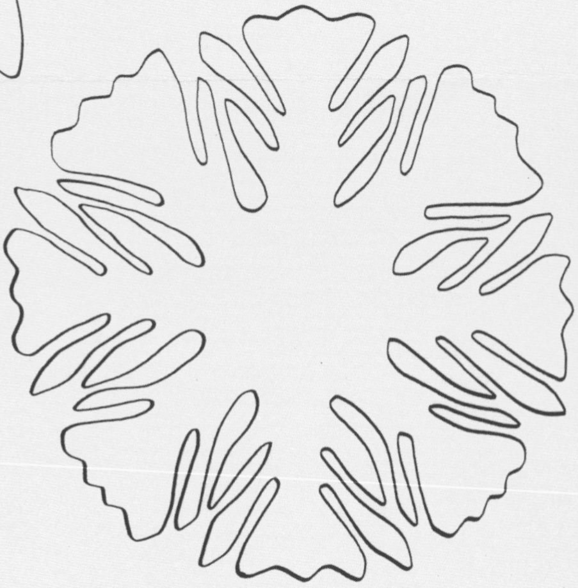

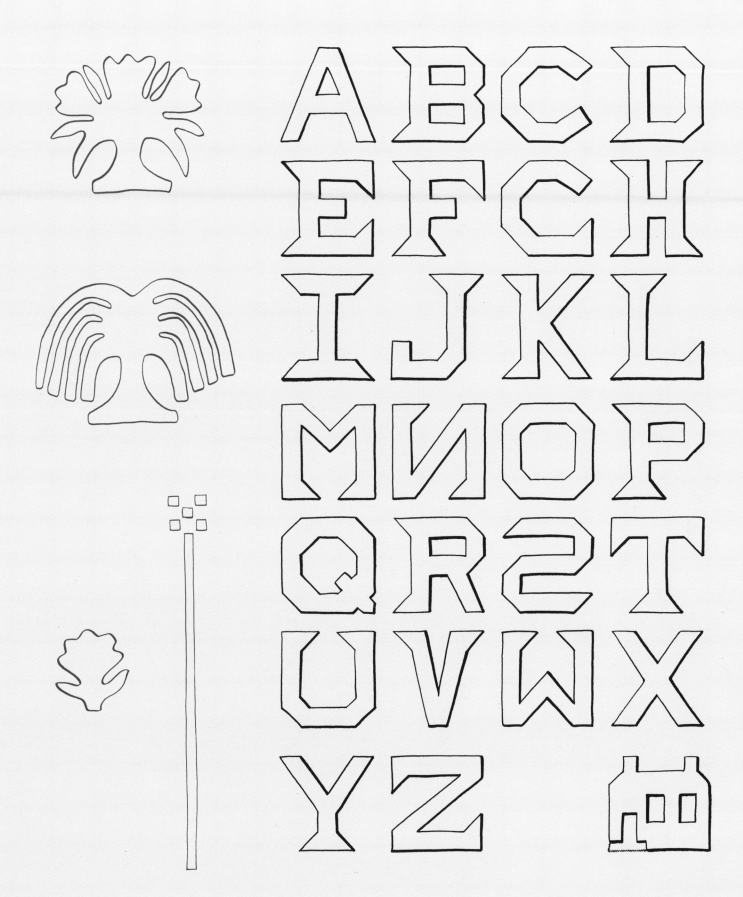

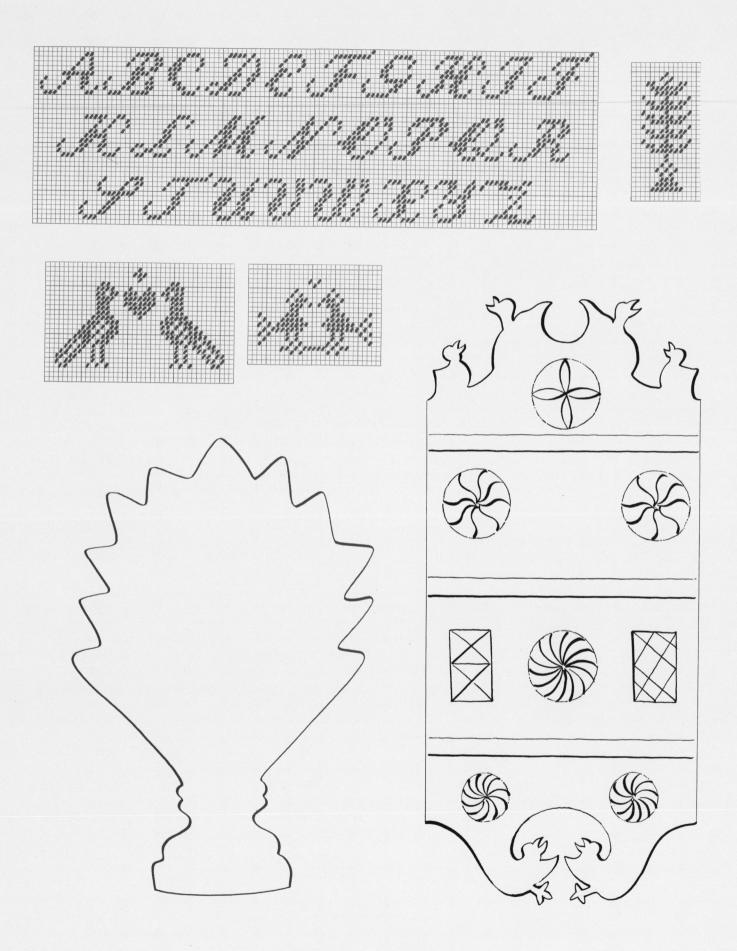

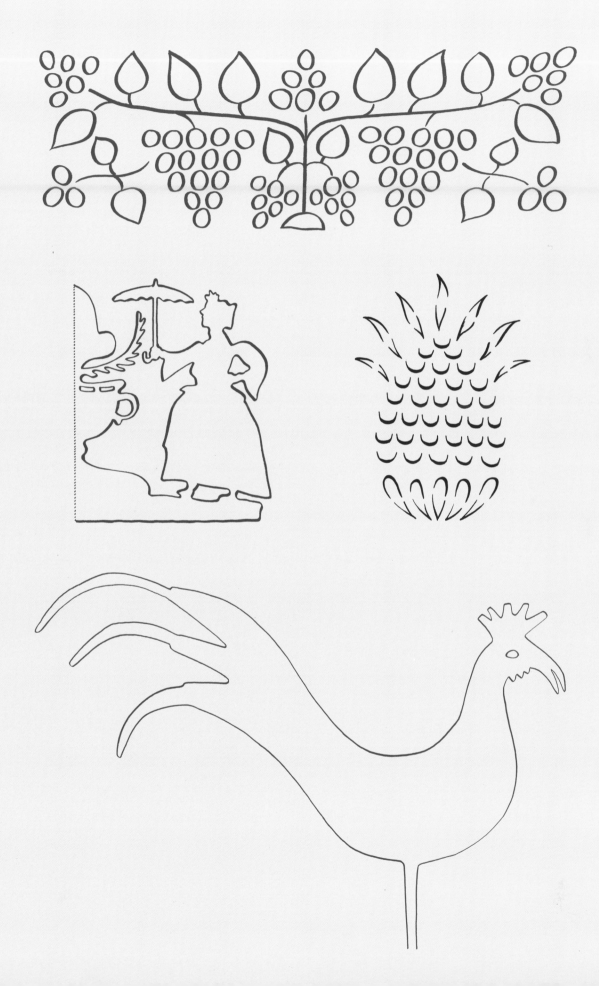

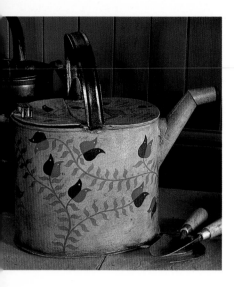

BUYING AND COLLECTING

A COLLECTION IS A PERSONAL STATEMENT AND THE CHOICE OF OBJECTS HAS TO BE YOUR OWN. WHEN LOOKING THROUGH THE EXAMPLES IN THIS BOOK YOU WILL BE DRAWN TOWARDS CERTAIN OBJECTS AND STYLES – MAYBE YOU PREFER A CERTAIN COMBINATION OF COLOURS OR TEXTURES. THERE IS NO POINT IN COLLECTING SOMETHING UNLESS IT HAS AN APPEAL FOR YOU BEYOND ITS MONETARY VALUE. THERE WOULD BE LITTLE SATISFACTION TO BE GAINED, AND THE MAKING OF A COLLECTION WOULD SURELY BE LESS FASCINATING IF IT WERE JUST A COMMODITY TO BE PURCHASED.

Unfortunately since the 1960s folk art has become fiendishly expensive, and the time for buying bargains is past. Even the smallest and plainest objects fetch large sums at auctions as folk items have gone from being considered quaint objects to serious works of art.

There are of course still treasures to be found in markets, junk shops and sales, but you should be realistic in your choice. If the objects are rare and highly sought after you will have little chance of buying them, and it would be better to visit museums and admire them there. It is, however, possible to find smaller, less flamboyant household items if you know where to look. By scouring sales you will develop a "selective eye" – this will enable you to spot a potential treasure under a heap of rubble. You may find this will turn into a time-consuming hobby that borders on obsession.

If you lack the time for this type of endeavour then you can buy from specialist shops. Many of these stores exist in big cities and there are also import shops which deal in folk art from all over the globe. These hand-crafted objects range from tribal art of indigenous peoples to ingenious toys. The recent revival of interest in folk art has meant that you can now find this style represented in many mainstream home furnishing stores. Equally, in America, communities such as the Amish still flourish and make their distinctive goods for sale in local markets.

Right: A collection of hand-carved sycamore spoons.
Top: Tulips are one of the most popular folk patterns.

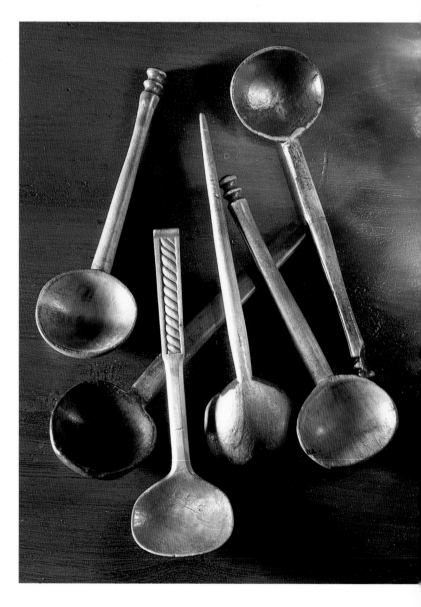

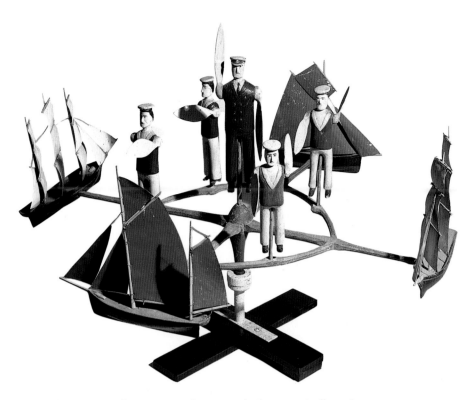

A late nineteenth-century weathervane, which was originally made to
stand on the roof of a seafarer's house.

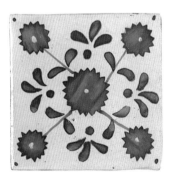 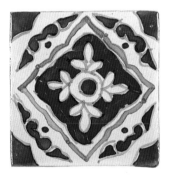 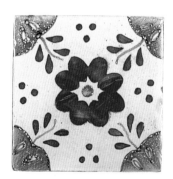

  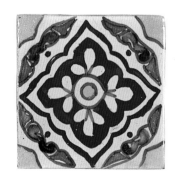

A selection of tiles from Mexico, with designs inspired by traditional
Spanish and Mexican patterns.

BIBLIOGRAPHY

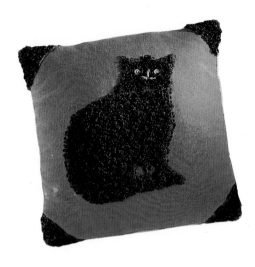

Cats are a popular subject in folk art.

Bishop, Robert. *New Discoveries in American Quilts*. New York: E.P. Dutton & Co. Inc., 1975.

Bishop, Dr. Robert. *American Folk Art – Expressions of a New Spirit*. New York: Museum of American Folk Art, 1982.

Creekmore, Betsy B. *Traditional American Crafts*. New York: Hearthside Press Inc., 1968.

Hornung, Clarence P. *Treasury of American Design*. New York: Harry N. Abrams Inc.

Kauffman, Henry J. *Pennsylvania Dutch American Folk Art*. New York: Dover Publications Inc., 1964.

Ketchum, William C. Jr. *All American Folk Arts and Crafts*. New York: Rizzoli, 1986.

Lewis, Felicity. *Needlepoint Samplers*. London: Studio Vista, 1981.

Lipman, Jean, Warren, Elizabeth, and Bishop, Robert. *Young America – A Folk Art History*. New York: Hudson Halls in association with The Museum of American Folk Art, 1956.

Lipman, Jean. *Techniques in American Folk Decoration*. New York: Dover Publications Inc., 1972.

McCauley, Daniel and Kathryn. *Decorative Arts of the Amish of Lancaster County*. Intercourse, Philadelphia: Good Books, 1988.

Pfeffer, Susanna. *Quilt Masterpieces*. New York: Hugh Lanter Levin Ass. Inc., 1988.

Plath, Iona. *The Decorative Arts of Sweden*. New York: Dover Publications Inc., 1966.

Rivers, Beverly (Ed). *Traditional American Crafts*. Des Moines, Iowa: Better Homes and Gardens Books, 1988.

Schaffner, Cynthia, V.A. *Discovering American Folk Art*. New York: Harry N. Abrams Inc. in association with The Museum of American Folk Art, 1991.

Seward, Linda. *Patchwork Quilting and Appliqué*. London: Mitchell Beazley, 1987.

Stewart, Janice S. *The Folk Arts of Norway*. New York: Dover Publications Inc., 1972.

Waring, Janet. *Early American Stencils*. New York: Dover Publications Inc., 1968.

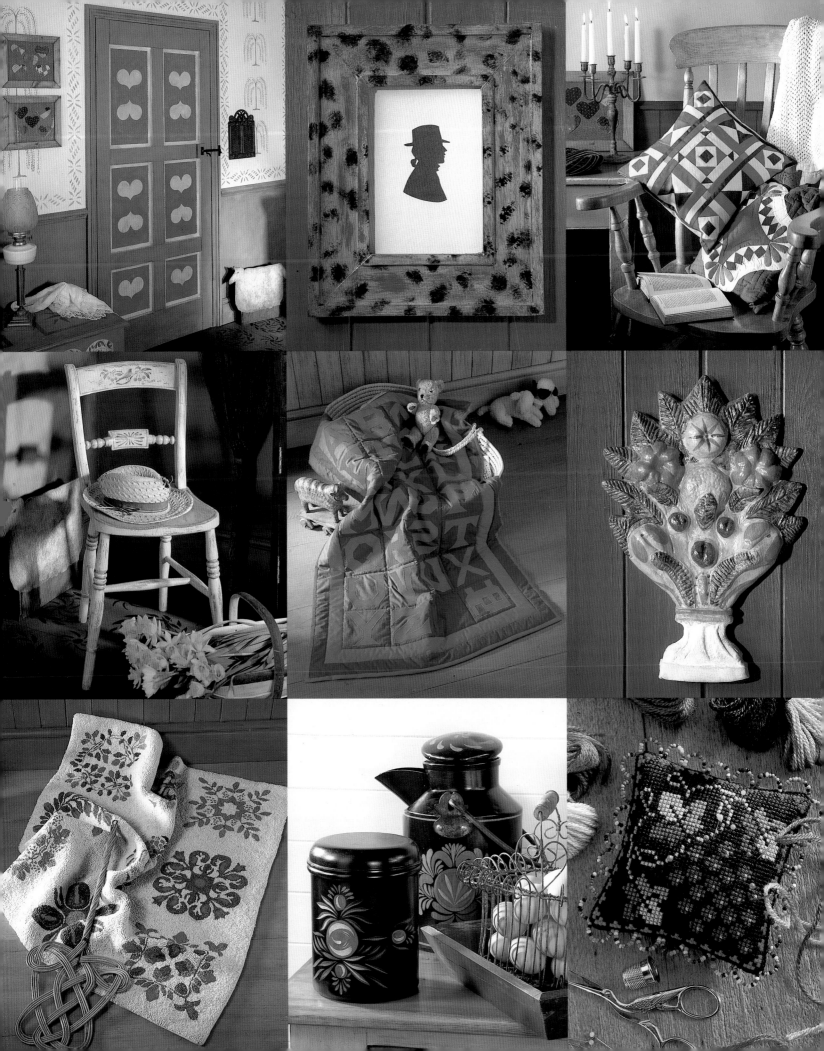

INDEX

ACKNOWLEDGEMENTS

AUTHOR'S ACKNOWLEDGEMENTS

We would like to thank Steve Tanner for his support and friendship – beyond the call of duty; Jonathan Reed, who assisted tirelessly in the studio; Sue Duffy for the styling; Tim Hickmoot of Farthings Pine, 18 Reginald Road, Bexhill-on-Sea, England, for his carpentry skills; and our family for keeping their demands down to a minimum.

CONTRIBUTORS

The publishers and authors would like to thank the following for their help with the projects: Annette Claxton, Pat Taylor, Jenni Dobson, Carole Hart, Jan Eaton, Jenni Stuart-Anderson and Ann Davies.

PICTURE CREDITS

The publishers would like to thank the following for their co-operation in providing pictures for use in this publication: Abby Aldrich Rockefeller Folk Art Center, Williamsburg, VA, page 8, 16 (top), 18 (right), 48, 60, 68, 97, 118 and 119; Cassell, London, page 7, 33 and 145; Ron Simpson Textiles, Grays Antique Market, 138 Portobello Road, London (Tel: 071-727 0983), page 79; Mittet Foto, Oslo, page 11 (right) and 19 (right); McWhirter Antique Furniture, page 21; Les Musées de la Ville de Strasbourg, page 6 (right) and 24 (right), 31, 34 and 71; Néprajzi Múzeum, Budapest, 6 (left), 47 and 51. Somerset Country Limited, 632 Fulham Road, London (Tel: 071-371 0436), page 15, 26 (top) and 145; Crane Galleries, London, page 14 (left), 133 and 137; Jenny Owen, page 102; Hermitage Rugs, page 103; Dalane Folkmuseum, Norway, page 25 (left); Fired Earth, page 11 (right) and 155 (below).

The publishers would also like to thank Adele Corcoran, Mrs Schaad, Rhode Design, the Shaker Shop, American Country Collection and the shops listed below, for their co-operation in loaning items for photography.

Appalachia – The Folk Art Shop, 14A George Street, St Albans, Herts (Tel: 0727-836796); page 13, 16 (below), 27, 85 and 105.

Folk Art, The Old Ropery, East Street, West Coker, Nr. Yeovil, Somerset (Tel: 0935-863026/2806); page 9, 12, 13, 20, 22 and 23.

Judy Greenwood Antiques, 657 Fulham Road, London (Tel: 071-736 6037); page 10 and 80 (left).

Peter Place Antiques, 636 King's Road, London (Tel: 071-736 9945); page 96 and 130.

Robert Young Antiques, 68 Battersea Bridge Road, London (Tel: 071-228 7847; page 11 (left), 19 (above), 46 (below), 59, 109, 111, 129, 131, 154 (below), 155 (above) and 156.

Tricia Jameson Design Ltd, 9 Pond Place, London (Tel: 071-584 7642); page 1, 14 (top), 17, 24 (left), 25 (right), 66, 80 (right), 80 (left) and 154 (top).